Advance Praise for Meaningful Marketing

"If I had to choose one book on which to base the entire marketing effort of my brand, this would be the one! The fundamental premise—shining through on every page of *Meaningful Marketing*—is that if you want to create a great business—figure out how to add real value to people's lives and then tell the truth about it. Through diligent research, the authors back this premise up with science, showing it to be a fact, not merely an opinion. This book proves that, in business, the smart thing to do and the right thing are one and the same. In doing so, it elegantly presents the true moral nature of capitalism. And for that, I consider Doug Hall one of its greatest champions."

Jon Butcher, CEO — The Precious Moments Companies

"This is a blockbuster work which skillfully blends research and practice. It is NOT another Marketing book to leave on a shelf. *Meaningful Marketing* instead, should sit on your desk, engines revving, until you pick it up and rocket down the road toward profit! The competition will eat your dust."

Arthur B. VanGundy, Ph.D. — University of Oklahoma

"Doug and Jeff are enlightening everyone to succeed meaningfully and to make a great, important, and lasting difference. Read this book and take action now."

Mark Victor Hansen, Co-Author — *Chicken Soup for the Soul*

"An extraordinary synthesis of the academic and the pragmatic—making this a 'Wheel of Marketing' for a new generation."

John Ruffley, Marketing Director — Masterfoods USA

"This book takes all of the mystery out of marketing and replaces it with a systematic and logical system. For anyone who takes their marketing role seriously, this book is a must read."

Kip Knight, VP International — E-Bay

"A great book. Powerful, practical ideas to market your business faster and more effectively than you ever imagined possible!"

Brian Tracy, Author — *TurboStrategy*

"*Meaningful Marketing* pulls together empirical findings from both scholarly and proprietary sources, mixes in a hefty dose of creativity, and then tempers the concoction with a strong sense of the pragmatic. The result is hundreds of insightful, usable ideas for stimulating sustainable sources of profitability. Kudos to Doug and Jeff for such a helpful contribution to our thinking."

Timothy B. Heath, Ph.D, — Miami University

"Doug Hall builds on his legacy as the hardest working, most passionate author touring America today. *Meaningful Marketing* features the richest research and deepest thinking on marketing ever found in a business book. Doug's tireless commitment to helping independent booksellers survive and thrive is unmatched by any business author."

Neil J. Van Uum, Owner — Joseph-Beth Booksellers

"Very rarely does a business book balance both theory and details, motivating readers to act. *Meaningful Marketing* covers both macro and micro topics in a way never before covered. I can think of at least 24 clients and friends who could immediately benefit from this book."

Roger C. Parker, CEO — New Entrepreneur

"This is the most complete and comprehensive book on what it takes to market your business. It's insightful about human behavior, pragmatic, and powerful. The concepts are simple; yet provide the answers to the many brain-torquing questions challenging managers today. This work is provocative, one reading is hardly enough. I view it as a handbook I will be walking around with for many years to come with many pages dog eared and scribbled on."

Ann-Marie Stephens, Sr. VP, Strategic Business Planning — Circuit City

"I absolutely love this book. It's been said that if one witnesses someone making something difficult look easy, then what one is actually witnessing is 'brilliance in action.' *Meaningful Marketing* is just that—Doug Hall and Dr. Jeffrey Stamp bring their collective brilliance to bear in a way that makes it easy for all of us to understand the difficult world of marketing and business success."

Tom Wilson, Ziggy Cartoonist — Universal Press Syndicate

"As a book-a-holic that loves to read the hot business book by the latest guru *Meaningful Marketing* messed up my pattern. I didn't read it. I tore it apart. We are already implanting the book's ideas with a type of confidence never before experienced. The book hit me with a 50-pound hammer of research to destroy my marketing prejudices and replace them with solid practical ideas. As a front line business owner there is no way I could have ever gained access to such helpful information and ideas."
Jerry McNellis, Founder — The McNellis Company

"*Meaningful Marketing* is fun to read, even though it has to be the equivalent of a university degree in marketing! It's an indispensable treasure trove of proven principles, practical insights and innovative ideas, all grounded in extensive research. It's certainly the only marketing book anyone would ever need."
Dr. Deanna Berg, President — Innovation Strategies International

"I couldn't put this book down! The advice Doug and Jeffrey dish out in *Meaningful Marketing* spoon-feeds those of us who are 'marketing-challenged.' Finally, I understand the power of an overt benefit-marketing message. In fact, I used their advice this very week to close new deals and launch an international staffing initiative!"
Patty De Dominic, CEO — PDQCareers.com

"Doug Hall, one of the world's most brilliantly creative minds, continues on his passionate mission to help businesses transform themselves from constantly battling for customers to creating a genuinely rewarding, profitable partnership with their customers. Reading this book is the smartest thing you'll do all year."
Dan O'Day — Radio Advertising Guru

"Setting the hurdle higher and then helping us clear it is a trademark of Doug's work. He doesn't settle for good work, he only settles for the extraordinary and it pays off in the marketplace."
Jim Figura, VP-Consumer Insights and Research — Colgate-Palmolive

"This is it—the complete marketing story, distilled to the essentials and presented with total clarity."
Copthorne Macdonald, Author — *Towards Wisdom*

"*Meaningful Marketing*'s data-rich content and innovative format brings together the art and science of marketing innovation to inform, reinforce, and educate. It's a masterful catalyst to just make you think!"

Peter J. Flatow, President — CoKnowledge, Inc.

"Forget half of what you've learned about marketing and be prepared to be surprised by the facts! *Meaningful Marketing* takes a pragmatic look at research that might otherwise gather dust in academic journals. I'm convinced that no business person will close the last page of this book without at least a dozen great ideas that can be easily executed to improve their company's bottom line."

Jordan Ayan, CEO — SubscriberMail

"*Meaningful Marketing* provides all managers—from small business owners to Marketing Vice Presidents—a plan of action to achieve sales and marketing success. This book takes the guesswork out of what does or doesn't work."

Allan Smith, CEO — Technology PEI Canada

"This book shoots down the conventional wisdom regarding sales and marketing. My own copy is completely dog-eared and covered with highlighter. I certainly hope my competitors don't get a hold of this, since I plan to use a lot of what I learned!"

Steve Miller, CEO — THE ADVENTURE LLC

"What I like best about *Meaningful Marketing* is its design: you can 'dip' in and out of it easily, digesting the 'chunks' of knowledge Doug and Jeff throw at you. I can actually visualize myself 'doing the ideas' and getting immediate benefits. This book lifts the veil over your eyes to reveal what you really need to do to improve your sales and marketing efforts. It debunks marketing myths and simplifies that which is often held out as complex. In my opinion, there is nothing else you can read that will have a more direct effect on your company's success."

Graeme Crombie, Partner — MATRIX, Ltd., Glasgow, Scotland

"*Meaningful Marketing* is the new and ultimate marketing reference book on how to create, develop, market, and manage brands strategically for the 21st Century. It details how to make a real difference in the marketplace and how to actively nurture brands for permanent growth. It's a masterpiece!"

Ilene Quilty, Group Director — Johnson & Johnson

"It has been my privilege to have worked with Doug Hall longer than anyone, other than his wife, Debbie. Doug is not one to dabble. He never stops working to get better at what he does. *Meaningful Marketing* represents the latest stage in his relentless pursuit to discover proven systems for growing sales and profits for companies large and small. I would say this book also represents Doug Hall at the height of his game, but that may be a bit misleading. Because he'll never stop raising the notches."
David Wecker, Co-Host, Brain Brew Radio Show, *Cincinnati Post* Columnist

"A must-read book on marketing. Some writers communicate with clear and interesting prose, some writers share profound thoughts, and some writers base their ideas on the most rigorous standards of truth. Doug Hall is one of the very few business writers who does all three well. Read this book right away and hope that your competition misses it."
Lynn Kahle, Ph.D., Professor — University of Oregon

"Finally, a reference book I can recommend to senior-level clients as well as students! The authors of *Meaningful Marketing* have clearly done their homework and made it so easy for the rest of us to crib the marketing truths and brilliant ideas to build our companies. This easy-to-read book contains top-notch marketing ideas that are based on solid truths derived from deep, valid, and reliable academic research. The reader strikes it rich with the 'marketing gold' dug, mined, and extracted by the authors from mountains of research. Their refinement makes this book 'worth its weight in' ... well, you know."
Jonathan Vehar, Sr. Partner — New & Improved® LLC

"For those who strive to be 'meaningful marketers' but who, like me, need guidance and inspiration, Doug and Jeff have done it again. This book is not a 'one-time read.' Keep it within reach and refer to it often ... for extraordinary results."
Jim Sullivan, CMO, Retail Services — Alliance Data Systems

"Very stimulating. *Meaningful Marketing* is provocative on a broad range of leadership issues. To think about marketing—as presented by this book—is to think about your core product, mission and relationships. For a university president, that counts as a good day."
H. Wade MacLauchlan, President and Vice-Chancellor
University of Prince Edward Island, Canada

"Memorize, mobilize, monetize. Pay attention to the simple principles in *Meaningful Marketing* to maximize your wins in the marketplace."

Paul Kurnit, President — Kurnit Communications

"For those of us with a short attention span, your new book, *Meaningful Marketing*, is a tremendous resource. You can pick it up for a few minutes and read a couple of pages. However, what I have found is that once I pick it up, I end up reading for an hour. Great stuff! I'm planning on using a couple of pages as an ice breaker and conversation starter for our weekly marketing meetings."

David Uible, Owner — Uible Management

"Even if you've created the best mousetrap, customers still have to find their way to your door. In today's world of a million doors, it takes *Meaningful Marketing* to connect with potential customers and lead them to your door. Finally, here's a book that cuts through the fog and tells you exactly how to make your new venture a success. Miss this one and you might as well throw handfuls of cash out the back door."

Joyce Wycoff, Co-Founder — InnovationNetwork

"Doug Hall and Jeff Stamp deliver an over-the-top primer for success. Turn to any page in this book, implement the wisdom shown, and you can immediately benefit your business. We're already planning on implementing at least twenty of the *Meaningful Marketing* Data-Proven Truths now and then adding one more every month for years and years of continual improvement. It's true—the keys to the kingdom are in your hands—read 'em and reap!"

Richard Hunt, President & Publisher — Emmis Books

"A few years ago I went to the largest ad agency in New York to pitch some ideas. In their lobby stood a massive sign exhorting their corporate motto, "TRUTH TOLD WELL," and ever since then I have been troubled. For we have become a culture disheartened by hype and spin. So, what on Earth does the truth have to do with marketing? Leave it to Doug Hall to remind us that we all are still on a quest for meaning in our daily lives. And that our customers innately divine truth from lies and vote with their pocketbooks when making their decisions. Anyone selling or promoting goods or services should read *Meaningful Marketing*."

Thane Maynard, VP — Cincinnati Zoo

Praise for Doug Hall & The Eureka! Ranch

"Eureka! Ranch's unconventional approach has won raves from some of the biggest corporations in the country."
   CNN

"America's #1 Idea Guru."
   A&E Top 10

"Eureka! Ranch ... has developed more new products (or off-shoots of existing ones) than any other organization in America."
   New York Magazine

"Former Procter & Gamble marketing whiz Doug Hall goes to any length to encourage a fresh perspective ... clients say it works."
   Wall Street Journal

"An entrepreneur who just might have what we've all been looking for, the happy secret to success."
   DATELINE NBC

"When Doug meets Disney, creativity ne'er wanes;
Our team explodes when he jump starts our brains!"
   Ellen Guidera, VP, The Walt Disney Company

"America's Top New Product Idea Man."
   INC. Magazine

"Doug Hall has a method to his madness, a rigorous, quantifiable process for inventing breakthrough ideas for clients. Unlike many creative gurus hustling ideation wares in the corporate marketplace, Doug makes it imperative that his Eureka! Inventing processes are quantified every step of the way.
   CIO Magazine

"Hall has a habit of thinking big. His credentials are impeccable."
   Unlimited Magazine, **Scotland**

Other books by Doug Hall

Jump Start Your Brain with David Wecker (Warner Books, 1995). An energetic excursion into the world of innovation, ideas, and radical thinking. It's a motivational anthem for those looking to think quicker, smarter, and more creatively.

Maverick Mindset (hardcover version; Simon & Schuster, 1997) and Making the Courage Connection (paperback version; Fireside, 1998). Both with David Wecker. Inspirational stories and ideas for helping you find the courage to journey from fear to freedom.

Jump Start Your Business Brain (Brain Brew Books, 2001). Foreword by Tom Peters. The Eureka! Ranch principles and techniques for helping businesses of all sizes win more, lose less, and make more money. The methods are brought to life through a multitude of small business case studies. A Book Sense™ National Selection (independent booksellers).

Meaningful
Marketing

Doug Hall WITH Jeffrey Stamp Ph.D.

Brain Brew Books
Cincinnati, Ohio
www.BrainBrewBooks.com
an imprint of F&W Publications

Meaningful Marketing. Copyright © 2003 by Doug Hall. Printed and bound in the United States of America. All rights reserved. No part of this book may be reproduced in any form or by any electronic or mechanical means including information storage and retrieval systems without permission in writing of Doug Hall, except by a reviewer, who may quote brief passages in a review. Published by Brain Brew Books, an imprint of F&W Publications, Inc., 4700 East Galbraith Road, Cincinnati, Ohio, 45236. First edition.

07 06 05 04 03   5 4 3 2 1
Cataloging-in-Publication data is available from the Library of Congress at <http://catalog.loc.gov>.
ISBN: 1-55870-681-X

Editor: Jerry Jackson, Jr.
Cover Design: Chris Cliebe and Clare Finney
Interior Design: Andrea Short and Clare Finney
Production Coordinator: Sara Dumford

Special Thanks

Complete lists of the many people who have helped with the creation of this book are included in the back of the book. However, a few people deserve special thanks up front.

Thank you, *Kari McNamara*—president of the Eureka! Ranch. People ask, How do you ever find the time with your busy work schedule to write a book? Our answer is simple—Kari. With skill and wisdom she focuses the company and our schedules on what is most meaningful.

Thank you, *Rose Randolph*—the research wizard behind this book. Her endless energy, attention to detail, and boundless intelligence are the foundation of this book.

Thank you, *Richard E. Petty* and *John T. Cacioppo*. Their academic article "Central and Peripheral Routes to Persuasion" was the stimulus that led to the discovery and articulation of the differences between Meaningful and Mindless Marketing.

Thank you, *David Lewis*, publisher. In our ten years of book writing, never has a publisher so quickly grasped and supported a vision for a book concept like David did of this one.

Thank you, *Jack Heffron*, editor. If the reading is worthwhile, it's because of Jack. If it's not, it's because we were too stubborn to listen.

Most important of all—thank you to our wives, *Debbie* and *Annabelen*. This book would not exist without your endless faith and support.

Table of Contents

Part III: Mindless Marketing: Data-Proven Truths and Practical Ideas

Foreword

BY SERGIO ZYMAN

Why am I writing a preface to this book? I'm writing it because it dovetails perfectly with my books, *The End of Marketing As We Know It* and *The End of Advertising As We Know It*. *Meaningful Marketing* is a proven playbook for surviving in the current world and for growing your business in general.

In the place of mindless gimmicks and tricks it delivers rock-solid data, insightful truths, and market-altering ideas that will help you get to your business destination.

This book shows you how to quantitatively tilt the odds of success in your favor. The book also documents practical ideas for making a measurable difference in your sales and marketing results.

In a nutshell, the book teaches what I preach, "How to sell more stuff, to more people, more often, for more money, more efficiently." It also does something that I like to do over and over again which is to blow up the black box of marketing and to replace it with proven principles. It proves clearly that marketing can and should be considered a hard science, not an artistic mystery.

Doug Hall and Jeffrey Stamp have done the work for you. Like business anthropologists, they have sifted through mounds of academic research and real world marketplace data so you don't have to. They've dug deep to quantify what really matters—what really works in today's market place.

Meaningful Marketing directly challenges conventional marketing wisdom. It backs up its challenges with hard data. Huge chunks of the book are counter-intuitive. And at the end of the day, you might think that this is just a trick to get your attention, but it's not. The counter-intuitive insights are proven principles that you need to understand if you want to make a real difference for your business.

In today's world, it's time for a major renovation in how we market and sell every branded product and service. It's time to start fresh. It's time to lay the policies and principles of failure aside. It's time to embrace a more scientific, data-driven approach where we "play with the odds" instead of "praying for long shots."

Meaningful Marketing is a blueprint for how I see marketing in the future. It's the kind of marketing that made me successful. It's a back-to-basics marketing focused on what really matters. It's about connecting customers and consumers with meaningful brands, products and services in order to get them to give us their hard earned dollars, yen, pounds, pesos and euros in return.

The data mining, statistical analysis and insight that *Meaningful Marketing* delivers are impressive. But the monumental aspect of the book is how Hall and Stamp have translated the data-proven truths into practical ideas, the kind of actionable practical ideas that have made their Eureka! Ranch legendary in the corporate world.

Never in business history has there been a greater need for revolution in how we approach sales and marketing. I've been talking about it now for years and have practiced it for many more years when I worked for the Coca-Cola Company. Now is the time for a more disciplined, factual, and measured approach. The discipline starts with a fundamental focus on meaningfully serving the real needs of our customers and our consumers. The time for creative geniuses comes after that. You have to have a strategy and a destination before you can start applying creativity to those strategies and destinations.

Meaningful Marketing is a book that beyond any doubts confirms what I have long believed: Marketing-centered thinking is and should be the engine of growth for your entire company, not just for your brands. Marketing thinking is too important to keep hidden in the sales and marketing department. Marketing is the fundamental promise of your organization. It is the glue that guides the direction and inter-relationships between all departments from finance to manufacturing and every other silo that you have on your organizational chart.

When I wrote *The End of Marketing As We Know It*, people wrote me and said, "Oh, wow! Now I get it. I understand what marketing is and now I want to start practicing it in a more scientific way." The two-page format of *Meaningful Marketing* screams at you to take action—to get up, get out and do something to make a clear difference for your company; a measurable difference for your company. The time for excuses is over. The time for action is now and I'm sure that after reading *Meaningful Marketing* many people will write to Hall and Stamp as they wrote to me, and they'll say, "Now I get it and I'm going to get it done."

Sergio Zyman
CEO, Zyman Marketing
Former Chief Marketing Officer
The Coca-Cola Company

June 13, 2003

Introduction

The purpose of Meaningful Marketing is to show you how to sell more with less effort.

Through immense investment of energy, sheer stubbornness, and relentlessness you can "make a sale" of just about anything. The purpose of our research and this book is to help multiply the impact of every dollar you invest and every hour you spend on sales and marketing.

Unlike many business books, Meaningful Marketing is based on hard data. The use of quantitative data (from both our own and others' research) as the book's foundation is your assurance that what you learn is reliable and reproducible.

By the time you've finished Meaningful Marketing, you will be better equipped to sell your ideas, your brand, your services, your products, or even yourself when looking for a new or better job.

The Concept of Meaningful Marketing

Meaningful Marketing is about honestly communicating to customers exactly how your offering will make a genuine difference in their lives. Alternatively, Mindless Marketing is about using sales trickery, the brute force of massive advertising campaigns or endless price manipulations to persuade customers to purchase.

Both Meaningful and Mindless Marketing can be successful in the short term. The difference between the two lies in longer-term success rates and profitability. A study of 901 new products found that when an offering was sold with a thoughtful, Meaningful approach, it was successful—as defined by five-year-plus survival in the marketplace—some 53 percent of the time versus only 24 percent when a Mindless approach was used.

Even more significant, the data indicates that when customers make thoughtful purchases, they are more loyal and less demanding of pricing discounts. The research found that 18 percent of brands sold using a Meaningful message were vulnerable to pricing pressures versus 90 percent of those sold using a Mindless approach.

Research also indicates that on average, new products that leverage Meaningful Marketing realize year-one sales results that are over

50 percent higher than for new products sold without Meaningful differences.

In short, Meaningful Marketing enables you to sell more with less investment of your time and money.

Mindless Marketing requires that you sell your product at a lower price, spend more on promotion and advertising repetitions, and hope for a Pavlovian response from customers.

A Meaningful Step Toward Stopping the Madness!

Like the best of new products and services, this book was born out of our frustrations with the growing failure of sales and marketing efforts behind new business initiatives.

> **MADNESS:** Failure rates in the grocery products industry have grown from 46 percent in 1961 to 65 percent in 1977 to 80 percent today.

> **MADNESS:** An estimated 90 percent of venture-capital-funded initiatives fail.

> **MADNESS:** Advertising testing has found that 66 percent of television commercials are 100 percent ineffective at growing sales.

This book is intended as a small step toward helping to stop this madness. To paraphrase Sergio, from the Foreword, Meaningful Marketing is designed to be a replacement for the policies and principles of failure.

Hard Data Enhances Reliability

On these pages we challenge you to make a major change in the way you think about sales and marketing. And of course, change requires courage. Fear of the unknown can make us cling to existing methods, no matter how ineffective they may be. It's human nature to think in terms of "better the devil you know than the devil you don't."

To encourage you to change, we've provided a veritable feast of data-proven truths and practical ideas for putting Meaningful Marketing to work for you. These truths are statistically proven with hard data.

Statistical data, impartially analyzed, allows us to separate illusions from reality. With statistics, we can quantify the likelihood that what we're observing is a reproducible and reliable truth versus a coincidental one-time random event.

Casino gambling shows what can happen to our human decision-making abilities when random events become mixed up with long-term trends. When we win, we often draw cause-and-effect conclusions that lead us to false truths about the factors that put a few bucks in our pocket. In our excitement, we try to make it happen again—whether by using a certain slot machine, standing in a particular location at the roulette table, or wearing a certain pair of so-called lucky socks. But in chasing these false truths, we quickly lose what we've won and then some. The long-term, statistical edge of the casinos is reproducible. Our short-term hunch is not.

Sir Isaac Newton once said, "If I have seen further it is by standing on the shoulders of Giants." In the case of Meaningful Marketing this was literally true, as we used academic journals in the fields of sales, marketing, and psychology as the primary source of data for this book (eighty-four of the one hundred truths).

We reviewed over two thousand academic articles as potential sources for data-proven truths. In the end, we used 179 articles to support the findings in this book.

Every month brilliant breakthroughs are published in peer-reviewed academic journals. Sadly, except for a lucky few that cross over to the popular press, awareness of these research findings never reaches the front-line business people who could really use them to grow their businesses.

Our primary criteria in selecting research articles to reference were their practical application to front-line sales and marketing managers.

Secondarily we screened articles for what we called "elegance of design and data output." As this book is intended for a broad audience, we had a bias toward those studies that could be easily explained in laymen's terms.

There are usually multiple studies that confirm each truth. To keep the text clean, we've chosen to highlight the one or two that we believe are the most representative of the academic literature and also the most easily understood.

We've supplemented the academic articles with results of our own previously unpublished research efforts. Original research efforts included analysis of commercially available data, like the panel data collected by IRI (Information Resources, Inc.) on the purchasing behavior of some fifty thousand households on over nine thousand products.

Original research also involved analysis of proprietary data sets. One such study involved the factors that separate new products that survive long term (for five-plus years) from those that fail and are killed (discontinued by the manufacturer). This study involved 901 new products and is called the Darwin 900 in honor of the famous naturalist Charles Darwin's theory of evolution by natural selection—that is, survival of the fittest.

The data analyzed for this book includes quantitative research on consumer, industrial and business to business marketing.

Measurably Smarter Data Demographics

1,337	Advertisements
12,424	Brands
4,129	Business-to-Business Customers
3,846	Industrial Customers
294,732	Retail Consumers
3,057	Sales Representatives

One Step Further Than Even Statistical Significance

As scientists, we knew that hard data would be our starting point. However, we also recognize that it's possible to manipulate data so to support a preexisting opinion. To reduce this risk, each of us independently reviewed the data sources based on the more challenging legal standard of "truth beyond a reasonable doubt." Specifically, we used the www.lectlaw.com Web site definition of it:

> **BEYOND A REASONABLE DOUBT:** *The level of certainty a juror must have to find a defendant guilty of a crime. A real doubt, based upon reason and common sense after careful and impartial consideration of all the evidence, or lack of evidence, in a case.*

Proof beyond a reasonable doubt, therefore, is proof of such a convincing character that you would be willing to rely and act upon it without hesitation in the most important of your own affairs. However, it does not mean an absolute certainty.

We challenged each other and ourselves with a very personal version of the definition above: "Is this truth of such a convincing character that we would be willing to rely and act upon it without hesitation in the most important of our own affairs?"

Even with this standard a few debates occurred between us. Resolution of debates was easy. As both of our names are on the cover, we both had to feel confident in all truths. In effect, on these pages we've done the research and the debating so that you can read and apply the truths and ideas presented with confidence.

We realize that it's always possible that new data may contradict our findings. We look upon potential future contradictions with anticipation, not fear. We love to learn. We welcome the submission of additional data and/or arguments that contradict our findings.

Readers are urged to examine our data references for themselves. And if you feel we've erred, please contact us and make your case. If you persuade us, we'll make appropriate revisions and publicly recognize your contributions both at the www.DougHall.com Web site (immediately) and in future editions (when published).

No Statistical Knowledge Required

We've translated all statistical terms into common English. The result is that even if you suffered from allergic reactions to high school math, you will easily grasp all truths on these pages.

You Will Win More Than You Lose

As Ben Franklin once said, "In this world nothing can be said to be certain, except death and taxes."

The truths detailed on these pages are proven probabilities. They are not black and white certainties. They have been proven statistically and, to us, beyond a reasonable doubt. However, while they are widely applicable they are not universally applicable. There will be situations in which they are irrelevant, or just don't apply.

Then, too, even truths with high statistical odds are not certainties. For a weather forecast of 80 percent chance of rain to be statistically correct, it must not rain about 20 percent of the time, or one out of five times.

With any individual event there is a chance that a truth may not apply. However, with repeated application, statistical forecasts become reality. Thus, if you apply the truths as we've articulated them here, you will win more than you lose.

We understand that some will consider our use of the term 'truth' to be somewhat presumptuous. We purposely decided to call our learning's truths based on our faith in statistics and in the integrity of our research sources. We have also done it because we believe that given the outrageous levels of sales and marketing failure, it's time that academics and others committed to quantification of learning, take stronger, bolder stands.

Fast Reading and Easy Application

To insure that Meaningful Marketing is indeed meaningful to you, we've kept the discussion of philosophy short and focused on providing scientific truths and practical ideas that you can immediately put to work.

The left-hand page details the data-proven truth, its essence distilled into a single sentence at the top of the page. The balance of the page provides an overview of the supporting research.

The right-hand page details a multitude of practical ideas for applying the truth to your sales and marketing challenges. We've purposely provided an overabundance of suggestions to guarantee that you'll find ideas to help you no matter what your situation.

We recommend that you not search these pages for the one answer to your problems. Rather, approach your search like you would a stock portfolio. Identify and apply a collection of practical ideas for improving your personal and professional effectiveness.

To keep the reading clean and uncluttered, we've placed all academic data citations in the Technical Appendix in the back of the book.

Within the truths and ideas you will find overlap. This is done on purpose to reinforce concepts and ideas that we feel are particularly important for you act on.

Sales and Marketing in One Book

We think of sales and marketing as variations on the same task—the art of communicating to customers what exactly distinguishes your product or service from everything else.

Sadly, often these two disciplines have an adversary relationship, resulting in a lack of communication and lost opportunities. We feel that sales and marketing need to see themselves on the same team and must coordinate efforts if they are to be genuinely successful.

Selling is about sparking an exchange of goods or services for monetary value. It involves knocking on doors and making phone calls, pitches, and presentations.

Marketing is about mass selling. It's about providing the field staff with ammunition that enhances their effectiveness.

At their foundation, both sales and marketing are about communications. They're about communicating the story of the great product or service that your company's research, development, and production groups deliver.

The Five Parts of the Book

PART I: MEANINGFUL MARKETING VS. MINDLESS MARKETING

This relatively brief section explains the strategic and tactical differences between Meaningful Marketing and Mindless Marketing. It's designed to provide you with a fresh perspective on how to perceive and pursue sales and marketing.

PART II: MEANINGFUL MARKETING TRUTHS AND IDEAS

Meaningful Marketing is the most effective approach for generating significant and sustained business growth. Part II details 80 data-proven truths and 315 practical ideas for using Meaningful Marketing to improve your sales and marketing results.

PART III: MINDLESS MARKETING TRUTHS AND IDEAS

Mindless Marketing is effective at growing short-term volume. This section details 20 data-proven truths and 87 practical ideas for using Mindless Marketing to jump-start your business. Just understand that customers who come to you mindlessly also leave just as mindlessly.

PART IV: BONUS TRUTHS AND IDEAS

At the Eureka! Ranch we guarantee that our services will exceed customer expectations. So while the cover promises 100 data-proven truths, in fact the book contains 103. The bonus truths include Truth 0—found at the front of Part II, detailing an important warning for all readers—and Truths 101 and 102 at the end of the book, in Part IV, providing additional perspective on all that you've read.

PART V: TECHNICAL APPENDIX

For those with a passion for original research and a desire to discover patterns amongst the messy chaos of customer data, this section is heaven. Here as we have documented in detail the sources behind each truth.

Our Promises to You the Reader

On these pages you'll find data-proven truths and practical ideas that will help you realize measurably improved sales and marketing results.

Some of what you read might be familiar in your mind but not in your actions. We hope that once you've seen the familiar restated with clarity, and backed by hard data, you will be motivated to take tangible action.

Some of what you read may be new or may even contradict your existing beliefs. Pay particular attention to these pages. The act of going against established beliefs can lead to great growth. Picasso said, "Every act of creation is first an act of destruction." So, too, your first step toward real growth may require you to abandon certain assumptions, beliefs, and habits.

The primary mission of this book is to help you. As you realize success, so will your company. In our experience, virtually all Meaningful change is driven by front-line people first.

In closing, the truths and ideas on these pages are designed to move you from chasing long shots to focusing your energy on measurably smarter methods. The bottom-line result will be a Meaningful improvement in your sales and marketing effectiveness.

Doug Hall
Jeffrey Stamp, Ph.D.
Cincinnati, Ohio USA
April 30, 2003

MEANINGFUL MARKETING
vs.
MINDLESS MARKETING

Meaningful Marketing vs. Mindless Marketing

Meaningful Marketing is about honesty.

Meaningful Marketing is about respecting your customers' intelligence.

Meaningful Marketing is about having the courage to focus your energies and resources on developing offerings that make a meaningful difference in your customers' lives. And because you are looking to make money, it also means having the courage to offer a product or service that is meaningfully different from what your competition offers.

Meaningful Marketing's focus is on the acquisition of new customers. This is because the acquisition of new customers has been found to be the key driver of long-term growth.

Mindless Marketing is the alternative to Meaningful Marketing. Mindless Marketing is about using sales and marketing tricks as opposed to the actual merits and virtues of your offering to make the sale.

Mindless Marketing is often easier to execute, as it involves changes to only your sales and marketing tactics. Meaningful Marketing is harder to execute, as it requires the support of your R&D, manufacturing, and operations departments in the design, development, and delivery of a product or service that provides a Meaningful difference versus competition.

Mindless Marketing is mass hypnotism. It is about getting customers to take the path of least resistance. It's also about coaxing entranced customers to follow your spell and do as you say. When under a trance, customers do the unthinkable—so long as the trance is not broken.

For example, when a teenager buys a bizarre piece of clothing because it's trendy, it's best that he not think about how it will look in his photo album years from now.

When parents pay too much for a hot Christmas toy, it's best that they not think about it rationally.

When you're buying a cool new car model—and paying above sticker price—it's best that you not make a rational evaluation of what the price does to your resale value.

When we blindly follow the latest business fad—without thorough evaluation of its relevance—we, too, are acting mindlessly.

With Mindless Marketing, customers are encouraged not to think.

They are encouraged to simply follow the persuasive marketing path laid before them like pigs to a slaughterhouse—following only the tail of the pig in the lead, never looking up and asking if the herd they follow is going to a place where they really want to go.

Meaningful Marketing is about having an adult conversation. It's about a dialogue between you and your customers regarding what they will receive, enjoy, and experience as a result of committing their hard-earned money.

Meaningful Marketing is about telling the story of your genuine patentable breakthroughs. Mindless Marketing is about exaggerating the performance of mediocre products or services.

Meaningful Marketing is a conscious choice. Mindless Marketing is impulse purchasing.

Meaningful Marketing is about fulfilling customers' needs. Mindless Marketing is about persuasion.

Meaningful Marketing leverages value. Mindless Marketing primarily focuses on price.

Meaningful Marketing leads to customers who become your biggest cheerleaders. Mindless Marketing purchases can lead to buyer's remorse.

The Third Option: Meaningless Marketing

Meaningful and Mindless define the two successful ends of the marketing spectrum. Below these two is a state called Meaningless Marketing. Meaningless lacks the substance of Meaningful Marketing or the clever trickery of Mindless Marketing.

Sadly, in many categories Meaningless Marketing is the primary form of marketing. Meaningless Marketing ideas hang in limbo with little power to genuinely attract or to persuasively spark your customer's attention.

In brief, Meaningful Marketing creates and nurtures long-term success. Mindless Marketing can be effective in the short term. Meaningless Marketing has virtually no chance of success.

Today's Customers Are Short on Bandwidth

The driving force for both Meaningful and Mindless Marketing is the overwhelming number of options today's customers have.

Today's customers are mentally overwhelmed. The average supermarket has over forty thousand different items in it.

The total of all printed knowledge is estimated to double every five years.

In 1993 the New York Times estimated that humanity publishes as many words each week as it did in all of human history up to 1800.

Three times as many magazines exist today compared to twenty years ago (fifty-five hundred consumer titles alone).

Over 120,000 new books are published every year!

A report by the 3M Company indicated the average adult is exposed to some three thousand advertisements a day!

The American Academy of Pediatrics estimates that children take in over twenty thousand television commercials a year.

With increasing numbers comes massive fragmentation. According to Nielsen Media Research, the number one network television show is viewed by ever-shrinking audiences. In the 1950s, the top show reached 62 percent of the adult population; in the 1970s, 31 percent; in the 1990s, 21 percent.

The prestigious McKinsey & Company consulting firm reported recently, "There has been an explosion in consumer touch points fueled by the Internet and other technology-driven channels like call centers, ATMs, WebTV, and kiosks. This has created an array of options for building brand presence. At the same time, marketing space everywhere has experienced increased clutter, narrowed audiences, and escalating costs."

Potential customers have limited capacity to perceive and process your message. They have only so many channels of mental bandwidth. It's estimated that customers use only 2 percent of the available information that presents itself each day.

When your customers' craniums are occupied with real-life deadlines and stresses, your message can all too easily fail to get honest consideration. Customers ignore Meaningless Marketing messages and focus their attention on either substance-rich Meaningful messages or the path of least resistance offered by Mindless messages such as low price.

Trends Driving the Importance of Meaningfulness

Three mega trends—increasing education, population aging, and growing free market access—make it urgent that you move your marketing from Mindless to Meaningful.

INCREASING EDUCATION: In 1960 barely four in ten Americans age twenty-five or older had graduated from high school. Today eight out of ten have high school diplomas. In 1960 less than one in ten Americans had graduated from college; today nearly three out of ten have.

With increasing education comes the ability and the desire to know more and to make more Meaningful purchasing decisions.

POPULATION AGING: Between 1960 and 2000, the number of adults age sixty-five and over has doubled from eighteen million to thirty-seven million. And it's expected to double again by the year 2040.

With increasing age comes greater experience in separating factual marketing messages from Mindless hype.

In the 1950s and 1960s, when television advertising was new, you could tell the youthful, uneducated American population to "buy this" and they would.

Today, an older, wiser population is more discerning. They want to know precisely how your offering will make a Meaningful difference in their lives.

GROWING FREE MARKET ACCESS: The last mega trend multiplying the importance of Meaningfulness is the true free market knowledge network created by the World Wide Web. The Web makes it easy for everyone to research, compare, and contrast purchase options. And when customers have greater access to information, they make more Meaningful purchasing decisions.

In the past, an advertiser could use Mindless Marketing tricks to generate significant sales before he was found out. Today, the Internet has improved customers' ability to quickly uncover the truth behind marketing hype and gimmicks.

Today, people routinely search the Internet when they consider a major purchase like a new car. In the future, as advanced computer intelligence systems become available, computerized "alter egos" will be programmed to think through and make many Meaningful purchasing decisions that we don't have time for.

A similar explosion in free market access occurred from 1870 to 1910 as 5.1 million phones were installed, the railroads developed into an efficient national network, and the concepts of "brands" and national advertising were born. In just four years, from 1871 to 1875, the number of brands with registered trademarks grew nearly tenfold from 121 to 1,138.

The net effect of this growth in free market access and the concurrent industrial revolution was a nearly 30 percent decrease in the consumer price index. As customers had more access to knowledge, manufacturers' prices went down.

Today, brands that don't offer a Meaningful difference are facing similar pressure on both their pricing and bottom-line profits.

Together, increased education, population aging, and growing free market access mean good news for manufacturers of products or services that make a Meaningful difference for customers. The same factors are bad news for those seeking to live on Mindless trickery and gimmicks.

The business world is becoming aware of the size of the shift that is occurring. Sadly, recent business books have been focused primarily on finding methods for more effectively "tricking" customers into purchasing. Business people are encouraged to build "buzz" by such methods as paying college students to order and "talk up" the virtues of various brands of alcohol. Marketers are being encouraged to trick customers into giving them "permission" to propagandize them—a modern version of the age-old "foot in the door" persuasion technique.

Mindless Marketing tricks can succeed for a short time. However, that period of time is getting shorter as knowledge access grows. The real return on investment with Mindless Marketing tricks is shrinking rapidly.

The Search for Mindless Marketing Tricks Is Endless

The search for new Mindless Marketing techniques is never ending. It's driven by the fundamental human desire to find a shortcut to success.

It's also driven by a lack of faith in a brand's fundamental value, quality, and virtues. In our experience, we've found a near one-to-one relationship between managers' faith in their brand and their pursuit of Meaningful Marketing communications.

A rich source of Mindless Marketing gimmicks is new advertising vehicles. The theory is that where you place your advertisement is more important than what you communicate. Common sense and academic research find this concept flawed. Direct mail, print advertising, and television advertising tests have repeatedly shown that what you say is more important than where you say it.

The search for Mindless Marketing tricks is nothing new. In 1983 advertising legend David Ogilvy wrote in *Ogilvy on Advertising* of the never-ending desire of the media and the advertising community to find the latest "hot marketing trend."

> *There have always been noisy lunatics on the fringes of the advertising business. Their stock-in-trade includes ethnic humor, eccentric art direction, contempt for research, and their self-proclaimed genius. They are seldom found out, because they gravitate to the kind of clients who, bamboozled by their rhetoric, do not hold them responsible for sales results. Their campaigns find favor at cocktail parties. . . . In the days when I specialized in posh campaigns for The New Yorker, I was the hero of this coterie, but when I graduated to advertising in mass media and wrote a book which extolled the value of research, I became its devil. I comfort myself with the reflection that I have sold more merchandise than all of them put together.*

Your choice is clear: You can be a "hip and cool" marketer, or you can pursue marketing as our friend Sergio Zyman, former chief marketing officer of the Coca-Cola Company defines it: "Selling more, to more people, for more money, more efficently."

The Evolution From Meaningful to Mindless

Virtually all businesses start out with a product or service concept that provides a Meaningful difference for customers. This difference is the basis for the creation of the new business venture.

If the difference in the product or service is sufficiently Meaningful and it is marketed with sufficient investment of time, energy, and money, the company thrives.

In a free market, as a company grows, it soon attracts opportunistic competitors with neither the imagination nor the courage to create a meaningfully different offering of their own.

The clones attempt to replicate the wonder of the original at lower prices. As they succeed, what started out as a Meaningful Market quickly degenerates into a game of Mindless price maneuvering.

We're advocates for competition. However, we'd like that competition to be customer focused, and that means thinking deeply about discovering and developing ideas that make a Meaningful difference for customers.

Innovation clones can be beat through a continuous commitment to innovation. As your competition works their way through the technical, production, distribution, marketing, and patent challenges associated with your current innovation, you bravely invent even more Meaningful products and services.

It's a simple matter of grow or die. If your offering today is virtually the same as it was twelve months or twelve years ago, your enterprise is dying. One day you will look up and discover the world has changed.

If your marketplace is competitive, you will see the change in your bottom line. Clones will eventually turn your Meaningful difference into a commodity, vanishing your profits.

If you have a virtual monopoly on your marketplace, it will happen much slower but it will be just as devastating. One day you will find that your monopoly in the world of buggy whips or stagecoaches has been made irrelevant by the train or automobile.

To survive and thrive in the world of business requires a continuous commitment to discovering new ideas that can make a Meaningful difference in our customers' lives.

Meaningful Loyalty

With Meaningful Marketing, customers consciously decide to purchase your offering. If their level of satisfaction with your actual product or service is equal to or exceeds their expectations, they develop trust.

With repeated satisfaction, further trust develops—until the customer arrives at a point of Meaningful loyalty. The customer has consciously made your offering her choice. She has meaningfully decided to forego future thinking and, from then on, as long as she's satisfied, continues to purchase your offering.

We often order a Coca-Cola, a Budweiser, ranch dressing on our salad, or cheesecake for dessert because we've made a Meaningful decision that they are our preferred choice.

We often stay at specific hotel chains, rent cars from a certain company, and fly specific airlines not by conscious choice; rather, we've made a Meaningful decision to commit our purchases to specific brands to grow our frequent-traveler accounts.

In the U.S.A., we often visit megasize stores like Wal-Mart and Home Depot because, through repeated experiences, we've proved to ourselves that "they're cheap" and/or "they'll have everything I'm looking for."

One research study found that nearly 80 percent of consumer purchases of laundry detergent were based on a Meaningful loyalty decision process. In-store observations revealed that customers picked up and examined only one product option and spent only thirteen seconds from when they entered the laundry detergent aisle to when they made a purchase.

On one hand, meaningfully loyal customers are a major advantage for incumbents who enjoy it. It's an annuity, which, as long as your quality is maintained and competition doesn't create a more Meaningful offering, pays dividends day after day, year after year.

On the other hand, meaningfully loyal customers are a major barrier to growth for new companies, products, or services.

Achieving Meaningful Loyalty

How easy it is to achieve meaningfully loyal customer relationships varies depending on your category and marketplace competitive set.

When customers have made numerous purchases and been satisfied with results, they will develop Meaningful loyalty.

When the risk of making the wrong choice is not large—and pricing differences are minimal—customers will often commit to Meaningful loyalty, based on historical brand choices, without thinking further.

When customers believe your category of goods and services is stable and unchanging, they will allocate less of their mental processing ability to making decisions and will repeat-purchase with Meaningful loyalty. Academic research has found that consumers exerted considerably less effort in choosing peanut butter than in choosing a pair of running shoes or an automobile.

When the risk of disappointment has a high cost, the consumer is making a decision for the first time in your category, or your industry is undergoing considerable change, then customers are less likely to give up their right to think. They are more likely to make purchases on a Meaningful basis.

Stealing Your Competition's Meaningfully Loyal Customers

Meaningful loyalty is similar to Mindless buying in that customers are on autopilot. The difference between the two is their level of conscious choice.

To steal your competitor's meaningfully loyal customers, you have to think big. You have to offer a big and bold, Meaningful benefit difference.

Starbucks broke the hypnotic trance that Folgers and Maxwell House coffee enjoyed, by delivering a superior total coffeehouse experience. Starbucks has thrived by changing the rules of coffee consumption.

Samuel Adams from the Boston Beer Company broke the trance that Budweiser, Miller, and Coors had, by delivering a lager with richer taste and greater hops content. Today, they've transformed an industry and continue to lead the craft brewing segment of the market.

Southwest Airlines broke the trance of the larger airlines through a spirited delivery of greater value. They even created a meaningfully different frequent-flyer program. Instead of making customers collect and redeem miles, Southwest keeps their Rapid Rewards program customer-focused and simple.

> *Rapid Rewards is the frequent flyer program you can use. Rapid Rewards is the only major frequent flyer program that doesn't limit the number of seats available for Award Ticket use. If a seat is available on the flight you want to take, it's yours!*

Fly just 8 roundtrips, and you receive a free ticket! Rapid Rewards counts credits, not long miles. If you take just eight (8) roundtrips (or receive 16 credits) within 12 consecutive months [you] receive a free Award Ticket on Southwest Airlines, no matter how far you fly or what fare you pay.

Meaningful Marketing Drives Your Sense of Mission

The purpose of most business enterprises is to realize profits for shareholders through the sale of a product or service that fulfills a need.

Thus, the Meaningful difference that is your primary marketing message is also the mission of your company. It's your reason for existence. It follows, then, that:

Gaining awareness of your Meaningful difference is the purpose of your advertising, public relations, sales, and marketing departments.

Production and delivery of your brand's Meaningful difference is the purpose of your product supply operation.

Protecting your brand's Meaningful difference from illegal copying by competitors is the purpose of your legal department.

Identifying new dimensions of your Meaningful difference is the purpose of your brand's research and development department.

Research finds that when new products are meaningfully matched to customers' needs, a chain reaction of synergies occurs from higher profit margins, to greater cross-department synergy, to faster development and delivery to the marketplace.

Srully Blotnick documented the opportunity for significant personal profits from the pursuit of meaningfulness. He studied the careers of 1,500 business school graduates from 1960 to 1980. At graduation, 1,245 of the students were categorized as being focused on making money, while 255 of the graduates were focused on pursuing something that was personally Meaningful to them. Twenty years later, there were 101 millionaires. One came from the first group, 100 from the second.

Mindless Marketing Tactics Work

Mindless Marketing is effective in the short term. It's also effective when you catch on to a customer fad. The fashion industry and television networks leverage fad chasing as their primary sales strategy. The challenge is to know when to stop. Fads tend to be replaced by other fads, and when they do, the decline in sales is often faster than the growth you realized. This phenomenon is readily observable in the discount bins of stores where stacks of yesterday's fads are sold for twenty cents on the dollar.

When you have an older, established brand with larger numbers of existing customers, Mindless marketing can be an effective way of exploiting that equity for profits. It can be effective until your competition learns and applies Meaningful Marketing to break your customers out of their Mindless trances.

Mindless Marketing can also be effective when you have a virtual monopoly. With a monopoly, customers mindlessly purchase the only option available. We use Microsoft Office—not because it's great; it's not nearly as fast or as reliable for book writing as the now dead Write Now program we used to use. We use Microsoft Office because it has a virtual monopoly on the business marketplace. But history tells us that, from the Roman Empire to the railroads to even the big three automobile producers, monopolies eventually crumble as new and more Meaningful solutions are invented.

There is no shortage of research validating the power of Mindless Marketing tricks to effectively manipulate customer behavior in the short term.

Mindless Marketing uses manipulative tricks—peer pressure, artificial scarcity, and psychological games that go by such names as foot in the door and door in the face—to generate customer purchasing, regardless of the product's or service's merits.

The theory is that you can use Mindless Marketing to "get a date" with a prospective customer, and then because of your "wow!" product or service, they will become committed to you.

Frankly, if you have a "wow!" offering, why not use that to make a Meaningful connection with potential customers? The transition from Mindless tricks to Meaningful authenticity is fraught with danger. If your customers realize they've been manipulated, the backlash can be painful and costly.

The Mindless Marketing Drug Addiction

The most popular method of creating sales from Mindless Marketing is through price promotions. Academic research and real-world experience shows that selling at a lower price than competition generates sales.

A large price differential can be quite successful in breaking the trance of customers who are mindlessly purchasing competitive products.

The challenge is that research also indicates that many customers who make a Mindless switch based on price stop purchasing when the price goes up.

A research study of major brands found that promotional events— price reductions, coupons, etc.—generated enough incremental profits to cover costs only 16 percent of the time.

Mindless Marketing through price promotions is like a drug addiction. It's difficult to stop, and when you do it's painful.

In a bold move in the 1990s the Procter & Gamble Company went to an everyday low pricing strategy and virtually eliminated temporary price reductions and coupons. The net effect was an effective increase in net price and an average 18 percent loss of market share across the twenty-four categories studied during a seven-year period.

Most grocery store packaged goods do not offer a Meaningful difference versus competition. Customers realize this. That's why, when the price of an item goes up and a less expensive alternative is available, a significant number of customers switch. In the case of Procter & Gamble, scanner data indicates this equaled 17 percent of their customers.

Interestingly, not all customers left at once. In the case of Procter & Gamble the vast majority of customers kept purchasing their brands—despite the effective price increase. These are the loyal customers that have been created over the years as a result of the Meaningful differences that the brands have historically provided.

Encouragingly, the decline that Procter & Gamble experienced was temporary. Their enhanced focus on Meaningful Marketing, through elimination of discounting, a new commitment to product excellence and Meaningful advertising led to outstanding sales and profit growth by the year 2003.

It's even possible to use massive advertising awareness levels to create temporary Mindless Marketing success. Massive investments of advertising can spark impulse purchasing for a period of time. But the effect is temporary. A study of fifty-five successful advertising campaigns found that when media spending in support of the commercials stopped, the incremental sales also stopped. In the year after advertising was stopped, 31 percent of the sales gained from the advertising was lost. In the second year 59 percent of the gain was lost.

And remember—this is for the successful commercials. As mentioned earlier, studies indicate two-thirds of all commercials generate no significant growth in sales at all. Net: Sustainable success through outspending, outshouting, and outpromoting your competition is a clear long shot.

By making your offering and your marketing message more Meaningful, a more genuine customer connection is established. You dramatically increase your ability to realize a sustainable return on your investment.

The Meaningful Marketing Ideal Development Cycle

In an ideal world, your offering will continuously offer a Meaningful difference versus competition. That's nice, but in the real world, customers, technologies, and markets are dynamic and, by design, changing. The reality is that you'll experience a never-ending succession of peaks and valleys in the normal cycle of innovation and competitive introductions.

In the peak times, you will have superiority. In the valleys, you will have parity or, worse yet, a deficit versus competition.

If you deliver a reliable pattern of Meaningful differences, most of your customers will remain loyal to you during the valley periods.

David Ogilvy neatly summed up the secret to new product success:

> *Most new products fail because they are not new enough. They do not offer any perceptible point of difference—like better quality, better flavor, better value, more convenience or better solutions to problems.*

Practical and Proven Wisdom To Help You Know More

While some managers are addicted to pursuing Mindless Marketing tricks, we're optimistic that within every corporation there are independent thinkers with a passion for doing work that matters.

When he appeared as a guest on our Brain Brew radio program, Drayton Bird, former vice chairman of the Ogilvy & Mather Direct Agency, defined the purpose of business learning this way:

> *Essentially what you want to do in business is to be able to go in every morning and say today I can do better than I did yesterday. And the only way you are going to do that is if you know more. And the only way you are going to know more is if somebody tells you more.*

Similarly, the pages ahead are designed to help you know more about how to design and execute Meaningful marketing and sales efforts that make a measurable difference for you, your organization and, most importantly, your customers.

MEANINGFUL MARKETING
Data-Proven Truths &
Practical Ideas

Three Methods For Using This Book's Wisdom

The format and content of this book was the result of feedback from hundreds of readers of early drafts. The depth and breadth of the book was driven by readers' requests for a comprehensive handbook on the science of sales and marketing. However, as the book's content grew, there was a desire for a "user's manual" of step-by-step methods for applying its wisdom. In response to our customer's requests, the following three methods are included to do just that:

METHOD #1: MEANINGFUL MARKETING QUICK START

If you're looking for a quick jolt to your sales and marketing results, focus your attention on Truths 1 to 10.

METHOD #2: "JUMP-STARTING" STAFF MEETINGS

This method was simultaneously discovered by a number of the book's early readers. When they had a sales or marketing meeting, they asked for a random number from one to one hundred. They then turned to that truth, paraphrased the truth and ideas, and then used that as a ten to twenty-minute "jolt" to their staff's thinking.

METHOD #3: THIRTEEN VIRTUES OF MEANINGFUL MARKETING

The third method is a longer term approach. It was inspired by a program Ben Franklin developed for personal improvement. Franklin distilled all he knew about life into thirteen core virtues. So too, we've synthesized the wisdom on these pages into what we believe are the Thirteen Virtues of Meaningful Marketing. We recommend that, as Franklin suggested, you focus your attention on one virtue each week—seeking to live it to its fullest (we've provided references to three key truths that support each virtue). Within a year, you will have completed four cycles and Meaningfully changed your approach to sales and marketing.

1. *Learn:* Every week become quantifiably smarter regarding your customers and your vocational craft. Truths 0, 27, 44.

2. *Pioneer:* Lead your marketplace and leave copying to those without the brains or courage to be original. Truths 1, 72, 76.

3. *Overtness:* Let a customer say no because what you offer doesn't apply to them. But never let a customer say no because they don't understand what overt benefit you're offering them. Truths 2, 35, 75.

4. *Clarity:* Strive for self-evident clarity in all communications. Truths 3, 7, 63.

5. *Focus:* Eliminate the irrelevant. Truths 6, 30, 67.

6. *Credibility:* Continuously enhance customer trust in you, your company and your brand. Truths 17, 18, 38.

7. *Authenticity:* Communicate with honestly and integrity. Truths 24, 79, 80.

8. *Demonstrate:* Let your product, service or idea talk for itself. Truths 10, 19, 28.

9. *Persistence:* Never, ever, ever give up when you are pursuing the right thing in the right way. Truths 8, 41 66.

10. *Measurement:* Quantify goals and systems. Truths 46, 59, 69.

11. *Service:* Dedicate yourself to serving the genuine needs of your customers. Truths 11, 32, 64.

12. *Write:* Use the written word to define and refine your thinking. Truths 1 to 100 show the power of putting facts and ideas on paper.

13. *Courage:* Be bold. Be brave. Leave a legacy. Truths 60, 61, 102.

The More You Know, the Less You'll Grow

The more advanced your prior knowledge of sales and marketing, the lower your chances of significant learning from this book.

Adult learning of new ideas is highly dependent on our level of motivation and our prior knowledge. Research has found that the more we think we know about something, the less likely we are to learn when someone tries to teach us.

This finding comes from three studies of the impact of prior knowledge on learning. In each study, adults were shown information on various new product concepts and then tested on what they had just been told. The research found that consumers with the least prior knowledge of the category gave the most accurate answers. Consumers with greater prior knowledge assumed that they already knew about the product category and thus didn't need to focus or concentrate on learning the information presented.

The same holds true for this book. Those who feel they know the least about sales and marketing are the most likely to read this book closely and to seek methods for direct application in their world.

Those who feel that they already understand sales and marketing are less likely to open their minds to learning. Instead of seeking ways to apply the truths, they will skim the material and process the learning in a shallow fashion. They debate and disprove truths that don't align with their beliefs or established ways of doing things.

As this truth indicates, you have a choice. You can humbly open your mind to new learning, or you can pat yourself on the back for your personal intelligence and endlessly repeat your cycles of success and failure. The choice is yours.

PRACTICAL IDEAS

A. Focus on Similarities, Not Differences

Everyone's company, industry, location is different. However, the dynamics of customer purchasing follow identical patterns. Customers give you money in exchange for your offering. The details differ but the strategic evaluation process is nearly identical. Instead of focusing on differences, focus on how you can test and apply the book's learnings to generate immediate returns.

B. Read With a Pen or Highlighter

As you read, highlight every idea, concept, or phrase that sparks a thought in your cranium. Read with the pen cap off. The physical act of highlighting will force you to think deeper about what you're reading. Each time you sit and read this book, challenge yourself to keep reading until you've found three concepts that resonate with you and your situation. And contrary to what your teachers used to tell you, feel free to write in this book.

C. Challenge Your Team to Think What If?

Have your business team or key advisors read the book as well. Once a week, gather to discuss three of the data-proven truths. Spend thirty minutes brainstorming ideas for applying one or more of the truths to your situation. Beware—some of the truths will be easier to apply than others. However, the most challenging ones may contain ideas that could make the biggest difference for you.

D. Dig Deeper

To help you think deeper about the data-proven truth, get copies of the actual research studies we describe. All references are listed in the back of the book. Your public library or corporation will probably have an online research tool that allows you to easily access most of the studies.

Be the First With Your Meaningful Difference

Being first to market nearly doubles your sales versus being the fourth to market.

Meaningful Marketing is about making a real difference. To break customers out of their hypnotic trance, you must offer something that is meaningfully different. Customers view change as risky. When you offer a Meaningful difference, they are much more likely to take a risk. Before they can assess meaningfulness, you must first be different—a pioneer, an explorer, a dreamer, the first at what you promise.

Research on the impact of order of entry for new brands quantifies the advantage of being first versus being a follower. On average, brands that are second to market generate 71 percent of the sales of the pioneer. Those that are third to market generate 58 percent and those that are fourth some 51 percent of the sales of the brand that is first to market.

By definition, the first to market is news. When you have news, then you have information to communicate, and as the first, you command a customer's conscious attention.

When you have a copycat offering, you are more likely to have to resort to low prices and other Mindless gimmicks to get customers' attention.

With "real news," the effectiveness of all your sales and marketing efforts is multiplied. A study found that advertising for new products—which by their nature offer greater news—was five times more effective at growing sales than advertising for more familiar or less novel established brands.

PRACTICAL IDEAS

1. Define Yourself From the Point of View of First

Look within your offering and find something that you are the first to offer. Ideally, this is a simple and dramatic statement—the first computer repair service that does house calls, the first beer with zero calories (we can dream, can't we?). Don't be surprised if you don't have something simple to claim. Most products and services don't. Don't despair, as you have other options.

2. Define First Versus a Limited Category

Define what you're the "first at" based on a limited subset. For example, we're the "first in our town to offer in-home repair of consumer computers." Or we're the "first in our industry to offer 24/7 customer service."

3. Define First as a Combination

Define what you're the "first at" based on a unique combination. For example, we're the "first to offer French cuisine dining in thirty minutes." Or we're the "first industrial lubricant company to offer twenty-four-hour delivery and credits for recycled oils."

4. Repeatedly Articulate What Makes You the First

Articulate your point of difference everywhere—at the start of every sales presentation, on every advertisement, on every brochure, on your voice mail message, on your business cards, on your letterhead, on every T-shirt, mouse pad, and coffee cup that you print.

5. Meaningful Difference Impacts Development Success

The lack of a Meaningful difference is a common reason why many managers have a hard time generating momentum on "small" ideas within their organizations. When you seek the support of fellow employees on an idea that is not meaningfully different, you are in effect asking them to make an operational change or disruption for no good reason.

Be Obvious About Your Overt Benefit

Being obvious about what overt benefit your customers will receive, enjoy, and experience increases your success rate by 75 percent.

Customers have little time to compare, contrast, and consider your product or service offering. The never-ending flood of voice mail, E-mail, and junk mail has caused customers to develop a protective barrier against your marketing message. To break through the barrier, you need to be direct and obvious about the customer benefit you offer.

Analysis of over 901 new products found that those with a benefit message that was overt and obvious were 75 percent more likely to succeed in the marketplace than those whose message was broad and indirect.

The more work required of your customers to translate your message into how it affects them and their lives, the less likely they are to notice, consider, and purchase what you have to offer.

Don't promise that your dog food has patented dental crystals. Be obvious: Say that your patented dog food guarantees fresh breath for twelve hours after your dog eats it.

Don't promise that your industrial lubricant is technically advanced. Be obvious: Say that your advanced lubricant reduces breakdowns even in seven-hundred-degree extreme heat.

Don't promise that your running shoe features rebound technology in the sole. Be obvious: Say that the rebound sole in your footwear reduces fatigue by 50 percent, meaning you can walk and run longer without getting tired.

Let a customer say "no" because they're not interested in what you offer. But never let a customer say "no" because they don't understand what you offer.

PRACTICAL IDEAS

6. Transform Features Into Benefits

Features are not benefits. Features are the facts, the technology, the "stuff" that makes up your offering. Benefits are what customers will receive, enjoy, and experience as a result of their purchase. It requires work on the customers' part to translate your features into what benefits they will receive. To improve marketing effectiveness, take the work out. Review all your marketing messages and ask, "Why should customers care?" Transform every feature statement into an overt benefit promise.

7. Use Your Voice Mail Messages as a Test Market

Articulate "what's in it for the customer" in an obvious fashion, and then script the voice mail messages you leave for customers. State clearly, "I'm calling about a new _____ we have that can help you (save 30 percent, increase quality by 20 percent, improve your direct mail response rates by 40 percent, create the most romantic Valentine's dinner)."

Make twenty-five calls and measure the number of callbacks. Then script another message and try again. When you get the right benefit and state it in an obvious fashion, you'll know it, because response rates will increase by 50 to 100 percent.

8. Model Your Message Based on the Great Masters

Direct response marketers (print, direct mail, infomercials) leverage overt and obvious benefit communication to drive response rates. To learn from these masters, gather a collection of great junk mail and/or set your VCR to record infomercials. Take a morning to tell your sales and marketing story in the format that the direct mail pieces or infomercials use. When a benefit claim is made, make a claim; when a testimonial is given, give yours. At the Eureka! Ranch, this technique has become a staple in our marketing invention tool kit.

DATA PROVEN TRUTH #3

Be Specific About Your Meaningful Uniqueness

Sales messages that are specific about your point of Meaningful difference have a 52 percent greater success rate.

Customers are creatures of habit. Breaking their buying habits requires you to overtly, specifically, and directly articulate the benefit of your offering.

To get customers to listen, you must give them a dramatic reason. A study of over 901 marketing messages for new products found that when the sales messages specifically stated the product's point of difference, those brands were 52 percent more likely to survive for five years or more than those that were less overt.

Customers are overwhelmed. It's estimated that they have over a million different purchasing options or SKUs (stock-keeping units) to choose from. The average large grocery store carries some five thousand SKUs. Contrast this with the fact that the average family buys 80 to 85 percent of their needs from just 150 SKUs. Customers simply don't have the time to seriously study every marketing message for every new product or service.

To cope with the marketing bombardment they face, customers have learned how to rapidly sort and categorize marketing messages as Meaningful or Mindless. Through thousands of purchase and usage experiences, they've learned how to identify the difference between a Mindless claim of "unsurpassed performance" and a specifically Meaningful one—"cuts your time in half."

Large corporations have trouble being specific about what they offer because of their highly conservative legal departments. Small businesses have trouble being specific because of their natural tendency to be humble rather than boastful. In both cases, the answer is not to overhype. Rather, it's to tell the genuine truth about what the customer will receive.

PRACTICAL IDEAS

9. Quantify Your Uniqueness

Factually and measurably determine what your advantage is over the competition. Is your product 50 percent more durable? Can it be installed in 30 percent less time? Do you have a customer service response time that is twice as fast? Is your service system three times more reliable?

If you can't quantify your advantage, then don't complain when customers go to a lower-cost competitor. Lower cost is a benefit that is specific and numeric. The only way to confront a specific price disadvantage is to offer your customers a specific and measurable value advantage.

10. Describe Your Offering With a Mind-Opening Thought

Find your point of drama and articulate it with clarity. Open your customers' minds by bluntly and boldly articulating how your product will transform their lives. What is your true point of drama? Seek ways to help customers see it more clearly.

11. Think Like a Member of the Media

What would be the headline to an article written about you and your company? What would be the "tease" on TV or radio? "Up next we have _____ with a remarkable new _____ that allows you to _____."

12. Speak of Your Uniqueness From the Viewpoint of New and Existing Customers

Use the words your existing customers use to speak about your advantages. Existing customers of your product or service have integrity and an honesty of perspective. Ask both long-established and new customers what makes you different. Ask them to quantify the difference. Ask them to compare and contrast their experiences before and after purchasing your brand.

DATA PROVEN TRUTH #4

To Sell a Lot, You Need a Lot of Customers

For mega growth the number of customers you have is almost three times more important than the amount you sell to each customer.

A common debate when attempting to grow sales is: Should the primary emphasis be on increasing the number of customers or on increasing sales volume with existing customers?

Common wisdom is that it's easier to build sales through increasing loyalty than it is by cultivating new customers. For small growth—1 to 20 percent—this might be true. But for mega growth—25 to 400 percent—the common wisdom is flawed.

This truth is based on analysis of 9,804 brands scanned by UPC (universal product code) numbers in grocery, mass merchant, and drug stores. A statistical model was created to explain total annual sales relative to the number of customers the brand had and dollars spent per customer over the year. Analysis found that the number of customers was 2.8 times more important in explaining big brand success than loyalty was.

As a secondary check, the nine-thousand-plus brands were divided into three equal-size groups based on total annual sales, and the relative importance of the number of customers versus loyalty was compared. Again the number of customers was found to be about three times more important than the amount purchased per customer.

Specifically, versus small brands, big brands had 978 percent more customers who purchased on average 331 percent more per year. Clearly both factors are important. However, if your resources are limited, the data indicates first priority should be on increasing your total number of customers.

Cultivating new customers is really hard—because customers are Mindless in most of their purchasing. To break the trance, we must articulate a difference that is genuinely Meaningful to them.

PRACTICAL IDEAS

13. Quantify Your Customer Count

Quantify how many customers you currently serve and determine if that customer base is growing or declining. Identify where they are coming from or where they are going. Set a numeric and specific goal for growth. With data, you can make quantitative progress.

14. Perpetually Focus on Finding New Customers

As part of every sales and marketing plan, devise an overt and specific program for bringing in new customers. Regularly seek referrals from existing customers. Hold educational seminars that demonstrate the virtues of your product or service.

15. Remember the Goal Is Total Customer Growth

Becoming really big requires more net customers. This means you must bring in more and not lose those you have. If you add one thousand and lose twelve hundred, you're not going to grow. As you focus on growth, be sure that you've committed the necessary resources to maintain vitality among existing customers.

16. Redefine Your Benefit to Broaden Your Audience

By redefining your benefit, you open yourself to new customers. Classical music concerts are usually thought of as entertainment for classical music lovers. The Indian River Festival of Classical Music doubled their attendance by redefining their events more broadly as experiences for nurturing romance—"Music You Can Hear With Your Heart."

17. Design Your Offerings to Grow the Category

If your category is small, growing new customers will require you to grow your category. You can design for category growth by developing new products or services that directly address the concerns or negatives that nonbuyers perceive.

When the Customer's Buying, Sell Lots!

To drive customer loyalty, the amount purchased per buying event is over three times more important than purchase frequency.

A customer's annual purchase volume is made up of the amount of times they buy and the amount they buy with each purchase. In the marketplace both strategies are pursued with brands offering frequent-buyer clubs as well as supersizes.

Statistical modeling of household purchasing data from over nine thousand consumer products found that volume per purchase is 3.5 times more important than frequency of purchase in explaining the total amount that a customer purchases each year.

Conceptually this makes sense. Competition is not static. Your competitors are perpetually making offers to entice your most loyal customers to give them a try—to experience and enjoy what they have to offer.

Think of customer loyalty as a giant roulette wheel. With more loyal customers, you have a larger proportion of the wheel dedicated to your brand. When customers make purchase decisions, they spin the wheel. With each spin of the wheel there is a defined opportunity to win or lose your customer's next purchase.

When a customer purchases twice as much as normal, you receive 100 percent of both the current purchase and the next purchase. This gives you a greater opportunity for that customer to notice and appreciate your Meaningful difference. And when the customer appreciates your difference, your odds of developing the most valuable of customers—a Meaningful Mindless customer—increases.

PRACTICAL IDEAS

18. Design Tangible Incentives for Volume Purchasing

When a customer is prepared to purchase, give them overt incentives to purchase more. Don't harass buyers. Rather, delight them with a tangible opportunity to make a larger investment in your brand through a discount on larger volume purchases.

19. Repackage—Supersize!

Repackage your product or service into larger sizes. If you market services, offer long-term contracts. If you sell products, create supersize versions. Increasing product package size increases both customer value and your profitability, as it rarely causes a proportional increase in your costs. The same is true for services.

20. Use Customer Service to Rewrite Purchase Orders

Use customer service visits, calls, E-mail, or direct mail to upsell. Give customers a special opportunity to "rewrite the purchase order" and extend their product or service usage. This has multiple benefits to you: (1) It provides you with direct customer feedback on quality; (2) it enhances customer perception of your commitment to them; and (3) it offers the opportunity to expand the customer's initial purchase.

21. Design Complete Solutions

Think hard about what else a customer needs to purchase in order to experience and enjoy your product or service more. Challenge yourself to create a complete-solution package so customers don't have to make a separate purchase.

22. Bundle Your Company's Brands Together

Bundle a collection of your company's products and/or services together to increase your share of the customer spending. This is a way to realize genuine synergy from owning multiple brands.

DATA PROVEN TRUTH #6

Do One Thing Great

When your message is highly focused, you have a 60 percent greater chance of long-term success.

Meaningful Marketing is about building a trust between customers and your brand. Trust is built on the belief that you and your company have a higher-than-normal level of expertise in a specific area. This trust results in greater customer loyalty and less price sensitivity.

A customer's trust in your expertise is dramatically enhanced when you focus on doing one thing better than anyone else.

Analysis of over 901 new products found that when the marketing message was highly focused on one benefit, the brand was 60 percent more likely to succeed in the marketplace than when the message was unfocused.

When you attempt to be all things to all people, you are perceived as a master of nothing. All brands have many dimensions. Most dimensions are simply the cost of getting in the game—not dramatic differences.

Think hard about your offering. What is the one element that, above all others, defines why someone should become your customer? What is the one Meaningful difference that is most Meaningful to your customers?

When your offering is highly focused, your word-of-mouth advertising is turbocharged: It's simply easier for customers to tell others about your virtues.

Today's customers have an overwhelming amount of information available to them. With focusing, you increase the odds that today's overwhelmed customers will detect and take action on what you really offer.

PRACTICAL IDEAS

23. Make Defining Your Brand an Urgent Priority

If you don't know what your brand stands for, there's little chance that your customers do.

Sadly, it is rare to find a brand that has a clear definition. We know this because when we conduct invention projects, we ask various members of management what their brand stands for. Usually not even 30 percent of the responses are the same. When we give lectures, we often ask for business cards and are shocked to see how few of them feature any articulation of what the brand stands for.

To define your brand, you must learn how to say "no." We suggest the following process: Videotape old customers, new customers, noncustomers, new employees, and old employees. Have the interviewees explain their relationship with the brand and then answer three quick questions:

- When you hear (your trademark) what comes to mind?
- What is the one thing that (your trademark) is best at?
- What is the one thing that (your trademark) does that no one else does?

Have the videotape edited down and then, with a team of managers, review the tape and write down what is said and what is not said. Play the tape three times. Then have your management team write down their own responses to the questions. Use all the responses as the basis for defining clearly what you want your brand to stand for in a customer's mind.

24. Publish Your Focused Brand Vision on Everything

Once you've clearly defined what your brand stands for, publish it everywhere. It should be on your business cards, your letterhead, and every other sales and marketing piece that you distribute.

Keep It Simple, Stupid

When your sales message is simple and easy to understand, you increase your odds of success by 70 percent. Ideas written at a fifth-grade level or less are significantly more effective.

When a group of people creates sales and marketing messages, the odds of complexity increase exponentially. Everyone has a little idea here, a small suggestion there. When all the "help" is added together, it's no wonder that the resultant message is confusing to potential customers. Two studies quantify the virtue of keeping your messages simple.

Both studies followed a set of 901 new products from introduction to at least five years later. The original marketing message was evaluated and the results compared in terms of long-term success or failure. Analysis found a 70 percent increase in success probability when a marketing message was clear and easy to understand.

Additionally, the marketing messages were evaluated using the Flesch-Kincaid reading complexity measure. Brands with messages written at a fifth-grade reading level or less were 25 percent more likely to survive than those with messages written at a higher level of complexity. This does not indicate that customers are functionally illiterate. Rather, it's quantification of the impact today's overstressed world has on potential customers.

The need for simplicity is true even when selling sophisticated technology. Within the corporate buying world you will find both technically literate and technically illiterate managers. To succeed, you must translate your technological wonder so that even the most technically illiterate manager can understand it.

PRACTICAL IDEAS

25. Use Nouns and Verbs, not Adverbs or Adjectives

- Tell customers what you will do for them.
- Speak the truth.
- Use adverbs and adjectives sparingly.
- Use nouns and verbs to tell the action you will apply to a person, place, or thing.
- Ruthlessly edit hype, hyperbole, and harangues out of sales letters, advertising, and presentations. Avoid sweeping or global generalizations that cannot be readily supported.

26. Explain Your Idea to a Fifth-Grader

Tell a child your sales and marketing story. Then ask him to repeat back what he heard. Correct the difference between what you said and what he said to sell more with less effort.

27. Focus on Exactly What Will Be Different

When customers purchase your product or service, what will be different? How will their lives be better? What exactly will they now experience that they didn't before?

Do the same with your annual sales and marketing plans. Ask your team, "What exactly are we going to do differently this year?" "We're going to work harder" is not an acceptable answer. Remember, to change results, actions need to change. If you can't define what will be meaningfully different at the start, chances are nothing will be meaningfully different at the end of the year.

DATA PROVEN TRUTH #8

Sell Complex Products and Services Differently

When the truth of your Meaningful difference is complex, never, ever, ever give up. Repeated exposure can help customers understand.

In an ideal world, our point of difference is simple and easy to understand. However, truth in today's technology-laden world is rarely simple. Today's products and services are often highly complex and not easily grasped in a simple sound bite.

Research indicates that the challenge of selling complex products becomes easier with patience and repeated exposures. Researchers showed 381 participants a series of advertisements for dresses that ranged from the very simple to the very complex. They were shown the designs once, twice, three, four times. They were then asked to rate how well they liked each on a set of three scales ranging from good to bad, pleasant to unpleasant, and likable to nonlikable. The average liking for complex designs rose steadily from 3.4 with one viewing to 4.3 after four viewings. Net: The more often customers came in contact with a complex concept, the more they started to like it.

Conversely, the very simple dress designs started with higher likability ratings, 4.2 with one viewing, and declined to 3.4 after four viewings. In effect, what started out as intriguing became less interesting or boring with each successive viewing.

At the Eureka! Ranch, we've noticed that initially, clients tend to gravitate toward ideas that are the most familiar and/or easiest to execute. To combat this, we force clients to suspend judgment for a period of time while they review the ideas multiple times. The net effect: What seemed a good idea at the start of a two- or three-day project often is considered boring at the end. What was unthinkable at the start becomes the chosen path at the end of the session.

PRACTICAL IDEAS

28. Plan for Repeated Exposures

Design your sales and marketing efforts such that they deliver multiple exposures. Define the big picture (dramatic difference) in the initial presentation or advertisement. Provide demonstrations, Web sites, and other sources of experiential learning. Provide follow-up information about the multitude of details that support your promise.

29. Compartmentalize Your Presentations

When presenting something that is highly technical, clearly state how you're not going to describe it in detail. Resist the temptation to explain everything. Instead, offer a "white paper" that defines your technology or method for later reading. Offer a Web site that has the complete details. Provide a video that tours the factory production process.

30. Be Open With Customers' Feelings of Fear

When what you offer is really new, be open about customers' feelings of fear. Instead of hard-selling, be patient and acknowledge that in some cultures and for some managers, it may take more time for them to accept the "new and different." Give customers an opportunity to "test-drive" for an extensive period of time.

31. Reduce Fear by Making a Pedigree Connection

Reassure customers by providing an analogy of how—even though your offering is dramatically different—it has a pedigree in another category. For example: "Our new engine system is based on the same technology utilized in race cars." Or "our new type of beer is number one in Germany."

32. Help Ease the Transition

Reassure customers that the change will not be difficult. Detail clearly how easy the transition will be from where they are now and overtly address their specific fears.

DATA PROVEN TRUTH #9

Target Customers Who Seek Meaningful Innovation

To speed success, focus your initial sales and marketing resources on those customers who are most open to trying new things.

Customers have varying levels of acceptance and interest in Meaningful Marketing messages.

On the cover of their book, *The Influentials*, Ed Keller and Jon Berry wrote, "One American in ten tells the other nine how to vote, where to eat, and what to buy." They make a compelling case for the existence of a group of thought leaders who have a disproportionate power to persuade the masses.

A research study on customers' attitudes toward innovative product concepts, conducted in Canada, France, and North Africa, classified roughly one-third of the population as innovators, those very open to new products and services. Two-thirds of the population was classified as imitators, those content with following later.

In general, the research indicates that those most likely to try new ideas tend to have higher self-esteem, are better educated, and are more informed than the average customer. The good news, according to Keller and Berry, is that when you make an impression on an influential, they are prone to vigorously spread the word about your product's virtues.

Limited sales and marketing resources are available. If we're not careful, we can use them up trying to sell to those who, frankly, no matter how hard we try, are not likely to purchase in the beginning. An important part of sales and marketing effectiveness is knowing when to stop chasing the potential customer who asks lots of questions, use lots of your energy, yet is highly unlikely to buy within a reasonable amount of time.

PRACTICAL IDEAS

33. Focus on Whom Your Difference Means the Most To

Step back and consider what type of customer can realize the greatest benefit from your offering. To whom will your difference be the most Meaningful? Identify them and write them a one-page letter proclaiming the good news of how you can make a real difference for them.

34. Leverage Your Fanatics

All business categories have fanatics. In the case of technology, it's user groups. With celebrities, it's fan clubs. With restaurants, it's their most frequent patrons. Identify and then leverage this group by giving them the first opportunity to experience your newest product or service. Afterwards, seek their help in spreading the word.

35. Fuel Influentials' Passion for Being Smarter

Influentials, fanatics, and other thought leaders have a natural passion for in-depth understanding. The masses are content with simple understandings of your technological wonder. Influentials love to be seen as smarter. Fuel this passion with detailed test results, technical schematics, and perspective on your development pedigree. Empowered with knowledge, influentials will spread the word to others.

36. Follow the Historical Thought Leader Patterns

Research indicates that high-performing salespeople tend to focus their attention on those customers with the ability to influence others. The quickest way to identify the thought leaders among your existing or potential customers is to research when they bought the most recent big innovation in your category. Those who led the last time are the most likely to be the thought leaders with your new offering.

Demo or Die

Sales or marketing presentations that offer a first-person demonstration as proof of effectiveness are nearly 50 percent more effective than simply relying on your reputation.

There is never enough time to make a presentation that covers everything we know. Deciding what to not say, present, or cover can be a real challenge. Whenever possible, include a first-person, sensory-filled demonstration.

The original marketing messages for nine hundred products were divided into four sets based on the type of credibility strategy used.

The baseline or "lowest success" occurred when the primary source of credibility was the established brand's or parent company's name and reputation.

The next best strategy was the new product's pedigree (21 percent more effective), that is, how it was created, its source of technology, components, or ingredients.

The next best strategy was the testimony (29 percent more effective) of customers, experts, and/or celebrities speaking of the product's effectiveness.

But the best strategy was the demonstration of the product or service itself (47 percent more effective) or a sensory cue (sight, sound, taste, touch) that provides first-person credibility of delivery of the benefit.

No amount of words comes close to the impact of firsthand experience with a Meaningful new product or service benefit. Don't blame your customer for not believing what you say. Prove it. Imagine Thomas Edison or the Wright brothers trying to "sell" a movie camera or airplane without a demo—impossible.

PRACTICAL IDEAS

37. Get the Customer to Test-Drive

Go to whatever length necessary to help your customer test-drive your product or service. Have them get inside and truly feel, experience, and enjoy the wonder of what you offer. One of the country's most successful car dealers has a weekend test-drive program that provides qualified customers with a car for the weekend. Once a customer has test-driven a car for a weekend, the dealer has a 90 percent close rate.

38. Show and Tell Your Demo

If you can't get the customers to take a test-drive, then bring your point of difference alive through show-and-tell demos. Let them see, feel, and/or touch the point of difference to make it come to life in their minds.

If your product has more of a special ingredient, bring samples of both your product and your competitor's. If your service time is faster, have the customer call your customer service line and a competitor's. Clock response times on a stopwatch.

39. Use Technology to Bring the Demo to Life

If you can't bring the real thing to life as a demo, then bring photos and video that show the points of difference. With today's digital photos and video cameras, there is no reason to not have excellent visuals. Let the customer "see" for himself how the Meaningful difference fits into his life.

40. Use Technology to Remind Customers of the Demo

When possible, take photos or video of your customers actually utilizing your product or service. Then send the images to them as a visual reminder of the feeling they experienced that day.

Meaningfulness Is About Genuine Attention to Details

When you align executional details on your singular message, you increase your odds of success by 63 percent.

When you are truly committed to making a Meaningful difference, you sweat the little details—because it is in the details that you convince customers of your commitment to making a difference in their lives.

A study of 901 new products found that the odds of success increased 63 percent when the details of name, graphics, packaging, and communication style were in sync with the core message.

Consider two pieces of furniture, one made by a factory and the other handmade by a craftsperson. On the surface, they look the same. However, when it comes to the details (details not visible on the surface), the craftsperson has invested the extra time and effort necessary to make a better piece of furniture because it is a statement about skill, not about simply making money.

Meaningfulness means worrying about the details that are not necessary "in the big picture." It's about taking pride in all that you do for customers. In a world of "same old, same old," a dedication to the details can have a dramatic impact on a customer's trust in you, your brand, and your company.

PRACTICAL IDEAS

41. Multiply the Number and Impact of Touch Points

Document every way your sales, marketing, and brand connect with customers. Look at each connection, from advertising-sparked information requests, to customer service phone lines, to after-sale follow-up. How can you multiply the impact of each connection?

42. Define Your Brand-Building Wish List

The pressures of profit building commonly causes companies to focus only on what needs to be eliminated. Take time to think in reverse. Consider what you'd like to add to build your brand: If you had surplus money, time, or resources, what would/could you do with them? Sadly, when we challenge brand managers to do this, they usually have no answers. Focus on those things that would reinforce a customer's satisfaction and build confidence that you will provide your Meaningful benefit.

43. Multiply the Impact of Your Sales Contacts

Review your Web site, your sales materials, your sales presentation. Are they all 100 percent in alignment? Do they say the same thing in the same way? If not, why not? Every time you add inconsistency, you create doubt. Align all sales and marketing materials with the same Meaningful difference and you will be selling more with less effort—100 percent guaranteed.

44. Review Transitions in Your Sales and Usage Process

Review the transitions that a customer's order must undergo as it moves through your company's systems. Often each department is effective, but something gets lost in the transition. Challenge yourself and your team to make customer transitions as seamless as possible.

DATA PROVEN TRUTH #12

Speak to Customers' Heads and Hearts

To reach all customers, in their preferred style, understand both the emotional and rational dimensions of your offering.

Customers' evaluation and thinking styles vary from emotional and inspirational to rational and logical. Research indicates that both of these approaches can be used successfully to sell your offering.

A set of nine hundred new products were divided into two sets based on whether the customer benefit communicated was primarily rational (save money, solve a problem, cure a pain) or emotional (enhance peace of mind, feel better, feel sexier, gain more personal confidence). The data indicated no significant difference: 33.1 percent of brands with a primarily rational benefit survived, and 32.8 percent of brands with a primarily emotional benefit survived.

As you make your sales pitch, keep in mind that as you move through the chain of command, odds are that you will meet people with a logical left-brain style as well as those with a more emotional right-brain style. When you reach the top of the chain of command, the general manager or CEO will likely be one of the 28 percent of the population with a whole-brain orientation—those with the ability to see both the rational and emotional perspective simultaneously.

Meaningful Marketing means connecting with customers based on their preferred communications style. When you speak to customers based on their preferred approach, you show respect to them as individuals.

Every product and service contains emotional and rational dimensions. When you open your mind to both aspects, you add richness to your mission and will be able to sell to more types of people with less effort.

PRACTICAL IDEAS

45. Express the Feeling to Find the Facts

To identify emotional benefits, think "before" and "after." How does a customer feel after using your product or service? Do they feel proud, happy, excited, or intelligent? What is the moment that a customers understands the real benefit of your product or service?

After defining the "feel" of the benefit, turn your attention to quantifying the source of the change in feelings. What specifically is the driver that sparked change? Rationally, what does your product offer? Search for the source of the feelings to identify the rationale for purchasing.

46. Define the Facts to Find the Feelings

Gather the charts, the data, the test results, and the economic projections that define your benefit. Define clearly the logical, rational benefit that your brand offers. What truly sets you apart from your competition?

Having defined the facts, now think about how they make you feel. When you step back from the facts, what is the feeling you are left with? How does the tangible benefit impact the experiences and feelings of the buyer?

47. Develop the Skill to Flip Between Rational and Emotional Thinking Styles

Practice the ability to flip between a rational and emotional perspective. This will help greatly when dealing with a multitude of customers and with ever-changing perspectives. Challenge yourself when you make a purchase: "I'm buying this because logically it will deliver _____." Also, challenge yourself to define the emotional aspects: "I'm buying this because I hope it will make me feel more _____."

Facts Are Meaningful to Left-Brainers

Use truth and knowledge to help logical left-brain customers understand why your offering is the smart choice for them.

Each customer has a distinct set of attitudes, personal styles, and beliefs. The more we can tailor our presentation to address them as individuals, the greater our chances of sales success. The largest group of adults is known as logical left-brain adults. They are best sold to with facts, data, and logical arguments.

This finding comes from a collection of studies on thinking styles. The largest study involved measurement of 311,207 adults. The research found that 44 percent of adults had a logical, rational, or, as it's known, left-brain orientation.

Additional research of business executives found that left-brain people respond best to presentations where the salesperson was more serious, very knowledgeable, and highly organized, with clear command of the facts and specific recommendations.

The greatest challenge with left-brain types is they are slow to change. By nature, they are highly conservative and skeptical. It can be particularly difficult to get left-brain types to stop and even consider new offerings.

The good news is that logical managers respond to factual truths. When they have made a commitment, they are more likely to remain loyal and are less likely to make a change based on an emotional impulse.

To find out where they stand, directly ask, "What do you think of our product compared to what you are using now?"

PRACTICAL IDEAS

48. Chart Your Differences Side by Side

Logical types love a side-by-side comparison. Chart what you do versus the alternatives. List the strengths and weaknesses. Be honest and straightforward. Left-brainers hate being hustled.

49. Stress Truth and Recognition of Your Client's Smarts

Logical types love being seen as smarter than others. Overtly praise them for the smart things they already do. Stress your search for truth and facts. Let them feel that they have intelligently discovered and deduced the right course of action.

50. Be prepared, on time, and well rehearsed

Make your presentation with professionalism, directness, and as little "fluff" as possible. Left-brainers make their first evaluation based on micro details. Spelling mistakes and math errors in presentations are to them evidence of weak thinking and lack of intelligence.

51. Stand Strong—and Never Duck a Punch

Logical types have a macho-ness that requires them to challenge your thinking. Confront their questions straight on. When you don't know, say so. Don't bluff. And don't allow them to make inaccurate statements. If you stand strong, you win their respect. If you are evasive or cowardly, you are dead.

52. Be Specific About What You'll Do, and Do That

End your meeting with a summary of the overt and specific next steps. Summarize with clarity what you will do—what information you will get them, what questions you will get answers for, when you will set up a test-drive, etc. Then do exactly what you promised.

DATA PROVEN TRUTH #14

Enthusiasm Is Meaningful to Right-Brainers

Right-brain customers respond best to presentations that are delivered with energy and enthusiasm.

Each customer has a distinct set of attitudes, personal styles, and beliefs. The more we can tailor our presentation to address them as individuals, the greater our chances of sales success. The second largest group of adults is known as emotional right-brain adults. They are best sold with energy, personal relationships, and emotions.

This finding comes from a collection of studies on thinking styles. The largest study involved measurement of 311,207 adults. The research found that 28 percent of adults had an emotional, people-oriented, or, as it's known, right-brain orientation.

Additional research of business executives found that right-brain people responded best to sales approaches where the salesperson was more humorous, animated, relationship-oriented, and focused on their personal needs more than their own company's needs.

The great challenge with right-brain types is that they are sometimes slow to make decisions. They love to "shop and talk," so closing the sale can be a challenge. The good news is that when they're committed to you, they tend to be vocal advocates, telling everyone they meet how great and wonderful you and your offering are.

To find where they stand, directly ask, "How do you feel about what I'm offering?" It is nearly impossible for right-brain people to not open up and tell you what's on their minds when asked.

PRACTICAL IDEAS

53. Trust Your Intuition

Emotional types continuously send out clues about their needs. Unlike left-brainers, who play their cards close to the vest, right-brainers are open with their feelings and fears. Listen closely; they are telling you what you need to know to succeed.

54. Build a Personal Relationship

Emotional types must like you before they can purchase your offering. They often don't trust their analytical skills when evaluating data, so instead they rely on their feelings about you as a person. When they connect with you, they connect with your brand.

55. Be Emotional and Passionate

Make your presentation with energy and enthusiasm. Right-brainers listen more to how you say it than to what you say. They have personal radar that searches your soul for genuine conviction.

56. Talk for as Long as They Want

Emotional types need to feel a sense of belonging and a sense that they are connected with others. This means they like to talk and talk and talk. Don't give them the slightest feeling that you are rushing them. Focus 100 percent of your attention on them. Be genuine. If you are shallow or deceitful, they will know and you are dead.

57. Make Frequent Personal Contacts

End your meeting by telling them how good you feel about the possibility of working with them. After the meeting, follow up with handwritten notes and personal contact. Keep in-depth records of their interests, and refresh your memory before each contact to maximize the personal nature of your interactions.

Balance Is Key for Whole-Brain Customers

Whole-brain customers respond best to presentations that balance inspirational vision with rational facts.

The last group of thinking styles is known as whole brain. This finding comes from a collection of studies on thinking styles. The largest study involved measurement of 311,207 adults and found that 28 percent of adults had a whole-brain orientation. They have a natural ability to see both the emotional and the logical side of each situation.

The great difficulty with whole-brain types is determining their perspective at a particular moment. One moment they can be delving into the nitty-gritty factual details; the next they can be thinking in what-if visionary dimensions. They love to look at both sides nearly simultaneously.

Whole-brain types see nothing wrong with switching from details to dreams in the middle of a conversation. In many respects they view thinking as a natural extension of the scientific method: Define the dream (visionary hypothesis) with the right side of their brain, then test the practicality (analytical experimentation) using the left side of their brain.

Whole-brain customers are the easiest to sell your new offering to, because they're not scared by change, facts, or thinking big. They are comfortable assessing the impact of multiple variables at once.

PRACTICAL IDEAS

58. Be Flexible

Be flexible in your sales and marketing presentation. Be ready to move and change in an instant from discussing the factual minutia to the long-term vision. As Ralph Waldo Emerson said, "A foolish consistency is the hobgoblin of little minds." With whole-brain customers, rapid change of direction is seen as a virtue, not a curse.

59. Nurture a Personal Passion for Facts and Emotions

Whole-brain customers have a natural passion for looking at the world from multiple dimensions. To them, a singular rational or emotional focus is limiting and one-dimensional. The more excited they get, the more likely they are to rapidly switch between the two perspectives. To make a Meaningful connection with them, nurture within yourself a genuine love for both facts and emotions.

60. Be Honest With Your Facts

When selling to whole-brain individuals, you need to fully understand the level of truth inherent in your claims. Do not overhype; be honest and factual. When you are certain, stand strong. When you're not, be open and honest. Whole-brain types are comfortable with uncertainty. They are not comfortable with those who attempt to declare truths as absolute. When you don't know, say so; don't try to trick them. They will see through you.

61. Be Genuine

Most importantly, be genuine in your presentation. Don't overhype or overthink. Rather, have a sense of balance and genuineness. Whole-brain customers respect those who are real and authentic in their presentations.

Expertise of People and Brand Quality

Perceived salesperson expertise is the number one driver of customer satisfaction with the supplier.

The most important sales and marketing fundamental may be as simple as learning more about what your product or service does.

A study of 172 industrial buyers was conducted to assess their satisfaction with various suppliers. Computer modeling found that the key drivers of customer satisfaction with a supplier were the salesperson's trustworthiness and perceived expertise. Of these two, perceived expertise was three times more important.

Customer confidence in your people's competence may well be a halo effect that carries over from your company's advanced expertise. The more knowledgeable your customers consider you and your people, the more confident they will be that you will deliver on your promises.

The importance of communicating the quality of your product or service offering was confirmed in a study of 1,209 industrial goods manufacturers. The research found that relative product quality was 9.2 times more important in explaining market share than relative price or spending on sales support.

Quality has long been known to be important. However, the relative magnitude of its importance is surprising.

As a sales and marketing manager you may not have direct impact on actual quality. But you can insure that your company realizes a full return on its Meaningful performance advantages by communicating them to customers.

When you know more, you have more confidence. Plus, when your offering itself is of higher quality than your competition's, then you are virtually unstoppable as a salesperson.

62. Become an Encyclopedia of Brand Knowledge

Become an absolute expert on the quality advantages of your product or service. Learn everything you can about what makes your offering meaningfully great. Then focus your thinking and the decision process of the customers on what makes your offering really great!

63. Use Your Product or Service, Exactly as Recommended, Side by Side With Your Competition's

Directly compare and contrast your offering with your competition's offering. Call your company and your competition with a question or complaint to experience the difference in quality of customer service. Use your offering as not recommended. Abuse your product and the competition's to test your product's durability.

64. Learn the Purpose of Every Item Listed in Your Ingredient Statement or Service Specifications

Take your offering apart and examine everything that goes into it. Learn why your company does what it does to make the product or deliver the service. Examine every item on your ingredient list or on your service delivery process and learn its purpose.

65. Be an Expert on Your Company's Comparative Quality

Understand fully the quality that your company's offering delivers relative to key competitors. Having absolute knowledge of quality is critical for those times when a customer looks you in the eye for assurance that he will really receive what you are promising.

66. Scream Loud When Quality Declines

It is the responsibility of the sales and marketing staffs to be the first-alert systems for quality issues. Your ongoing customer communications should give you news of quality problems long before they become a major issue.

Provide Real Credibility Substance

Providing real credibility to support your Meaningful difference claims increases your success rate by 40 percent.

Customer trust is at an all-time low. The public opinion pollster Yankelovich found that 93 percent of customers have no confidence in the advertising messages of major corporations. Being overt and obvious about your unique and Meaningful benefit will get customers to notice you. Providing a real reason to believe will help you increase confidence and close the sale.

Analysis of the marketing messages of nine hundred new products found a 40 percent greater chance of success for those who provided clear support for the promised customer benefit.

Today's customers are media savvy. They've learned to discern the difference between "smoke and mirrors" and real substance. Positive proof that the Meaningful difference you are promising will be genuinely delivered is critically important.

Proof can take many forms, from demonstrations to clinical test results to common sense explanations like "faster service because we have service locations in all parts of the region."

When you deliver a sales or marketing message in person—to customers or other managers—you need to understand that your reputation has a direct impact on customers' trust in your message. When customers believe in you as a person, they also tend to believe in what you're saying about your brand's offerings. In fact, the overt benefit to your company of a human sales force is the enhanced credibility that develops from their relationships with customers.

67. Role-Play the Part of Defense Attorney

With another marketing or sales manager, role-play the part of an attorney defending your brand's claims of benefit. Make your statements and then have your partner drill you on the truth of your claims. Encourage them to push you beyond general claims to specific facts, truths, and tangible substance.

68. Plan to Exceed Customer Expectations

Dramatic customer credibility is built when their experiences exceed their expectations. Design pleasant surprises into your brand experiences, like personally showing up to help with their installation of new products—even though it's not in the contract. Give free upgrades, extended warranties, or personal phone calls after purchase to check on satisfaction and answer any questions.

To measure the true health of your brand, ask customers, "Did the product/service experience meet or exceed your expectations?" With one question, you'll know where you stand.

69. Use Overt Honesty to Build Your Credibility

Your credibility is built from honesty. When an offering is not right for your customers, tell them so. When you don't know the answer, don't bluff; tell them you'll research it, and find the answer.

70. Use Shared Understanding to Build Your Credibility

Your credibility is built from shared understanding. Nurture a healthy curiosity about how your customers do things, why they do things, what they fear, and what they value. Visit their facilities, tour their factories, see and learn how things really get done. The more effort customers see you expend to try to understand their situation, the more they will trust your recommendations.

Tightly Link Benefit and Credibility

Direct synergy between the benefit promise and credibility results in a 74 percent greater chance of long-term success.

Marketing is about storytelling. It's about telling how your Meaningful difference will improve and/or enhance customers' lives in some way. Your Meaningful benefit difference is what customers will receive. Your credibility is how you will deliver on that promise. Your ultimate success is determined based on the synergy between what and how.

Analysis of 901 new product marketing messages found a 74 percent greater chance of success when there was strong synergy between the Meaningful difference and credibility.

Great marketing tells the whole story and tightly links the benefit with credibility: "We're the first brand to offer (Meaningful benefit difference) because we (real reason to believe)."

When you catch your customers' attentions with a Meaningful benefit difference, a natural anticipation builds of how you will make their lives better. That soon gives way to a fear of being once again disappointed. Customers have been burnt so many times that, while they are excited about your product's potential, they are simultaneously suspicious of being disappointed.

The amount and type of credibility needed is directly related to the magnitude of your Meaningful benefit difference. Claims of small improvements in performance require little support. Genuinely new-to-the-world advances, on the other hand, require substantial support.

PRACTICAL IDEAS

71. Audit Your Meaningful Benefit Claims for Honesty

Don't overhype. Most sales and marketing credibility problems are self-inflicted. Overstating what you really can do is a sure way to hurt credibility. Remember, trust in you declines every time a customer makes a purchase and is disappointed.

Look carefully at all your selling claims and ask yourself, "How do I know that this claim is absolutely true?" If you can't defend a claim easily and without question, consider modifying or eliminating it altogether.

72. Focus on Simple Storytelling

After reviewing all printed materials, step back and tell a trusted friend, an innocent child, or a wise elder the story of your offering. Record what you say and then review the recording and edit until it's a comfortable story.

73. Speak Directly to Your Meaningful Benefit Difference

Challenge yourself to find simple, solid, natural credibility-building factors that link directly to the benefit. If you have a collection of customer testimonials, use the ones that speak directly to your Meaningful difference. For example, if your benefit is about reliable, speedy service, use testimonials that show how, even during a major snowstorm, you still delivered the work on time.

74. Preemptively Confront Customer Skepticism

Left to themselves, customers can imagine all sorts of reasons not to believe you. Preempt this negative spiral by overtly confronting the skepticism. Say without hesitation, "We can do this because . . ." or "What makes this possible is . . ." By overtly confronting the issue, you help turn skeptics into converts. If they then have to "sell" others within their company or family, you've given them the ammunition they need to convert others.

DATA PROVEN TRUTH #19

Better Results Start With Better Forecasts

To make measurably more accurate sales forecasts, visit fifty or more potential customers.

Success in sales is a relative concept. It's relative to how much you've sold versus a predetermined objective. Most managers have an intense personal interest in results relative to the objective because that's usually the basis of personal commissions and bonuses.

Sadly, sales usually fall short of the forecast. A study of fifty-three new products found that the average sales forecasting error was 65 percent, and that the median error (middle value) of sales forecasts was a 26 percent shortfall. In effect, if you miss your objective by less than 26 percent, you are doing better than half of the researched companies.

A study involving 103 computer software firms was conducted to determine the traits of companies with higher versus lower sales forecasting accuracy. The companies with more reliable forecasts created their forecasts after conducting more customer interviews. The data finds a clear improvement after interviews with a few potential buyers (91 percent confidence level) and even greater improvement with fifty or more potential buyers (97 percent confidence level).

Many factors classically assumed to impact forecast accuracy showed no significant impact: judgment of founder, judgment of industry experts, competitive analysis, and market research concept tests.

Net: To increase forecast accuracy, talk to more customers to determine their real needs.

PRACTICAL IDEAS

75. Get Out and Talk to Fifty-Plus Potential Buyers

When it comes to forecasting customer interest, nothing beats the value of face-to-face conversation, and the more, the better. Instead of debating the merits of your offering in your internal conference rooms, go out and talk with real customers face-to-face. As you talk, listen and learn innocently. Don't try to persuade; rather, listen and understand what customers perceive. Remember, customers are far more likely to act on their perceptions than on your view of truth.

76. Talk to Customers in Different Ways

You can maximize the reliability of your customer feedback by providing them with multiple perspectives of your offering. Provide customers with the facts and the feelings of your new offering. The more they can honestly analyze, feel, and experience what you have to offer, the greater the accuracy of their feedback.

Provide customers with a real demonstration. If that's not possible, provide them with a clear, honestly written description of how your offering will impact their lives or business.

77. Don't Hide Your Negatives

Detail the strengths and weaknesses of your offering. Be honest with your customers. Detail every trade-off you've made in your product or service design and why you feel those were the correct decisions. Customers understand that 200 percent greater performance at 20 percent of the cost is rarely reality. Explaining trade-offs in a calm and confident manner removes the chances of emotional overreaction.

78. Document Your Past to Prevent Repetition

Review what you did to generate your past sales forecasts. Document the methods used and the accuracy of the results. Then estimate the real cost of forecasting errors. This figure provides the necessary data to support additional forecasting research before the next new product or service is shipped.

Be Overt in Claiming or Disclaiming Your Pedigree

Your company pedigree is a strength or a weakness, depending on the magnitude of your Meaningful difference.

The growth of any business involves the development of new ideas; some are variations on existing businesses and some offer bigger, bolder, and more Meaningful differences.

If your Meaningful benefit difference is similar to the existing brand, as in "even more powerful, more effective, or more dramatic" than the existing brand, then it's best presented as an upgrade or replacement for your existing offering.

If your offering is a variation of your existing brand, then the decision as to whether you should market it as a new brand or a variation of the parent brand is dependent on the level of Meaningful benefit difference.

Statistical modeling that compared the success of new brands against established brand line extensions or flankers found that at low levels of Meaningful difference, concepts utilizing an existing brand name were twice as likely to succeed as the same product with a new brand name.

At high levels of Meaningful difference, the use of a new brand name offers a higher probability of success. When your new offering is unique or more distinct, the use of an established brand name reduces your odds of success because customers inherently relate it to the old product.

A separate study of ninety-six brands over thirty-eight years confirmed this finding. During the initial years of really new products, the data revealed that brands with new names were 24 percent more likely to succeed. Later, when the market was more mature, offerings carrying established brand names were 60 percent more likely to succeed.

A new brand name is a public statement that a new and more meaningfully different offering is available.

PRACTICAL IDEAS

79. Push Your Ideas to Bipolar Opposites

Evolve your idea to be the best possible reinforcement of your parent brand's core message. Make the concept a driver of brand enhancement as well as incremental volume. Then, turn it 180 degrees and transform it into something radically unique in its benefit offering. Transform the core idea into a true new-to-the-world wonder.

Evaluate both ideas as distinct options. Evaluate the costs and profits associated with both paths. Note: Remember to assume significantly higher (two to five times) cannibalization of parent brand volume to the new item when the idea is less new and different and uses the established brand's name.

80. Tell Your Story Line Directly

When your offering leverages existing brand equities, say so directly: "For fifty years we've been your trusted source for _____," "As the number one most popular brand, we know _____," or "You know you can trust us for _____." Overtly make the direct link between the parent and new item. Don't assume that customers will "get it" themselves.

When your offering is genuinely new, then be equally overt in your communication: "For the first time ever _____." "Announcing a revolutionary new _____." "A patented scientific breakthrough now makes it possible to _____." Again, be overt about the magnitude of the revolution. Make your sales presentations and marketing materials look and feel as unique as the offering you bring forward.

81. Use Your Name as a Source Mark When Necessary

When your big brand name is not a good fit with a new product or service, for whatever reason, consider using it as a "source mark." In this case, the brand is sold as "From the makers of _____." In our experience, the use of a source mark provides virtually all the credibility benefits of branding the offering with the big brand name yet fewer risks.

Be Patient With Mega-Meaningfully Different Ideas

Mega meaningfully different products or services take on average six years before sales volume takes off.

Mega meaningfully different—new-to-the-world—ideas face significant challenges as they move toward profitability. The development investment is usually large and the desire to realize a return on the investment even larger. The natural tendency of sales and marketing professionals is to be aggressive with objectives. However, the data indicates that, with really big ideas, it takes an average of six years before they take off.

This finding comes from a long-term study of thirty-one mega innovations such as automobiles, color TVs, camcorders, compact disc players, cellular phones, direct broadcast satellite TV, and home VCRs. Modeling of volume by year found that on average it took six years before volume grew rapidly. Further, there was very low volume for the first few years with an average of only 1.7 percent of customers having purchased by the six-year point.

Clearly, when your ideas offer mega change, you need patience. Really big ideas take time to educate the marketplace and to gain customer trust. It's possible that with a huge advertising budget you can break the cycle of history. However, the probabilities are clearly against you.

The data also indicates that price is a key challenge with really new technologies. On average, the price at the volume takeoff point is 63 percent of the introductory price. And many items have a price when sales explode that is near one of these three specific price points: $1,000, $500, and $100.

PRACTICAL IDEAS

82. Focus on Niche Markets to Reduce Discouragement

Focus your sales and marketing efforts in the first few years on niche markets where the point of Meaningful difference you are delivering is most highly valued. These markets will be less price sensitive to your initial high cost. And by staying focused on a market where you can "win," you will reduce the chances for emotional wreckage and discouragement caused by your mega meaningfully different idea taking time to generate major volume.

83. Be Cautious With Early Investments and Forecasts

When your company's development investment has been big, the tendency is to be aggressive with early investments and forecasts. Be cautious. Set up a conservative introductory sales and marketing program that you can clearly "win" at. Then separately, conduct investment tests in smaller markets to validate that a bigger investment will deliver a favorable return.

84. Reassure Customers of Your Staying Power

Reinforce the long-term viability of your company and offering. Research on customers' perceptions of major innovations finds that beyond key benefits, customers are also concerned about long-term viability. Reinforce that your new product, service, or company is here to stay.

85. Be Prepared to Survive on Low Volume Levels

There is a good chance that volume will be a fraction of what you anticipate. Plan how you will make adjustments if the initial volume is smaller and growth is slower than expected. In the calm before introduction, you have significantly greater ability to develop smart and effective contingency plans.

DATA PROVEN TRUTH #22

The Importance of Nonloyal Customers

First-time and one-time customers represent over one-third of sales and profits.

Virtually all businesses have the perception that some 80 percent of their business is a result of just 20 percent of their customers. In response to this, companies commonly spend significant resources on customer loyalty and retention programs, as opposed to helping short-term/one-time customers become loyal customers.

The reality is, that in most cases, at least one-third of sales and profits come from nonloyal customers.

This finding is confirmed by two separate studies.

The Scanner 9000, a data set of 9,804 brands that have been tracked by UPC numbers in grocery stores, mass merchants, and drug stores, found that 62 percent of the average brand's customers and 34 percent of annual volume came from those who made only one purchase during the year.

A two-year tracking study of a mail-order catalog found that 47 percent of its customers and some 38 percent of its profits came from short-term, nonloyal customers.

Short-term customers are critical to accomplishing annual sales goals. First-time customers are also the source of all future long-term customers.

Many short-term customers are Mindless buyers; they're attracted by a promotional offer or simply an impulsive desire to try something else. Our challenge is to be sure they are aware of our Meaningful difference so that they fully notice and appreciate it, thus laying the basis for developing a Meaningful connection with our brand.

PRACTICAL IDEAS

86. Make It Easy for Customers to Impulse Purchase

Make purchasing for new customers as easy as possible. If you have a Web-based business, remove lengthy sign-in processes. If you offer a product or service, streamline paperwork and remove credit checks on small orders. The benefits in increased sales and profits will more than make up for the few losses from fraud.

87. Continually Test New Customer Segments

Dedicate a portion of your time and resources to discovering unexpected customer segments and business opportunities. When you do direct mail programs, test new mailing lists. When you work a trade show, focus extra energy on those who don't currently buy from you. Place your products in unexpected retail locations and track reactions.

88. Issue Direct Marketing Challenges

Overtly challenge nonbuyers to give you a try. Communicate your advantages persuasively through side-by-side demonstrations and testimonials from customers who've recently switched to buying your brand.

89. Celebrate the Arrival of New Customers

Define special methods for handling new customers' needs. Provide special instructions, guidance, and help with their "rookie" needs. Warmly welcome them to your brand and your people.

90. Create Special New Customer Follow-up Systems

Have a defined follow-up process to learn your new customer's satisfactions and dissatisfactions with your product or service experience. Overtly ask for another sale and if it's not appropriate at that time, define when in the future you should contact the customer again—then do it.

DATA PROVEN TRUTH #23

Incentives Motivate, But Customers Can't Be Bought

A financial incentive can stir a customer to action. However, more money won't turn a noncustomer into a customer.

Offering customers a modest financial incentive to try your product or service can have a dramatic impact on trial rates. Incentives can take the form of free samples, coupons, or straightforward discounts on initial purchases. However, more money is not always the smart choice. The return you realize from additional money has clear limits.

Researchers mailed a survey on group health insurance to twelve hundred members of an industry trade association. Incentives varying from $1 to $40 were offered to complete the survey. The results indicate that compared to the no-incentive control group, a $1 or $5 incentive doubled the response rates; however, higher incentives had minimal additional impact.

Survey Response Rate

No Incentive/Control. . . . 21 percent
$1 Incentive . . . . 41 percent
$5 Incentive . . . . 51 percent
$10 Incentive . . . . 44 percent
$20 Incentive . . . . 54 percent
$40 Incentive . . . . 54 percent

The control group grew to a 52 percent response rate, a rate similar to the incentive rate, after three additional mailings to those not responding. Similarly, you can achieve higher trial rates without the use of incentives. However, additional contacts and sales efforts will be required.

When introducing a new product or service, a modest incentive to early customers can be a wise investment. However, as you'll learn later in this book, accelerating early trial rates through discounts may not be the smartest long-term action.

PRACTICAL IDEAS

91. Provide an Incentive to Try But Don't Give It all Away

An incentive to try can be effective. However, giving everything away at the start establishes that your product or service is worthless. Giving an "early buy" discount for a limited time establishes the value of your offering.

92. Offer Limited-Use Samples

When possible, give a small-size sample of your offering—a taste, a test-drive, a sample financial plan. Don't be surprised if, even when your sample is free, you have a hard time getting takers. Studies tracking usage of free product samples have found that even with targeted mailing lists, it's not uncommon for only 50 percent of free samples to ever be utilized by customers.

93. Offer an Incentive for Sales Demonstrations

Create a value from the sales presentation itself. Incorporate real learning value into your marketing. When customers experience genuine learning during the sales process, they develop confidence in your skills and abilities.

94. Stand Strong and Confident

Price discounting is often driven by a lack of confidence. Salespeople who don't believe in the merits of their offering will resort to discounts and incentives to make up the difference. Sadly, the discounting can backfire, as it signals to customers that the offering must not be worth the price. And when customers start to doubt, no amount of discounts can motivate them to purchase. When you have a Meaningful offering, establish a no-discount policy. Stand strong, and when pushed for discounts reply that the money that would have been available for discounts has been invested in higher product/service quality.

DATA PROVEN TRUTH #24

Honestly Articulate What Customers Will Receive

Marketing is most effective when it creates expectations that are consistent with actual product performance.

The objective of Meaningful Marketing is to honestly articulate exactly what customers will realize when they make a purchase.

A professor provided study participants with a marketing message that either (1) accurately articulated performance, (2) understated product performance, or (3) highly overstated performance. A control group was provided with no marketing message. Based on the marketing description, participants rated their expectations of the product. After viewing and sampling the item, participants rated the product again.

The group receiving an accurate marketing description had similar ratings before and after product experience, 8.9 and 9.1 respectively.

The group receiving a marketing message that badly understated the product's performance provided a initial low rating of 3.2. After use, the rating rose to 6.6. However, this is still below what was independently determined as the accurate rating of around 9.0. Understating your marketing message leads to customers perceiving your product—even after use—at less than its full value.

Having no marketing message generated a product rating after use of 7.7. This is better than the poor message, but still below the 9.0 that is considered truth.

Participants who were presented with a statement that highly overstated the product gave a high initial rating of 16.7. However, after use, the rating declined to the truthful rating of 9.0. Note: Overhyping the offering did not create an enhanced perception of the product. Instead, it resulted in a customer who clearly understood that he had been tricked by marketing. This is not the path to a Meaningful customer connection.

PRACTICAL IDEAS

95. Use Customers to Enhance Marketing Accuracy

When you understate your offering's performance in your sales and marketing message, you run the risk of having customers understate its performance even after they've experienced it.

When you overstate your offering's performance in your sales and marketing message, you run the risk of having customers feel that they've been tricked. This has the potential of creating a negative impact on their perception.

Involve customers in marketing evaluation. Present a set of customers with your message. Have them utilize your product in a real-world setting. Then ask them to evaluate your marketing message based on their experiences. Seek their help in precisely articulating your message by listening to how they talk about it.

96. Involve Technology Experts in Marketing Development

Those who invented, designed, and developed your product or service often have a deep understanding of your offering's true strengths and weaknesses. The challenge is that they often speak in a technical language that is not customer friendly. Teach them to speak in simple, friendly terms and you will have a valuable resource to use.

97. Quantify Your Offering Versus Expectations

Ask customers to rate how interested they are in purchasing your product or service on a scale of zero to ten (zero equaling definitely not buy, ten equaling definitely would buy) based on reviewing your marketing message. After use, have them rate it again. Average the pre- and post-use ratings across fifty to one hundred customers. Compare the pre- versus post-use ratings. When your scores are within one point of each other, you have achieved balance between your marketing promise and actual performance. Note: As a general rule, when using a scale like this, average scores should be above five and ideally above six.

DATA PROVEN TRUTH #25

Timeless Fundamentals of Successful Selling

Successful sales and marketing requires a simple and Meaningful focus on your customer's true needs.

Selling to a consumer is considered to be different from selling to an industrial customer. However, research indicates both types of salespeople agree that certain fundamentals are critical to their success.

Researchers surveyed 170 consumer and industrial salespeople about a list of eighty-four different sales strategies and tactics. Both groups identified the following tactics as being most important in their sales efforts:

Personal Observation: Look and listen.

Ask Questions to Learn: Ask prospects direct questions to learn about their situation and needs.

Benefit Focused: Overtly state the benefit of your offering.

Keep It Understandable: Use short nontechnical words in sales presentations.

Direct Answers: Provide specific responses to exact questions from prospects.

Direct Close: Ask for the order in a straightforward manner.

Follow Up After the Sale: Check with the customer after the sale to ensure the customer is satisfied. Where necessary provide training on how to best utilize the product.

The top-rated methods are simple. They focus on understanding your customers' genuine needs and then fulfilling them with integrity.

Importantly, sophisticated closing gimmicks, dramatic showmanship, fear-focused sales tactics, and even the telling of jokes were not seen as important when it came to selling.

PRACTICAL IDEAS

98. Drive the Fundamentals

Get back to basics. Focus your energies on the fundamentals of successful sales and marketing.

Personal Observation: Get up, go out, and spend time observing real customers using your product or service. Watch for moments of delight and moments of frustration.

Ask Questions to Learn: Make a list of twenty-one things you think you know about how customers use and abuse your product. Then assess how absolutely certain you are of the factual nature of each statement. Rate them on a 0 percent to 100 percent scale with 100 percent being absolute and complete factual truth. Take the seven statements with the lowest certainty and ask your customers for their perspective.

Benefit Focused: Challenge yourself to identify the benefits of each feature listed in your sales materials and advertisements.

Keep It Understandable: Explain your offering to a fifth-grader.

Direct Answers: List your customers' most frequently asked questions. Then challenge yourself to answer them in the most direct fashion possible.

Direct Close: Take three customers who are in the process of "thinking over" your offering and politely, yet directly, ask them to make a purchase.

Follow Up After the Sale: Call your last dozen customers and ask them how they're doing and what you can do to help them.

DATA PROVEN TRUTH #26

Learning From Other Types of Salespeople

Industrial and consumer salespeople each have distinct tactics that hold potential for use by the other.

Industrial and consumer salespeople have much in common, as stated in Truth 25. However, they also have some significant differences that hold potential for cross leverage.

As mentioned before, 170 salespeople were surveyed on a list of eighty-four different sales strategies and tactics. Both consumer and industrial salespeople were researched and their ratings of the importance of various approaches compared.

Industrial salespeople consider the following techniques significantly more important than consumer salespeople do.

Propose Trial Use: Industrial salespeople are more likely to overcome objections by suggesting the prospect use the product or service offering on a trial basis.

Customize Sales Presentations: Industrial salespeople are more likely to fully or partially customize their presentations to match each customer.

Personal Observation: Consumer salespeople consider the following techniques significantly more important than industrial salespeople do.

Seek Referrals: Consumer salespeople are more likely to ask customers for the names of other potential customers.

Send Thank-You Notes: Consumer salespeople are more likely to send a letter of appreciation to the customer.

PRACTICAL IDEAS

99. Leverage Industrial Techniques With Consumers

Find ways to get your customers to experience your product first-hand. If that's not possible, build simulations that you can take with you to help them experience your Meaningful difference.

Leverage technological tools to customize your sales presentations. One-to-one database tools make it possible for you to mass customize your responses to consumer inquiries at a reasonable cost.

100. Leverage Consumer Techniques in Industrial Markets

By the nature of the business, an industrial salesperson's customers are often each other's competitors. Thus, there is a natural reluctance to overtly ask for referrals. However, in today's economy, movement between competitors by employees is frequent. Customers are therefore more open to providing referrals to salespeople, as the customers often view the salesperson as a tool for helping them network for new or better jobs.

In today's less personal, less connected world, a handwritten thank-you note can have a huge impact. A note from you to your customers conveys their importance to you.

101. Let Go of Ego and Become a Learning Sponge

A confident ego is valuable when presenting to skeptical customers. However, it's a negative when it comes to learning more about how to think quicker, smarter, and more creatively about your sales and marketing methods. Release your ego to learn. Challenge yourself to discover and apply at least one new method or idea each month.

Consider Yourself an Educator

Meaningful Marketing is about educating customers on your virtues as opposed to tricking them into buying.

In simple terms, the role of sales and marketing is to educate customers about the good news regarding what your product or service can do for them.

The more customers are educated regarding your offering, the more likely they are to purchase. A research study found that customers' purchase intent ratings, as well as their attitude toward a brand, were significantly higher when they experienced the product firsthand or watched an in-depth fifteen-minute commercial as opposed to a brief one-minute advertisement.

The more you educate and teach your customers about your true merits, the more likely they are to actually buy from you. This is in contrast with the accepted belief that customers don't have time to read or learn. The work of David Ogilvy and others in the field of direct marketing have shown clearly that, oftentimes, longer copy has more of an impact and is more persuasive than shorter copy.

A separate study of a technologically advanced product category found that customers with high category knowledge assessed options with double the accuracy of those with low category knowledge.

Customers with high levels of product understanding are able to translate product attributes into personal benefits. They have the ability to adapt what you claim into fulfillment of their needs.

Customers with little understanding see only your features and attributes. They mainly judge your product based on the direct application of what you describe.

Meaningful Marketing is about teaching customers the true virtues and applications of what you offer.

PRACTICAL IDEAS

102. Teach Differently to Different Target Audiences

One of the first rules of teaching is to understand the skill level and motivation of your students. Think deeply about your marketing message and sales approach. Force yourself to customize your communications to the most-educated and the most-novice customers. Having defined the two ends of the spectrum, you can now blend and adjust your message for those customers in between.

103. Education Starts With "Why Should I Listen to You?"

Before any pitch or presentation can be made, your sales prospect must stop and listen. This means you must articulate your news in a simple direct fashion. For maximum "stopping power," focus your headline statement on the Meaningful difference you offer. Be bold about how you can make a major difference for your customers.

104. The Second Question: "What's in It for Me?"

Now that you have the customer's attention, overtly articulate what your customer will receive, experience, and enjoy from using your offering. Focus your communication on your customers' needs, not your personal preferences.

105. The Third Question: "Why Should I Believe You?"

The last part of education is explaining how you will accomplish what you promise. The level of credibility required depends on the breadth of your promise. With a small promise, little doubt is created and thus little credibility is required.

106. Be Prepared for Honor Students

Some customers love to be challenged. Challenge these "honor students" by asking, "Is there anything else you'd like to know?" If you engage, challenge, and respect their thinking, honor students will become your brand's biggest fans.

DATA PROVEN TRUTH #28

Where You Are Is What's Most Meaningful

Few things are more powerful than in-person, face-to-face appeals.

Today's world makes it possible for us to more easily connect to many people, in many places, quickly, whether by mail, E-mail, cell phone, conference call, or videoconference.

In this time of electronic communication, don't forget the impact of old-fashioned face-to-face conversation. When you take the time to drive or fly to a customer's office, you are telling him that you value him and his business.

A study of response rates from 497 independent research surveys found that in-person requests were successful 82 percent of the time versus 47 percent for surveys sent by mail.

Another study was conducted to measure the effectiveness of various methods of encouraging households to recycle. Households who were not recycling were given a persuasive marketing message on the importance of recycling and were also given some recycling bags.

One group had the materials left on their front doorstep. The other group had them personally delivered by a neighborhood block leader. If the block leader couldn't make personal contact after a number of tries, the block leader left the materials with a personal note.

The weekly average recycling rates over ten weeks was 12 percent for those who had the materials left at their door versus 28 percent for those who had been personally contacted.

Clearly, making a personal contact makes a Meaningful difference.

PRACTICAL IDEAS

107. Examine Your Calendar to Assess Your Priorities

Review your calendar for the past six months. What percentage of your days did you spend face-to-face with customers? What percent was spent with existing customers? Looking even deeper, ask yourself what percentage of your days was spent learning about your marketing craft, your brand, or your industry?

As a basic rule of thumb, we feel that sales and marketing executives should spend 25 percent to 50 percent of their time either connecting with current or prospective customers or learning more about their craft. To marketing managers who see this as unrealistic, we challenge them to show us their success rate with business development initiatives. The first step toward reducing failure is to know more—and nothing beats personal contact for increasing knowledge.

108. Jolt Your Business Success With a Traveling Blitz

Spark positive sales momentum by hitting the road and visiting twenty current or potential customers. The more concentrated the period of time, the more impact it will have on your wisdom, perspective, and results. An alternative approach is to work the front lines of a trade show or the front of your retail store.

As you visit with customers, listen naively. Instead of defending and debating, listen with awareness and empathy. Seek to identify opportunities for growth. In fact, ask customers and potential customers directly what you can do to win more of their business.

109. Invite Them to Visit You

Create and host events for your customers. Events can include user conferences, technology demonstrations, or even educational seminars. By planning and hosting an event that is Meaningful for your customers, you demonstrate your knowledge and commitment.

DATA PROVEN TRUTH #29

Meaningfully Reduce Customers' Purchasing Delays

The reasons that customers delay making purchasing decisions can be directly addressed through Meaningful Marketing.

By understanding why customers delay purchasing decisions, we can learn how to improve our marketing effectiveness. By giving customers the information they need at the beginning, we reduce the amount of effort it takes to turn customer interest into a closed sale.

A series of research studies was conducted on why customers delay making purchase decisions. A total of eighty-one different reasons were identified. Mathematical modeling identified the following five factors as the critical causes of delays:

Too Busy to Devote Time to Evaluating Options: Customers don't feel they have the time to make a smart decision about what to purchase.

The Buying Process Is Unpleasant: Customers don't like the process of buying and making decisions.

Fear of Making a Bad Decision: Customers feel that the product might not work as advertised, based on the poor performance of similar products they've experienced in the past.

Need More Information: Customers feel a need for more information on other options and/or feel a need to get someone else's opinion.

Pricing Concerns and Changes: Customers are not only concerned about their ability to afford the item but that the price may drop soon after purchase.

PRACTICAL IDEAS

110. Make Your Benefit Personally Meaningful

When customers claim they don't have time to evaluate your offering, what they are really saying is that they don't anticipate a benefit worth investing their time in. The more personally Meaningful your overt benefit is to customers, the more open they will be to giving you their time. Challenge yourself to be more direct about how your offering will personally transform their lives.

111. Make the Process Painless for Customers

Review your buying process from start to finish. How can you make each step easier for your customers? Challenge yourself to find three Meaningful changes that can reduce the effort required by customers to learn about and purchase your offering.

112. Quantify Credibility

Fear of failure is reasonable. Provide measurable, tangible proof of how your product or service will deliver as promised. Show them your patent, your factory, all the details of how you are able to fulfill your promise to them.

113. Make It Easy to Gather More Information

By detailing your offering relative to a competitor's, you defuse issues about "needing more information." In addition, it allows you to determine the relevance and importance of various comparison criteria.

114. Give Customers Assurances of Long-Term Price Value

The biggest thing you can do to provide assurances of pricing stability is to have a firm pricing policy. When a customer perceives that your pricing is open to discussion, they immediately assume that discounting is in the future. Stand strong regarding the value of your proposition.

Reduce Options to Increase Sales and Profits

Simply cutting your product or service options by as much as 50 percent can, by itself, result in total sales increases of 10 percent or more.

The easiest way to increase sales and profits may be to discontinue 50 percent of your offerings and variations. Classic thinking is that offering a multitude of product and service options will help you increase sales because you'll reach a broader range of customers.

Three separate studies indicate that, in truth, reducing the number of options you offer can have a dramatic positive impact on sales. It appears that more options result in more customer uncertainty and consequential delay of decision making and purchasing.

> *Study 1:* Retail stores eliminated 10 percent of the least popular items in eight categories from their shelves. This alone resulted in a 4 percent increase in category sales.

> *Study 2:* The bottom 54 percent of products were discontinued across forty-two categories of an Internet-based retailer. This resulted in an average 11 percent increase in sales.

> *Study 3:* Consumers were offered samples of twenty-four or six flavors of jam to taste and purchase. When twenty-four flavors of jam were offered, 2 percent of customers purchased. When six flavors of jam were offered, 12 percent of customers purchased.

Basic production economics tells us that low-selling options are a dramatic drain on profitability. Yet, often we fall into the temptation of offering something for everyone.

PRACTICAL IDEAS

115. Get the Real Numbers

Assess your business situation with mathematical honesty. What are the real sales and real net profit of each and every product variation or option you offer? Look at the long-term trends and identify those offerings in long-term decline.

Examine the bottom 50 percent of your offerings. If you were to eliminate them, what percentage of the volume would shift to other offerings? What cost savings could you realize?

116. Evaluate for Meaningful Differences

Review your brand's offerings and classify them according to their Meaningful benefit difference to customers. Challenge yourself to articulate, in writing, the tangible difference of one option versus another. Review your marketing materials for the clarity of your differences. Ask your customers for their understanding of the differences between your offerings.

Having made your evaluations, make courageous cuts in the variations and permutations you offer. Items that offer the same basic benefits are excellent candidates for elimination.

117. Collapse Services Under an Umbrella Message

By its nature, companies offering services provide a multitude of options to fulfill customer needs. If we're not careful, we start selling the suboptions as separate choices, creating customer confusion. Instead, keep your focus on the bigger picture— Meaningful difference— and use customization to each customer's needs as part of the sales process— after customers have "purchased" your Meaningful difference.

Focus Promotions on New Users

An estimated 84 percent of sales increases in heavily price-promoted categories come from stealing customers from competing offerings.

Customers are creatures of habit. They mindlessly purchase from a small set of acceptable options. They can be shifted away from their current choice when provided with a Meaningful difference or when presented with an even easier and more Mindless option due to a temporary price reduction.

Mathematical modeling was undertaken on the source of weekly sales increases for various brands of coffee among one hundred households over a two-year period. The results indicated that more than 84 percent of sales increases were due to brand-switching (noncurrent customers switching to the promoted item), 14 percent from purchase acceleration (current customers repurchasing sooner than normal), and 2 percent from stockpiling (current customers buying more than normal at one time).

Clearly, when an industry is heavily promoted, like the coffee category, a large segment of the population becomes trained to purchase only when the price is reduced.

The Meaningful Marketing challenge is to find ways to convert the price switchers into deeper and more loyal customers. This requires customers to first notice and then value our Meaningful points of difference.

PRACTICAL IDEAS

118. Be Relentless in Articulating Your Differences

In the face of perpetual discounting, you must become relentless in articulating what makes your product offering unique. Communicate your distinctiveness even when articulating price discounts. Through continuous communication, you will eventually build awareness that your offering delivers value, not just low price. You won't reduce the need for discounts totally. However, even a small shift can create a big improvement in your bottom-line profits.

119. Leverage Customer Purchase Cycles

Understand the purchasing cycles of your customers. Arrange your follow-up E-mail, direct mail, and personal contacts to maximize your chances of making connections just before a new purchase is required. As you're planning, don't be shy about directly asking your customers when they anticipate making another purchase.

120. Segment Your Offerings for Extreme Differences

Challenge yourself to strip your offering to the absolute lowest possible cost. Consider the unthinkable. Eliminate packaging, options, variations, and "nice" extras. Focus this stripped-down version on those customers motivated by price alone.

Push your offering to the ultimate in service. Provide added value to those customer segments that value Meaningful differences.

121. Use Endorsements to Talk of Differences

Use endorsements to articulate the dramatic differences that customers have experienced as a result of switching to your offering. Better yet, leverage testimonials that speak of the value customers have received from repeated use of your product or service.

Leverage Failure as a Meaningful Opportunity

Customers who experience a problem that is satisfactorily addressed become more satisfied and more likely to tell others of your greatness.

Customer complaints offer an opportunity for you to showcase your Meaningful difference. Your attitude, attention, and commitment to resolving customer complaints can have a huge impact on customer satisfaction and increase the likelihood of them recommending your company to others.

A study was conducted of some 1,356 bank customers over twenty months. Customers were asked a series of questions regarding their overall satisfaction and their intentions to recommend the bank to their friends.

Analysis found that when customers had a problem and it was handled in a positive manner, their overall satisfaction ratings increased by 22 percent and their attitude ratings on giving positive word-of-mouth recommendations increased by some 58 percent.

Conversely, when customers' problems were handled in an unsatisfactory manner, their overall satisfaction ratings declined by 31 percent and their attitude ratings on giving positive word-of-mouth recommendations declined by some 16 percent.

Importantly, customers have a limited tolerance for repeated failures. Customers who complained twice about the same problem rated the bank very low despite two successful handlings of the same problem. (Overall satisfaction ratings declined 51 percent and word-of-mouth ratings declined by 47 percent versus the ratings provided before either problem occurred.) Net: A customer respects you when you satisfactorily address a problem, but they have no tolerance for repeated incompetence.

PRACTICAL IDEAS

122. Make Customer Service a Prime Marketing Tool

Consider customers who complain as a prime marketing opportunity. Explore their needs and issues. Resolving their problems with excellence lays the groundwork for future business from them. Listening closely to the problems they articulate also helps you identify product design and quality issues that others may also be experiencing yet are too timid to say anything about.

123. Encourage Complaints

Go out of your way to encourage customers to tell you about anything and everything that might not have been as good as they expected. Research indicates that nearly 70 percent of customers who experience problems with products do not complain to the seller.

Empower everyone to gather, record, and communicate customer impressions. Often customers will informally vent their concerns with receptionists or product delivery or installation staff yet not make formal complaints.

124. Search for Root Causes of Failure

When a failure happens, identify if it's a one-time honest mistake or a systemic flaw of your system or product. The only way to accomplish this analysis is to have a written record of customer issues and impressions. Create a system that signals an alarm when a repeated failure occurs.

125. Reward Speed of Recovery

Track speed of resolution. The faster you and your staff can resolve a little problem, the less likely it will become a big problem.

DATA PROVEN TRUTH #33

Smart Ways to Steal Competitive Volume

It is significantly more effective to emphasize performance differences when comparing against similar offerings. And it's more effective to compare similarities when comparing against dissimilar categories of offerings.

A classic method of growing sales of a product or service is to advertise and sell it for new usage occasions or purposes.

The target competitor that is to be the source of the new volume can have a product form that is similar yet whose characteristics are different from yours. Alternatively, the product can have an end use that has characteristics common with the parent brand, yet a product form that is very different.

Two research studies were conducted involving a total of 460 customers. Customers were asked their likelihood of using various promoted brands in various extended usage occasions.

When the products were similar (unsweetened dry cereal versus crackers), consumers were significantly more likely to say they would use cereal in place of crackers if the marketing message focused on points of difference (less fat, less expensive).

When the products were more dissimilar (unsweetened dry cereal versus cookies), consumers were significantly more likely to say they would use cereal in place of crackers if the marketing message focused on points of similarity (tasty, crunchy, fun to eat).

To change customers' attitudes and generate Meaningful substitution, focus the customers' attention on one dimension of change—either the product differences versus existing competitors, or the opportunity for new dimensions by using one product in place of an established option.

PRACTICAL IDEAS

126. Identify and Target Categories That Are Similar

Identify competitive product categories that have the most similarities to yours. Next, make a list of your Meaningful differences to theirs. For example, if you sell steak sauce, you might compare it to catsup and then identify your Meaningful differences as (1) has a marinated taste, (2) gives a tangy "kick," or (3) adds excitement to a simple hamburger.

127. Identify and Target Categories That Are Dissimilar

Identify competitive product categories that are more dissimilar to yours. Next, make a list of your Meaningful similarities to theirs. For example, if you sell liquid bleach, you might compare it to liquid cleanser and identify your Meaningful similarities as (1) is convenient to use, (2) disinfects, and (3) is powerful.

128. Direct Challenge

Make a direct challenge against a competitor's product, be it a side-by-side taste test, an in-home usage experience, or simply a paired comparison of your system versus the competition. Direct comparisons have a level of boldness that breaks through the clutter of daily life.

129. Competitive Testimonials

Raise doubt and uncertainty in the minds of buyers of the competition by featuring former users who've converted to your brand. A seemingly never-ending progression of switchers undermines the confidence of your competition's users.

130. Become a Bridge Builder

Find ways to engineer connections between your offering and other categories of products or groups of customers who are not being served. Modify your offering as necessary to enhance the fit with and value perception of new customer segments.

Reducing the Impact of Competitive Reactions

Strategic targeting can reduce competitive reactions to your business-building initiative.

New business initiatives have high failure rates. The two primary causes of failure are a product's or service's lack of Meaningful difference and unforeseen competitive reactions.

A study of 249 managers' experiences with competitive reactions to new products identified four strategies that reduce their speed and size:

Pursue Major Product Innovations: When you pursue Meaningful product differences, it takes significantly longer for the competition to react. The more unique your new offering is, the more time and skill it takes your competition to design, develop, and produce a comparative offering.

Attack Larger Companies: The larger your key competitor is, the slower their response will be. Quite simply, very large companies tend to face inertia and inflexibility. Additionally, they often have large investments in established ways of production and are reluctant to self-cannibalize.

Pursue Markets With a Few Strong Competitors: Markets that are crowded with a few strong competitors are significantly slower to respond to competitive introductions. It appears that when there are only a few strong competitors, each reacts slowly to avoid sparking an all-out war within the category.

Avoid Fast-Growing Markets: The faster a marketplace is growing, the more likely that competitors will view it as being of major strategic importance. Markets that are old and growing slowly are more likely to be ignored by major competitors.

PRACTICAL IDEAS

131. Pursue Meaningfully Different Ideas

The more dramatically different your idea is compared to established practices, the less likely you'll be copied quickly. Find the courage to do the unthinkable. Identify your competition's greatest source of manufacturing or production skill. Then create ideas that make this asset irrelevant to customers.

132. Attack the Biggest Competitors

Orient your competitive and comparative marketing against the largest competitors. If you can't find one giant, focus your energies where there are a few giants that display low levels of direct conflict. The bigger the company, the more likely they are to ignore smaller competitors and the longer it will take them to copy you.

133. Pursue the Wal-Mart Strategy

Wal-Mart was built into the U.S.A.'s largest retailer by first opening stores in rural markets were there was no retailer activity, no retailer excitement, and no retail growth. After the company achieved tremendous volumes and economies of scale, it then opened stores in the more competitive urban markets.

134. Pursue Markets That No One Wants

Who are the customers that no one wants? What are the most "boring" categories and industries? Who are the most difficult customers to service? The less interesting the opportunity looks on the surface, the less likely it is that the competition will defend, copy, or attack your introduction.

135. Leverage the Patent System vs. Big Competitors

Patenting an invention can take years. However, while the patent application is in process, you can state "patent pending" and the patent itself remains secret. If you make a big deal about your patent, you can create significant uncertainty.

The Power of Preventing a Loss

Avoiding a loss can be more motivating to customers than realizing a gain.

Classic marketing theory is that it's more effective to position a product or service as providing a positive benefit than as preventing a loss.

A broad collection of academic studies finds this to be wrong. As an example, one study involved college-age women who were encouraged to follow the American Cancer Society's recommendations for breast self-exams.

Those who were presented with the positive benefit message received the following kind of message: "By doing breast self-exam now, you can learn what your normal, healthy breasts feel like so that you will be better prepared to notice any small, abnormal changes that might occur as you get older."

Those who were presented with the loss prevention message received the following kind of message: "By not doing breast self-exam now, you will not learn what your normal, healthy breasts feel like and you will be ill prepared to notice any small, abnormal changes that might occur as you get older."

The research found that those who read the loss prevention message had significantly higher attitudes and intentions toward doing breast self-exams. And a four-month follow-up study found they were also significantly more likely to actually perform breast self-exams.

When you overtly discuss how your offering reduces the chance of loss, you amplify the customer's focus and attention on your Meaningful difference.

PRACTICAL IDEAS

136. Define Your Benefit as Preventing a Loss

Define what you offer first as a positive benefit to your customers. Then define your offer as a means of preventing a loss of freedom, money, health, or whatever is your primary marketing dimension.

Once you've defined your benefit as both a positive and as a method for preventing a loss, test both methods in market research, voice mail you leave for potential customers, or as part of your next direct mail campaign. Quantify the difference and act accordingly.

137. Quantify the Long-Term Costs of Nonaction

Document what the cost is to a customer of not using your product or service. Quantify the tangible loss they will suffer if they continue using your competitor's offering instead of yours. Dimensionalize the long-term impact by multiplying the effect over many usage experiences and/or years.

138. Articulate Fears and Doubts

Identify the "soft cost" losses that customers will experience if they don't purchase your offering. Articulate the lack of peace of mind, the uncertainty, and the lack of confidence that can develop as a result of poorer quality and poorer performance.

139. Put a Face on the Loss

Make the loss that a customer could experience as real as possible by telling the personal story of one or more customers who have suffered it. The more you can help customers see, feel, and relate to someone who has suffered the loss, the more motivating the preventive power of your offering will be.

Your Name Is Who You Are

Aligning your name with your benefit doubles a customer's recall of who and what you are.

Your brand name defines who and what you are. The more your sales and marketing message offers a Meaningful difference that aligns with the suggestive nature of your brand name, the more likely customers will recall and remember it.

Researchers showed 160 adults a series of marketing messages and brand names. Two days later, they were asked to recall the various messages. Suggestive brand names generated correct recall of the marketing messages 33 percent of the time. Nonsuggestive brand names generated only 15 percent correct recall.

Your brand name is a clear and overt declaration of what you offer. The more related and synergistic your name is with your message, the more effective your marketing will be.

A separate analysis of some 901 new products found that the odds of long-term marketplace survival were 34 percent greater when the new product's brand name evoked the benefit instead of being an abstract or unrelated name.

A major challenge with naming is the need to balance descriptiveness with distinctiveness. Trademark law does not allow for the use of descriptive names. To acquire trademark protection, you must have a fanciful name that uniquely identifies your brand of products or services. It can be suggestive. However, the more it describes the product form or usage, the less you will be able to prevent others from using a similar name.

PRACTICAL IDEAS

140. Think Literally

Remove from your mind anything you think and know about your brand. Look deeply at the literal collection of letters that are your brand name. Look in a dictionary and a thesaurus for direct meanings and synonyms. If your name is truly fanciful and not in any dictionary, then explore the meaning of the root components that make up the name.

Challenge yourself to speak of your product or service in terms of the literal meaning of your brand name. Create sales and marketing materials that help customers make direct connections between your name and your benefit.

141. Articulate Your Trademark's Genealogy

Review your history. Where did your name come from? What did it originally mean? What are its roots? How has it evolved over the years? In an appropriate manner, share this history with your customers. When a customer understands your history, you create deeper connections.

142. Think Graphically

Repeat the process detailed above with your graphical identity. Review your colors and any icons or symbols for potential connections with your brand's values and/or core benefit. Bring the connection to life for customers through direct education of the history and purpose behind your graphic identity. Once you've "connected the dots" for customers, they will always associate your graphics with your core business message.

143. Explore Sensory Cues

Explore using sound, taste, and smell cues to connect your brand with your benefit. At the simplest, link a piece of music or an audio sound bite with your brand offering. At the Eureka! Ranch, the music is classic rock 'n' roll. On our radio show, it's Celtic.

DATA PROVEN TRUTH #37

Meaningful Difference Defines Your True Sales Mission

A clearly defined sales mission is 2.4 times more important than overall job satisfaction when it comes to defining the potential for performance burnout.

The selling process involves high levels of self-confidence and self-awareness, which are eroded away when the salesperson's energy is distracted. Like a car that's running low on oil, a salesperson is who is running on or near emotional exhaustion delivers significantly lower performance.

A study of 203 field salespeople was conducted to determine what dimensions correlated with emotional exhaustion or burnout. The research found that when it came to defining the potential for performance burnout, role clarity was 2.4 times more important than the simple question, "Are you satisfied/happy with your job?"

Successful selling requires more than simply calling on customers and closing sales to achieve a numerical goal. For full satisfaction and continued motivation, it must also involve a cause greater than commercial success—helping make customers' lives better.

Money can motivate in the short term. However, for sustained success, there needs to be a sense of serving others, of helping make customers' lives better. And that means a clear understanding of the Meaningful difference that your offering will make in customers' lives.

When people are uncertain of the true impact an offering has—or don't believe in their offering—they waste energy chasing fears, doubts, and imaginary concerns. Over time, they lose confidence and effectiveness.

PRACTICAL IDEAS

144. Define Your Meaningful Mission in Writing

In simple words, clearly define how your brand makes a Meaningful difference for customers. Be sure that everyone understands and agrees on this as the core reason for your brand's existence.

145. Be Clear About Who You Serve

As Ben Franklin once said, "A man with one watch knows what time it is; a man with two watches is never sure." So, too, is the uncertainty, conflict, and ambiguity that a salesperson faces when serving multiple masters—customers, manufacturing, marketing, shareholders, etc.

The primary focus of sales should always be on the one with the money, the customer. It is the salesperson's job to match the company's offerings with the customer's needs. Everyone else within the organization should be aligned in support of the sales department.

146. Provide a Set of Numerical Goals

Define your sales mission as a set of specific goals to accomplish. Alan Chambers, the first Englishman to walk to the North Pole without resupply, defined it to us this way: "Instead of focusing on the hundreds of miles, I focused on each day, each week's goal. With each accomplishment, my mental confidence grew despite the weakening of my physical conditioning."

147. When Change Is Needed, Be Quick and Overt

There will be times when a change in the sales mission is necessary due to competitive reactions or new strategies. When the change is inevitable, be quick, direct, and overt about it. Make it clear that "today our sales mission is different." Mean it and stick to it. This approach will help reduce the potential for uncertainty, ambiguity, and burnout of the sales staff.

DATA PROVEN TRUTH #38

Guarantees With Strings Attached Deliver Little Impact

Every time you add conditions, issues, and fine print to your communications, you decrease your impact.

One of the most powerful ways to increase a customer's confidence that what you promise will become a reality is to offer a warranty.

A series of five experiments was conducted to determine the relative impact of various factors on a customer's perception of financial risk with various warranty options.

The research found that a no-excuses, top-quality warranty significantly reduced a customer's perception of financial risk.

Alternatively, a moderate warranty had the same impact as a poor warranty or no warranty at all.

Limited warranties, warranties requiring the customer to pay a portion, or even having the warranty come from the leading company with a long established reputation had no impact on a customer's financial fears.

Customers have become highly educated in their understanding of marketing tricks. They know the difference between a real warranty—made by a company that has no doubts about their offering—and a fake warranty being used as a trick just to sell a product.

The nonimpact of company reputation is a fact of life in today's world. Brand trust is based on what you are promising now—not what you did for my father and his father before him.

PRACTICAL IDEAS

148. Stand Behind Your Offering

Take a personal stand for integrity and honesty. Be overt in all sales and marketing claims. Check that your statements are honest both literally and in what perceptions they evoke. Go beyond legal definitions of truth to the standard of "beyond a reasonable doubt" as we've outlined in the opening of this book. By taking a stand that transcends your competitors, you build your trust account with customers.

149. Guarantee Your Offering

Boldly guarantee that you will deliver what you promise. Guarantee your product or service without any fine print. If you have concerns about offering such a guarantee, then you have bigger problems to address than sales and marketing.

150. Respect Your Customers' Intelligence

Today's customers understand the games marketers play when it comes to product and service claims. They understand when you are hyping, tricking, and misrepresenting your claims. Rework your advertising and sales presentations to be "literally" credible, even to yourself.

151. Reduce Complexity and Confusion

The more effort it takes for customers to understand what you are offering, the less they trust you. Put away your advertising copy and your prepared sales presentations and talk to your customers in simple language. Tell them what Meaningful difference your product or service will make in their lives and how you are able to reliably deliver on your promise.

Context Has a Major Impact on Purchasing

When you offer customers the opportunity to choose between three options, they are significantly less likely to select the cheapest one.

The tradeoff of value versus price performance versus cost is one of the most common decisions buyers have to make. In the interest of focus, many companies offer only a basic and deluxe version of their product or service. Academic research indicates that it's smarter for a company to offer three different options.

Research was conducted among 229 participants on the selection of various brands of watches. Three watches, a Casio at $29.99, a Citizen at $44.99, and a Seiko at $59.99, were reviewed.

In one test, the watches were shown in pairs and the participants were asked to make choices on each set and then a final selection from the three. In the other test, customers were simply shown the three options and asked to select across the three without focusing on pairwise choices. When the watches were compared as a set of three, the percentage of customers selecting the lowest-priced watch declined 36 percent versus when they were shown pairs of two.

Another study on pricing context found that customers judged a new product as less expensive when it was shown after viewing a higher-priced option than they did when first seeing the lower-priced option.

Context impacts a customer's price perception. They judge price relative to options. When provided with a choice of two, they are more Mindless in their selection and naturally gravitate toward the cheapest offering. When they are provided three choices, they become more Meaningful in their decision making and are more likely to avoid the lowest-priced option.

PRACTICAL IDEAS

152. Package and Price Your Offering Portfolio Smartly

Use a set of three options to move customers from the lowest to the middle price range. The benefit of this is that you often realize a dramatic increase in profit margin. As you think about the three price options, define them with clarity.

Lowest Cost: The absolute lowest priced model. This offering is for those who consider price by itself as the most important issue. They are open to trading off some ease of use and other features in order to get the lowest price. The profit margins are usually lower for this option, but the volume is usually higher.

Highest Performance: The most advanced and deluxe performance model. This product is for those who require or demand the highest level of performance. The profit margins are often very high; however, the volume itself is often low.

Smartest Price/Value Trade-Off: This offering is in the middle of the price range. It's about maximizing what customers receive relative to the price charged. Often this option provides higher profits relative to the lower cost option and greater volume versus the highest performance option.

153. Think Beyond Your Set of Options

As you price and promote your offerings, think beyond your offerings to those of the competition. If your company cannot or does not want to offer the lowest price or highest performance but your competitors do, then use them as a point of comparison and as one of the three options. This has the advantage of helping you focus on doing one or two things great as opposed to trying to cover the entire price range.

When You Have Substance, Reduce Flash and Sizzle

The more you have a Meaningful difference to communicate, the less you should distract customers with flash, fluff, and sizzle.

The goal of Meaningful Marketing is to get customers to purchase products that can make a real difference for them. The more your offering is genuine and real, the more you should reduce stylistic distractions from your marketing messages and sales presentations.

Customers have only so much ability to process information. The research indicates that when they are bombarded with engaging, exciting, or entertaining stimuli, they are less able to process, digest, and recall important sales messages.

Research was conducted with 324 adults to measure their ability to recall various advertising messages broadcast in three types of television program environments—extreme violence, sexually explicit, or neutral content.

Twenty-four hours after seeing one of the shows, participants were asked to recall what brands had advertised during the television show. Those in the neutral program control group were able to recall 4.7 of the 9 brands. Those watching the violent show recalled 3.0 brands. Those watching the sexual show recalled 2.8 brands.

A separate study in Italy found that about half as many men could remember a television news story reported by a very attractive female than could remember it if reported by an average-looking reporter.

It appears that the more customers direct their attention toward the television show, the less likely they are able to perceive and comprehend the marketing messages.

PRACTICAL IDEAS

154. Help Customers Focus on What's Meaningful

The more you have a Meaningful difference to communicate, the simpler your marketing communications should be. This was confirmed in a study of print advertisements. When the brand had a Meaningful message to communicate, it was more persuasive when the ad was shown in black and white, with color used only to highlight the important differences.

Cut out meaningless distractions from your sales and marketing messages. Simplify your marketing presentations to make your Meaningful difference the "hero" of your message.

155. When You Have Nothing, Distract Customers

When you don't have anything Meaningful to communicate to your customers, then your odds of success are greater if you turn up the flash, sizzle, and hype. But beware, in the long term, this is a losing strategy. At best, it can work for a short time. But with today's public knowledge access, it's just a matter of time before your trickery is exposed.

156. Slow Down Your Communication

We know our offering inside and out. Often customers do not. If we're not careful, we will talk too fast for customers to comprehend. Be sensitive to your customer's level of understanding. Offer to provide a step-by-step explanation or to provide documents or Web sites for teaching customers the same fundamentals that you know.

157. Show Your Product

Many advertising and sales presentations feature lots of talk and little product. If you have a meaningfully great product, show it. Make the product the center of every piece of customer communication. Stop reading now and check all your materials for photos of your product as the core of your marketing message.

DATA PROVEN TRUTH #41

The Power of Three Sales Pitches

The optimum number of marketing pitches to a new customer is three.

When first exposed to a new product or service, customers have an initial tendency to be hesitant. They develop negative counterarguments because they do not fully understand how the new idea can make a difference to them.

A series of consumer research studies has found that it's during about the third exposure that the number of positive thoughts outnumber the negative ones. By the third time people are presented with the marketing message, they are prepared to more fully and fairly assess the offering's merits. Another study found it takes an average of 4.6 face-to-face calls to close the typical industrial product sale.

A separate research study found that customers' first opinion about a new product offering has a surprising amount of error in it. Customers were shown pictures, descriptions, and pricing for new products and asked to rate each product on a 0 to 10 scale.

In 809 cases where customers voted 0 (i.e., that there was absolutely no chance of them purchasing), some 144, or nearly 1 in 6, actually did purchase the product in the following six months.

In 246 cases where customers voted 10 (i.e., that they were definitely likely to purchase), some 128, or a little over half, actually did not purchase the product in the following six months.

It appears that a customer's first instinct is a directional, yet not an absolute, prediction of their ultimate purchasing behavior.

PRACTICAL IDEAS

158. Keep Pitching

While a good first impression is important, it is not a death sentence when a customer turns you down. With each customer interaction, be sure to leave yourself an opening for another presentation. Guide your prospect away from making firm and fixed "no" decisions. Define the gap between your customer's "no" and your Meaningful difference. Then address this gap with each additional presentation.

159. Don't Rest

Remember, when a customer gives you an absolute "yes," there is still a 50 percent probability he will change his mind. When you get a "yes," move rapidly to close the sale. Maintain excellent customer service and commitment to deliver a Meaningful difference after the customer has said "yes"—and after he's made the purchase.

160. Stage Your Three Pitches

In some sales and marketing presentations, you can stage the three exposures. In this case, the first could be designed to provoke curiosity. The second is to develop understanding. The third encounter is to encourage a decision. Each stage can provide additional information.

- *Curiosity:* Articulate a "mind-opening thought" that causes the customer to stop, listen, and think.
- *Understanding:* Confirm how the promise as first communicated works and how you accomplish it.
- *Decision:* Reinforce the Meaningful difference, address any key concerns, and ask for the sale.

161. Let Follow-Up Correspondence Pitch for You

After each presentation, send follow-up notes thanking the customers for their time and feedback. Detail clearly what you are going to do to address their issues. Be clear and specific to demonstrate that you were really listening to them and value their opinions.

DATA PROVEN TRUTH #42

The Fundamentals of Industrial Marketing Success

Industrial marketing success is about communicating customer benefit, uniqueness, and value in an easy-to-understand presentation.

Within the world of marketing, consumer marketing tends to dominate the academic literature and popular press books.

This truth shows how the basic principles of Meaningful Marketing also hold true in industrial product marketing. A study was conducted of 103 new industrial products in the U.S.A., Canada, and Europe. For each initiative, a total of 298 variables were measured. The four most important measures for predicting success were:

- Important Customer Benefit
- Unique Performance
- Benefits Easy to Communicate
- Good Value for the Money

Unsuccessful products in the study had significantly lower values on each of these top success variables.

The keys to success are easy to articulate. The road to industrial marketing success is not hard: Provide your customers with a Meaningful benefit difference, keep it easy to understand, and provide them with a lot of value for their money.

It's easy to delude ourselves into thinking that we are delivering against these dimensions, when in fact, we are not. The natural tendency is to exaggerate benefits, points of difference, and value perceptions. Don't. In the world of industrial marketing, the community of buyers is small. A charlatan is quickly identified.

PRACTICAL IDEAS

162. Focus On What Excites or "Wows" Your Customer

Learn how to sell new customers by listening closely to your current ones. Ask those customers most familiar with your offering what excites them the most about your product or service. Compare what they say with what you say in your marketing messages. Listen closely to how they explain what is important to them. The language of customers often has a level of genuineness that no brochure from the "home office" can ever match.

163. Find Your True Difference

On one sheet of paper, list the overt benefits of your new offering. Then cross out all those that can be found from another broadly available competitor's alternative. Those left are your Meaningful benefits.

164. Tell Your Story to the Uneducated

In industrial markets, our education can often be a barrier to our marketing communication skills. If a technical briefing, marketplace survey, and/or industry dictionary is needed to understand your point of difference, then your odds of success are poor. Also, it's likely your customer's management team has significantly lower understanding of technical details. Define and refine your message until you can explain it clearly to someone who is not in your industry. It will then be ready for customer presentation.

165. Define Why Your Value Proposition Is Great

Stress what customers receive for their money. Make sure that customers fully understand the depth and breadth of your quality. In today's marketplace, costs are rarely random. If your offering costs more than others, there is often a real reason. Higher absolute cost can be due to the use of better-quality ingredients, a higher commitment to customer service, or a greater research and development investment for creating more-effective product or service designs.

The Fundamentals of Meaningful Sales Success

Salesperson success is powered by passion, planning, persistence, people skills, and product knowledge.

The five Ps of successful selling are a whole-brain blend of left-brain discipline—planning, persistence, product knowledge—with the right-brain emotional dimensions of passion and people skills.

These results come from a quantitative study of ninety-one sales managers on forty-six different aspects of sales success, sales failure, and the root causes of success versus failure.

Respondents had an average of thirteen years experience in sales management. Prior to being a part of sales management, the respondents had spent an average of eight years working as field salespeople.

The top five drivers of success were passion/ambition (3.8 out of 4.0), good planning/organizational skills (3.6), people skills (3.4), persistence (3.3), and product knowledge (3.3).

Focusing on a Meaningful benefit difference energizes all five dimensions. A Meaningful difference fuels a natural passion in you to help other people. You will now concentrate on how you can make a real difference in your customers' lives instead of how to use Mindless sales trickery on them.

A Meaningful difference fuels your personal persistence and your natural curiosity to gain product knowledge and plan your efforts. You will have a level of depth and caring that is driven by integrity and authenticity.

PRACTICAL IDEAS

166. Passion

Seek passion in your heart, not your mind. Passion can't be faked. It comes from a deep belief that your offering will make a real difference in customers' lives. Passion comes from a spark of rational thought that has been swept up in emotional faith. Live and breathe your offering. Become fully immersed in its merits.

167. Planning

Set clear and specific objectives. Then create a Meaningful plan for accomplishing those objectives. When you don't know what to do, then say so. Don't lie to yourself with false objectives. Instead of acting blindly, make learning and testing the objectives you pursue. You fuel your passion when you are confident that your objectives are real and sustainable.

168. Persistence

Anything that is new creates tension and uncertainty for customers. This is not a reflection of your offering's merits, just a marketing fact. Persistence is easy to access when you genuinely believe in the merits of your offering.

169. People Skills

People skills are the natural outcome of an attitude of service. When your focus is on fulfilling your customers' true needs, your people skills are genuine and long lasting. Alternatively, when your focus is on simply being a "buddy" to your clients, the relationship is often shallow and short lasting.

170. Product Knowledge

Sales is about knowledge transfer. Each month, every month, commit yourself to at least one significant learning experience. Learn more about your customers' needs and your company's offerings.

The Power of Humble Curiosity

The more educated and experienced you are, the greater your chances of misunderstanding your customers.

Wisdom comes from direct and experiential education. When we first start on the job, our wisdom resources grow rapidly with new knowledge and experiences. In time, we become a source of wisdom for others.

The risk with stored wisdom is that if it's not continually refreshed and reviewed, it can become out-of-date with today's reality.

A study was conducted of 540 industrial product buyers along with the sales representatives who called on them. It found that those salespeople with the most accurate understanding of their customers' true expectations were significantly more successful salespeople.

However, the study also found a negative correlation between accuracy of knowledge and experience in the industry, age, and formal education level. This suggests that while younger and less experienced salespeople have less overall wisdom, what they do have is a more accurate perception of the marketplace.

A separate study by AT&T found that salespeople are often poor judges of their customers' opinions. The researchers showed four new product options to salespeople and their customers. The salespeople were instructed to respond the way they thought their customers would. Sadly, the results varied widely. The collective opinion of the sales force was not at all predictive of their customers' true opinions.

We start out our careers as wide-eyed and innocent. We're sponges—soaking up knowledge and wisdom. If we're not careful, as we age, we end up arrogant and out of touch with the reality of our marketplace.

PRACTICAL IDEAS

171. Observe How Customers Really Use Your Offering

Experience firsthand the usage of your offering. Follow your offering from the moment of purchase to end consumption. Do this on a real-time, first-person basis. Ignore findings that confirm your perceptions. Look instead for knowledge that contradicts your preexisting thoughts.

172. Set Up Annual Vision Meetings With Customers

Set up annual reviews with customers to discuss their situation. Review where they are now and where they see their business going. Listen closely to what they say and more importantly what they don't say. Often it's what customers don't say that reveals the most about their challenges and opportunities.

Before these meetings, use the Internet to read the latest news stories about your customer's company. Read closely what senior management is saying in their briefings with financial markets. The more aware you are of these issues, the more freely your customers will help you "connect the dots" and understand how the broader company's vision may or may not impact you and your company.

Share with customers your company's long-term vision as well. In particular, paint a picture of hope. Define clearly your long-term commitment to growth and development.

173. Stop Assuming

When your company's management has questions about the impact a new initiative will have with customers, hesitate. Don't automatically answer in your usual way. Rather, hit the phones and the street to ask customers their opinions. Ask clearly and listen openly to what the real experts—your customers—think and believe.

DATA PROVEN TRUTH #45

Meaningful vs. Mindless Loyalty Programs

Meaningful loyalty programs are built on sharing news and building connections, not simply delivering discounts.

In 1981, American Airlines invented the world's first frequent-flyer program. Within seven days, United Airlines introduced a program of its own. Before long, it became the cost of doing business, and all airlines had some form of a frequent-buyer program.

Industry data indicates that once customers join a loyalty program, they tend to increase spending on that brand by an average of 27 percent. Furthermore, 43 percent of members say that loyalty programs lead to more frequent purchases, and 16 percent said a loyalty program causes them to choose one option exclusively. These numbers are clearly significant, yet they are not startling when you consider the total cost of these programs.

Loyalty programs are most effective when you have a fundamentally Meaningful offering and you are seeking to build a deep connection with your customers.

Loyalty programs can become financial nightmares when their sole purpose is to deliver Mindless discounts. In these cases, they increase the perception of your brand as a common commodity and are primarily centered on "trapping" customers into purchasing.

At the end of 2001, it was estimated that the world's airlines had given out nearly twelve trillion frequent flyers miles, with two-thirds of those miles as yet unredeemed. This is a huge unfunded liability.

Just like marketing can be Meaningful or Mindless, so, too, can loyalty programs deliver either substance or simply a complicated discounting plan.

Meaningful loyalty programs can offer price discounts. However, that is rarely their primary reason for existence. Rather, they are geared toward communicating news and information to their members.

PRACTICAL IDEAS

174. Leverage Special Access Loyalty Programs

The simplest and maybe the least expensive benefit you can offer to loyal customers is special access and priority service. The travel industry does this well. Car rental agencies and airlines offer express services for check-in and free upgrades when available. The offer of special access is the ultimate thank-you to customers for their loyalty. Explore opportunities to provide preferred shipping, ordering, or delivery to your most loyal customers.

175. Leverage Special Knowledge Loyalty Programs

Loyal customers have an advanced understanding of your product or service. Open a system of dialogue with loyal customers. Encourage advanced discussions on a two-way basis. Give them access to the leading edge of your company's thinking. And listen to their ideas. The greater the interaction between your company and your customers, the tighter the loyalty bond.

176. Leverage Collector Loyalty Programs

Collector loyalty programs can be very powerful. Collectors exist for everything from dolls to stamps to antiques. To encourage collecting, empower secondary markets and offer products that lend themselves to collectibility.

177. Your Approach Is as Important as What You Give

Maybe the most important thing to consider regarding loyal customers is how you treat them. A simple thank-you and remembering their names are at least as important as what you give them. This is not always easy, as loyal customers are also the ones most likely to voice their suggestions for improvement. Over time, their suggestions can sound like complaints and you can start consciously or subconsciously treating your loyal customers badly.

Meaningful Marketing Is About Measurement

When you set numerical sales and marketing goals, you take a meaningful step toward realizing them.

Meaningful Marketing is about measurement. It's about quantifying the tangible benefit difference that you offer customers. It's also about measuring response rates to all sales and marketing initiatives.

The most fundamental measurement is to set a personal goal for your own results. The beneficial effect of goal setting for task performance is considered one of the most robust and replicable findings in psychological literature.

By goals, we mean challenging, tough-to-reach, specific goals. Not easy, see-what-happens, give-it-a-try goals.

The very act of writing down a challenging goal has a near magical ability to make it a possibility.

A study was conducted of 491 independent salespeople who had recently started a new job. The salespeople were surveyed on their personal, self-set sales goal for their first year:

- 60 percent reported setting no goal of any kind.
- 32 percent reported setting a general earnings goal.
- 8 percent reported setting a specific annual dollar earnings goal.

The level of goal setting had a direct correlation with earnings. In contrast to those salespeople who set no earnings goal, those who set a general goal earned twice as much, and those who set a specific goal earned nearly three times as much.

When you define on paper your clear and concrete objective, you fuel your internal motivation. You are, in essence, challenging yourself to grow and achieve your own standards.

PRACTICAL IDEAS

178. Develop a Plan for Meaningful Growth

What is your past six-month, twelve-month, or two-year trend? Write it down. This is your natural momentum. Now, calculate what a doubling or tripling of your growth trend looks like. What will it take to deliver this kind of growth? If your sales are declining, what will it take to turn your sales around? Write it down.

Simply "working harder" is unlikely to be the answer. Rather, you will need to make a significant change in your sales and marketing. You will need to change your message, how you deliver your message, or the frequency of your message delivery.

179. Always Quantify Advertising Effectiveness

Measure every new piece of advertising and every media vehicle. Include a toll-free phone number or Web site for more information or special offers. Always collect and analyze your response rates. Great advertising immediately generates customer interest. Identify a specific customer mailing list or television, radio, or print advertising vehicle to conduct your tests with. The more tests you run, the greater your understanding.

180. Always Quantify Media Efficiency

The cost of space in print media or airtime on television or radio varies according to the quality and quantity of impressions delivered. The choice of media vehicle should be based on cost efficiency. By researching the relative response rates of various media options, you gain leverage in negotiations. If one vehicle generates half the response rate, then you can push hard for a significantly lower price.

181. Stay Honest to Milestones

Develop a "shipping" mentality whereby your organizational culture prides itself on not missing key milestones no matter what. When a salesperson gives his word to the customer that a new product or service will be delivered, he's speaking for everyone.

You Sell More When You Compete More

Competition by internal and external forces fuels a passion for winning more sales.

The importance of business competition is controversial. Some see competition as an evil, a force that disrupts interpersonal teamwork and creates negative energy. Others see it as fundamental fuel for a free marketplace economy where winners and losers are clearly identified.

Research was conducted with 158 business-to-business salespeople. As expected, it found a direct relationship between those who set high personal goals and those with the greatest sales success.

The research also sought to understand what the compelling reasons were for a salesperson to set higher personal sales goals. Modeling of goals found that the following variables were the most predictive.

1. Self-Confidence: This is the confidence a salesperson has in his personal skills and abilities.

2. Personal Competitiveness: This is a love of interpersonal competition and a passion for winning and being better than others.

3. Organizational Competitiveness: This is a culture that encourages and rewards interpersonal competition.

The research found that all three dimensions were significant and interrelated reasons when it came to setting high personal goals.

Interestingly, when one component is missing, it directly impacts the others. For example, a confident and personally competitive salesperson will tend to set lower goals if the work culture is not perceived to be competitive.

When it comes to making a Meaningful difference, competition on both the individual and organizational level is effective.

PRACTICAL IDEAS

182. Leverage the Rhythms of Sports Teams

Sports teams have a rhythm. They practice and prepare for a season that builds to a championship. Then they take a little time off and start the cycle again. You can create a similar momentum for your sales and marketing team. Develop a rhythm of rest, preparation, competition, and going for the championship.

183. Overtly Build Sales Self-Confidence

Research has identified three tools for improving sales self-confidence:
  • Training and teaching sales skills
  • Achieving sales success
  • Modeling actions based on a proven success model

184. Recruit Competitive People

Look for competitiveness in the backgrounds of prospective salespeople. Examples include participation in competitive sports, events, and activities. Overtly ask prospective employees if they consider themselves to be highly competitive. Ask what fuels their competitiveness. Ask for examples of times when they tried and failed. Then ask how they felt about losing. Look for a healthy level of competitive frustration with the loss. It's highly probable that those with no problem losing will have no problem not winning for you as well.

185. Overtly Develop a Competitive Organization

Empower healthy competition between divisions, departments, and regions. Direct the competition toward the one thing that matters the most. Make sure everyone understands the rules of competition and that everyone plays fair. Recognize those who assist, by awarding "best supporting actor" to encourage full participation.

DATA PROVEN TRUTH #48

The Five Decision-Making Styles of Buyers

Research indicates there are five distinct styles of decision makers: charismatics, thinkers, skeptics, followers, and controllers.

A two-year research project was conducted involving some sixteen hundred executives across a broad range of industries. The research identified five distinct types of business-to-business customers. By understanding who you are dealing with, you can modify your marketing approach to make it more Meaningful for that customer.

1. *Charismatics* (25 percent of executives): These are the visionaries who quickly grasp concepts and get excited about big ideas. When it comes to making a final decision, they often have a short attention span and need a balanced perspective.

2. *Thinkers* (11 percent of executives): These are the toughest executives to persuade. Thinkers are intellectual decision makers who dislike being forced into making decisions.

3. *Skeptics* (19 percent of executives): These are aggressive, instinctive executives. They distrust data, especially when it contradicts their beliefs and natural instincts.

4. *Followers* (36 percent of executives): These are the most conservative of executives. They live a life of fear. They trust past precedent, previous experience, and the recommendations of other managers.

5. *Controllers* (9 percent of executives): These are the most fact driven and fear adverse of all decision makers. They distrust ambiguity and uncertainty.

PRACTICAL IDEAS

186. Selling Charismatics

Focus on the most important and most dramatic "big picture" bottom-line benefits first. Leverage visual aids and minimize the use of catchwords and stereotypes. Keep your presentation fast and fluid. Be prepared to shift from the long-term vision to executional minutia and back to vision again in seconds. Be sure you really believe in what you're selling and have absolute knowledge of all details.

187. Selling Thinkers

Provide an open and honest presentation of all the data. Utilize market research, cost-benefit analysis, and details on past precedents. Thinkers love a frame of reference, so provide tons of side-by-side comparisons. Focus on the facts and just the facts. Empower and guide, but don't force thinkers' decisions. Learn to pause and ask for their viewpoint before summarizing to build support.

188. Selling Skeptics

Prepare yourself emotionally for a demanding and disruptive presentation. Methodically build trust. Focus on why your offering is meaningfully different. When you're attacked, keep your cool and stay focused on your Meaningful difference to rise above skepticism.

189. Selling Followers

Show how what you have to offer reduces their chance of failure. Detail clearly the pedigree of all that you're recommending. Overtly explain how your recommendation is the path that many others are following. Detail clearly how large the potential gain is and how minimal the risk is.

190. Selling Controllers

Be the expert. Present your facts in a straightforward linear fashion. Don't hesitate or show weakness of any kind. If you stand strong and confident, you'll reduce their fear.

The Three Cultures of Business Buying

Research indicates there are three distinct cultures of organizational buying: entrepreneurial, planning, and bureaucratic.

The organization that a buyer belongs to can have a direct impact on how he processes and proceeds with purchasing decisions. By understanding the different types of cultures, you improve your chances of making a Meaningful and successful connection.

A study of 109 business buyers identified three core types of large company decision cultures, along with a collection of methods for selling to them.

1. *Entrepreneurial:* These types of organizations often have no formal buying policies. Decisions are highly decentralized with one or two people making decisions. Decision making is dependent on personal intuition and judgmental evaluation procedures. Entrepreneurial organizations can be easy to make a sale to but very difficult to maintain as they are just as likely to change vendors at any time without good reason.

2. *Planning:* Planning organizations make decisions based on long-range considerations. Decisions are a result of a careful assessment of the organization's needs. Consensus across departments is a critical part of the decision process.

3. *Bureaucratic:* Decisions are based primarily on past precedents and the official rules and regulations of the organization. Forms and procedures are critical. Buyers are more managers of the process than they are independent decision makers. Change is seen as an evil because as it disrupts the flow of Mindless consistency. At first, sales can be difficult with bureaucratic organizations. However, the good news is, once sold, they are slow to change again.

PRACTICAL IDEAS

191. Selling Entrepreneurial Cultures

Be simple and straightforward. The buyer is inclined to make independent decisions. Focus on building trust with the customer and yourself, your offering, and your company. Empower the decision maker to just say "yes." If your offering is complex or hard to understand, then you will lose the advantage of spontaneous decision making that entrepreneurial cultures love. Focus your presentation on the innovative nature of your offering and why it's such a smart decision. Stay in touch by asking, "what's new," and build trust by keeping up with changes.

192. Selling Planning Cultures

Concentrate on the technical facts of your product's performance and compatibility. Leverage team-selling by bringing a marketing and product technology expert with you to presentations. Match up your company's experts with their experts. Define clearly the strengths of your processes and quality control systems. Focus your presentation on the systemic and "total solution" nature of your product or service. Stay in touch regularly to reinforce your commitment.

193. Selling Bureaucratic Cultures

These are the most Mindless of all buyers. You need to make them aware of your services, but it's hard to sell them. Rather, the process usually involves your writing formal responses to their requests for proposals in the exact manner as presented. Be as competitive as possible on price as there is a good chance that it will be the primary, if not the only, decision criteria. Focus your presentation on your flexibility in adapting to the customer's specifications and your systemic and long-term price advantages. Stay in touch by using testimonials from other users. Bureaucrats love to follow others.

DATA PROVEN TRUTH #50

The Three Sources of Trust

Research indicates there are three distinct sources of customer trust: company, salesperson, and product.

Trust is a belief that the benefit being promised will be reliably delivered. Building the trust required to spark a purchase is a never-ending challenge.

Through thousands of disappointments, customers have developed high levels of distrust for new offerings. A primary job of sales and marketing is to build bonds of trust with new customers.

Research was conducted with 568 purchasing managers to quantify the core source of customer trust. Computer modeling identified that trust was dependent on three factors: (1) trust of the company, (2) trust of the salesperson, and (3) trust of the product's performance.

Most importantly, it was found that each of the three dimensions had a direct and highly significant correlation with bottom-line sales success.

Further modeling identified the relative importance of each of the three sources of trust. On a relative basis, the company's reputation was the most important and the specific new product was the least.

Relative Importance

Trust in Company. 1.9

Trust in Salesperson 1.7

Trust in Product 1.0

Buyers understand that products come and products go. Consequently, they base trust on something more sustainable—their perception of the level that the company and the salesperson will stand behind the product in the event of problems.

PRACTICAL IDEAS

194. Build the Corporate Brand

Leverage your company's historical pedigree of success. Articulate the corporate culture, people, and processes that stand behind everything you do. Clearly and overtly explain how your new offering builds on your company's commitment to making a Meaningful difference for customers. Literally wear your brand on your sleeve. Embroider and imprint your corporate logo everywhere.

195. Provide Leadership to Your Industry

Participate in your industry trade association on key committees. At industrywide trade shows, make a major statement about your commitment to the industry and your customers. At industry conferences, provide keynote speakers and seminar leaders with publicly release research that can help the industry grow.

196. Build Personal Trust By Being a Raving Company Fan

Be open and overt about your absolute trust in your corporation and its offering. Be a raving fan for your corporation. Stand solidly behind the virtues and meaningfulness of what your company offers. Customers observe your attitude toward your company. The more you believe in your company, the more they will, too.

197. As a New Company, Confront Your Disadvantage

As a new company, your lack of corporate pedigree is an immediate and considerable disadvantage. Confront this directly by linking your company's credibility with the credibility of your corporate founders or parent company. Offer introductory extended warranties, on-site technical assistance, free samples.

198. Let Your Product Do the Talking

Let your product do the talking: Challenge customers to participate in real-world product demonstrations.

DATA PROVEN TRUTH #51

The Three Stages of Brand Trust

Research indicates that the three most important stages of brand trust are brand satisfaction, brand predictability, and brand expertise.

The purchase and usage of a new brand either creates or destroys customer trust. Research among 280 customers found a significant correlation between level of brand trust and customer loyalty. Loyalty in this case is defined as agreement with statements such as "I intend to keep buying this brand," "I often tell my friends how good this brand is," "If this brand is not available when I'm shopping, I will wait to get it or search for it somewhere else."

Mathematical modeling of what drives customer trust identified three stages of trust:

1. *Brand Satisfaction* (importance score 0.46) The first and foremost stage of building trust is your performance versus expectations. No amount of marketing hype can overcome the importance of product performance.

2. *Brand Predictability* (importance score 0.21) The second stage of building brand trust is continuation of the satisfaction delivered during stage one. When customers experience reliable delivery of their initial satisfaction, they develop sustainable trust.

3. *Brand Expertise* (importance score 0.11) The third stage of building brand trust is the big-picture view of the brand's level of overall competence. It's about the brand's expertise relative to the offerings of competition. When customers believe that you are best in class, their loyalty becomes Meaningful, Mindless, and unquestioning.

PRACTICAL IDEAS

199. Consider Your Stage of Trust With Each Customer

Organize your customers based on what stage of trust they have in you and your brand. Develop sales and marketing programs that help each customer move to the next level of Meaningful trust.

200. Insure Brand Satisfaction

Brand satisfaction is about having a healthy balance between marketing promises and real performance. It's our opinion that the most successful marketing sets an expectation level that is about 80 percent of reality. This leaves 20 percent above and beyond the marketing promise for exceeding customer expectations.

201. Insure Brand Predictability

Ship quality predictably. Maintain open and frequent communication with customers to insure no surprises for the customer. Predictability means communication, not Mindless consistency. When even the simplest improvements or changes are made— from packaging to formulation to performance—be overt in communicating the changes.

202. Insure Brand Expertise

Communicate clearly the Meaningful skill your company has in discovering, developing, and delivering world-class products or services. Provide technical seminars and newsletters discussing ongoing research efforts. Proudly share reviews and endorsements by industry thought leaders and the media.

203. Consistency Builds Trust

Monitor all communications of the brand with respect to the three factors just described by focusing on consistency. Once Mindless tactics take root, they are hard habits to break. Adopt a quality control mentality with regard to communications so that your brand's credibility doesn't erode with Mindless inconsistencies.

DATA PROVEN TRUTH #52

The Core Sources of Personal Trust

Customer trust of a salesperson is based on (1) dependability, (2) honesty, (3) customer first, (4) competence, and (5) likability.

Cultivating personal trust among customers is of critical importance to sales success. The common stereotype is that of a salesperson seeking to become the most likable of friends with the customer.

Research indicates that while likability is the most often developed trait, it's also the least important when it comes to nurturing customer trust with you as a salesperson.

Researchers asked 187 industrial buyers to rate the most recent salesperson who had called on them. They provided eight different ratings of their trust in the salesperson, along with ratings on a series of diagnostic dimensions.

Results and importance versus likability were as follows.

1. *Dependability* (320 percent greater than likability): Following through on promises and being reliable.

2. *Honesty* (130 percent greater than likability): Telling the truth, not exaggerating, and being open about strengths and weaknesses of his offerings.

3. *Customer First* (80 percent greater than likability): The buyer's perception that the salesperson puts the buyer's true needs ahead of making a sale.

4. *Competence* (30 percent greater than likability): The salesperson's knowledge about his company's products or services.

5. *Likability* (Control): How friendly and approachable the salesperson is. Likability was the least important trait and also the most likely trait, with nearly twice as many salespeople being rated highly on likability than the average for all trust traits.

PRACTICAL IDEAS

204. Dependability

As the classic saying goes, "Say what you do and do what you say." Let everything else go crazed but insure that your word is good. Create a pattern of dependability by making small promises and overdelivering on results.

205. Honesty

Honesty is about being frank and truthful. It's about being real and genuine. Instead of being a "professional pitchman," be an honest advisor. Present both the strengths and the weaknesses of your offering. It's better for customers to learn about your weakness from you now than to discover it themselves later.

206. Customer First

You cannot serve two masters. And long term, the way to best serve your company is by putting your customer first. You may lose the sale today, but long-term rewards are orders of magnitude greater.

207. Competence

No one should know more about your offering and your competitor's offering than you. Knowing more means an understanding of both the factual technology of your offering and the practical application of it. Continually test your mastery to build confidence.

208. Likability

Likability is about connecting to customers on a personal level through common interests and goals. It also means common courtesy—making efficient use of the buyer's time, being courteous and polite.

The Power of a Market-Driven Learning Orientation

When you and your company are market driven instead of production-efficiency driven, you realize significantly greater growth, profitability, customer satisfaction, and new product/service success rates.

In the quest for profits that fuel growth, companies can be loosely segmented into two distinct types of organizational focuses—those that are market driven and those that are driven toward production efficiencies.

A market-driven orientation is characterized by a focus on discovering, developing, and delivering superior value for customers.

A production-efficiency orientation is focused on maintaining lower costs and lower pricing in an effort to increase unit sales.

In-depth research conducted in Australia found that those companies that were market driven had significantly greater sales growth, profitability, customer satisfaction, and new product/service success rates.

A key determinant in identifying each company's style was in how they approached the gathering and sharing of customer information.

Market-driven companies in this study were significantly more likely to gather information both formally and informally about their competition, their marketplaces, and their customer needs.

Market-driven companies were also significantly more likely to share market learnings across departments.

The facts stated above address individuals as well as corporations. When you are market driven, your individual effectiveness and competitive performance also grows.

To be clear, listening and learning can initially be inefficient uses of your time. However, continued effort deepens your ability to rapidly capitalize on market trends and opportunities.

This Australian study is the basis for the next few truths.

PRACTICAL IDEAS

209. Learn and Talk More About Your Competition

Overtly ask questions about how your offerings compare with those of the competition. It's almost certain that when a customer purchases your product, they will do so in place of something else. Often your perceived market competitor is different from the actual competitor your customers switch to.

210. Read More About Your Customers and Industry

Today's electronic information systems offer a wealth of information opportunities for those with the patience and commitment to learn. The more you read and learn, the greater your likelihood to be among the first to identify Meaningful opportunities.

211. Ask Key Customer Groups Where They're Going

Directly ask customers what their greatest challenges are and what their vision for the future is. In particular, listen closely for differences in opinions between your most loyal and least loyal customers. Even though they both are purchasing your product, their motivations, beliefs, and attitudes could be very different.

212. Keep Asking What's New

Make it a habit to ask your customers and your own company staff, "What's new?" In our compartmentalized world, we have a tendency to assume that everyone is aware of all changes. In truth, information flow tends to be slow and inefficient. By informally asking, "What's new?" you increase your odds of knowing more than your competition.

213. Keep Listening After the Sale

Maintain your market-driven orientation after the customer has purchased to look for any inconsistencies between your marketing process and product delivery. Differences in impressions before versus after purchase can be helpful in optimizing your marketing.

DATA PROVEN TRUTH #54

The Power of Meaningful Market Research

The capability to conduct Meaningful market research is a critical business success skill.

Companies that are serious about growth are always on the search for competitive capabilities that separate them from their competitors. An Australian research study found that companies that had greater sales growth, profitability, customer satisfaction, and new product/service success rates also had significantly stronger market research abilities.

These customer-driven companies leveraged their market research abilities in finding new customers, improving their marketing programs and communications, and in guiding their product development offerings.

The core of Meaningful market research is a focus on understanding the customer's perceptions from an "outside-in" viewpoint.

The leveraging of market research requires courage and curiosity.

Courage is required as one must be open to being surprised. It's easy to stand in judgment of what is right and what is wrong. More difficult is having the courage to really learn from your mistakes.

Curiosity is required as great research starts with articulating a question to be explored. From this question, the scientific method of testing and learning is applied with discipline.

Critical to great marketing research is an understanding of and comfort with disciplined statistical analysis. Statistics are required if you are to make decisions that are reliable and reproducible. Research without statistics is about as reliable as your horoscope.

PRACTICAL IDEAS

214. Measure Importance to Find What's Most Meaningful

To take a simple measurement of the relative importance of various customer benefits, make a list of five things you communicate to customers. This could include things such as your quality, service guarantee, variety options, etc. Next, draft a simple E-mail and ask customers to rank the dimensions from one to five, with one being the dimension that is most important to them. When the E-mails come back, simply average the scores for each dimension and you have an instant understanding of relative importance.

215. Focus Groups Have Been Validated as Not Accurate

A simple measurement of what consumers actually say gives you insights into perceptions, attitudes, satisfaction, and disappointments. But the qualitative feedback from focus groups should not be used to generalize the whole market. Rather, use focus groups and personal observation as an exploratory step to develop hypotheses that can be validated in reliable quantitative research techniques.

216. Look for Both Forms of Customer Opportunity

When looking for Meaningful differences the starting point is often quantifying the customer need. This can be done by identifying how big and how frequently various problems occur for customers. Survey them in person, via mail, or via E-mail. Ask customers to rate the frequency (number of times a year, month, or week) that they encounter each of a set of problems and ask them to rate on a scale of one to ten how big of a problem each is when it occurs. To understand the market opportunity, ask them also to rate from one to ten their satisfaction with currently available solutions for each problem.

Compare the problem magnitude (frequency times intensity) versus satisfaction gap (ten minus satisfaction score) to identify Meaningful benefit opportunities.

The Power of Meaningful Pricing

Pricing management is a critical business success skill.

A broad-based empirical research study targeted Australian companies to discover the performance advantages of market- and
nonmarket-driven firms. Analysis revealed that companies with
greater sales growth, profitability, customer satisfaction, and new
product/service success rates also had significantly stronger pricing
management skills.

With Meaningful Marketing, communicating the value you offer
potential customers is the most important task. The second key issue
is properly setting your price.

Setting price is part science, part art. It's about being sensitive to
the multidimensional nature of customers' price perceptions.

In a free market, the price you set is a clear assessment of what
you believe to be the value of your offering. Cheap products are cheap
products. Products that are of higher quality and that offer Meaningful advantages over the competition usually cost more.

When you can actually achieve a pricing premium compared to
competition, it becomes one of the best measures of your brand
because it is free market testimony to your customers' commitment.

Pricing wisdom is also about understanding your competition's
costs. When you know your competition's fixed and variable costs,
you can better understand what, if any, leverage you might have in
pricing.

The most important dimension of pricing is profit margin. The
greater your margin, the greater your ability to invest in Meaningful
R&D, pay shareholders a reasonable return, and have flexibility when
competitors attempt to become more competitive with their pricing.

PRACTICAL IDEAS

217. Meaningful Pricing

Being open and honest about your pricing will win more sales than playing pricing games. Be direct about what value customers receive and what it costs. Give them confidence in the stability of your pricing.

One of the most important issues for customers is to feel that they got the best price possible from you. If you have one price and only one price—with no price negotiations—customers may not like it, but they feel satisfied that they didn't "overpay." Contrast this with situations where price is negotiated—causing customers to leave the transaction with a sense of apprehension that they may have paid too much.

218. Understand Volume vs. Price

As you set your prices, be sure that you understand how volume impacts your cost structure. It could be that, at a higher volume, your cost of production drops dramatically as you move to lower-cost production methods. However, it's just as possible that a higher volume will not have much of an impact. By understanding the impact of volume on pricing, you can better manage customer expectations and your own with regards to pricing in the future.

219. Where Are Prices Going?

Price changes represent significant sales opportunities. During inflationary times, special sales opportunities exist prior to increases. In technology products where raw costs are regularly decreasing, sales opportunities exist around each decline. By understanding the momentum and timing of pricing changes, you are better able to meaningfully advise your customers.

The Power of Meaningful Product/Service Development

Product/service development is a critical business success skill.

An Australian research study found that companies that had greater sales growth, profitability, customer satisfaction, and new product/service success rates also had significantly stronger product development abilities.

Skill in development of new offerings is not about technological wizardry. Globally, research shows that great development skill is about being able to translate scientific knowledge into Meaningful products and services.

The great developer of new offerings has the ability to see both sides—both the technological truths and the customers' needs.

As discussed earlier, customers have no interest in new technology for the sake of the technology only; rather, they seek satisfaction of their wants and needs. And great development skill blends an understanding of what's technically possible with what's desirable by your customer.

Great product developers are skilled at adapting and adjusting until they achieve a healthy balance of technical implementation to customer requirements. They look for elegant product designs that make powerful high technology solutions simple and customer friendly.

Increasingly, product developers are challenged to keep a keen eye on leveraging technology to discover ways to recoup all or part of the incremental costs for their technology enhancements so to achieve superior customer value. Note, if you increase the benefit by $100 and charge $100 for the improvement, you have made no Meaningful value improvement.

PRACTICAL IDEAS

220. Meaningful Product/Service Development

Be the voice of the customer in all product and service development discussions. Challenge development people to explain in one simple sentence how a new technology will make your customers' lives better. Have them quantify how the incremental cost is less than the incremental benefit perception.

221. Define Technology Claims Early in Development

When a new technology starts gaining development momentum, quickly turn it into customer-friendly words—brochure copy, Web site copy, or a simple industry press release. When you put the customer proposition in writing, you define with clarity the project's development goals. And even more importantly, when you put it in writing, you expose the flaws of weak thinking.

222. Use Adventure Teams to Enhance Entrepreneurism

A study of seven hundred firms in the United States identified the existence of factors in companies that were successful in product innovation. An advantage was found in firms that applied an entrepreneurial approach to new product development teams. Put together capable cross-functional "adventure teams" from R&D, marketing, manufacturing, sales, and management that can rapidly create, market, and test prototypes with customers. Our favorite timing is the biblical "forty days and forty nights."

223. Make It Less Fuzzy

Often considerable confusion occurs at the "fuzzy front end" where new marketing ideas are fed into the corporate commercialization machine. Sorting ideas by degree of Meaningful difference can be a powerful tool for prioritizing projects. Make two-dimensional plots of technology cost estimates versus Meaningful benefit difference to identify opportunities that are both customer Meaningful and cost effective.

DATA PROVEN TRUTH #57

The Power of Meaningful Channel/Distribution Management

Channel and distribution management is a critical business success skill.

In an earlier truth, one of the keys to Meaningful sales growth was finding more customers. To deliver to new customers requires performance advantages in managing distribution channel logistics. An Australian research study found that companies that had greater sales growth, profitability, customer satisfaction, and new product/service success rates also had significantly stronger channel and distribution management abilities.

Channel and distribution management is about understanding the relay chain between your company and the end consumer of your offering.

Think of a pipe with a series of valves in it. On one end, you load your offering into the pipe. At the other end of the pipe is the end consumer of your product or service. In between you and your end consumer are a series of valves representing such dimensions as distributors, the media, your sales force, your customers' buying departments, and retail store staff.

When your offering comes to a closed valve, it is stopped. To achieve success with channel and distribution management, it is critical that you deliver value to each member of your distribution pipeline.

A common mistake is "wishing" for distribution support. Instead of treating each valve with respect, you assume that through sheer customer suction from the end of the pipe you can force the valves open. Get over it. Each valve is a customer. Each customer has distinct needs. Each customer needs to be sold as an individual. Do not try to sell the customer at valve three in the distribution pipeline the benefits that are important to the customer at valve four.

PRACTICAL IDEAS

224. Meaningful Channel/Distribution Management

Define your distribution pipeline. What people or organizations are critical for your success? Create a simple visual chart that lays out your distribution process. Openly assess your status with each valve of your distribution pipeline and determine if you and your company are welcomed as a valuable partner. If not, why not? Challenge yourself to articulate clearly the Meaningful benefit difference that you provide to each valve along your pipeline.

225. Develop the Performance Advantage of Speed

Discover better ways to support your pipeline to leverage time as a competitive advantage. The old adage "time is money" never goes out of fashion. Your speed of reaction means less inventory, less costs, and better customer service for everyone.

226. Explore Distribution Changes as a Source of Difference

Every valve in your distribution pipeline offers opportunities to enhance your Meaningful difference. Explore ways to adapt, adjust, and alter what is done at each step in the process. A powerful customer-driven trend is the shift of portions of manufacturing and/or product assembly from the factory to closer to the end customer so to enable customization and personalization.

227. Lead New Customers to Open Markets

Collaborate with channel partners to create new avenues and opportunities for your products or services. Look at the behaviors of your target customers and find new places to be where they are. Look for relevant but unexpected ways to fulfill customers' needs.

DATA PROVEN TRUTH #58

The Power of Great Customer Communication

Great skill at customer communication is a key to success.

The goal of creating greater customer value is becoming a worn cliché. To move past the cliché, identify key variables that actually impact bottom-line results.

An Australian research study found that companies that had greater sales growth, profitability, customer satisfaction, and new product/service success rates also had significantly stronger customer communication abilities.

Customer communication skill is about a commitment to speaking to customers in a Meaningful and motivating manner. It's also about committing the resources to actually get your message heard.

The style and format of communications varies according to industry. In industrial markets, personal selling face-to-face is the primary communication system. In mass consumer markets, advertising and promotions are the primary forms.

No matter what your market, you need to be able to overtly communicate your message in a concise fashion. In industrial settings, the focused message is often used as part of voice mail or E-mail to prospects. In these and all cases, tight messages focused on your Meaningful benefit are important for getting the customer's attention quickly.

To articulate the message requires a commitment to viewing your offering "from the outside in"—the perspective of the customer. To think in this manner first requires you to have a clear understanding of who your customers are, how they think, and what really motivates them.

PRACTICAL IDEAS

228. Learn to Listen Closely

The path to great communication is listening. The more closely you listen to customers, the more accurate and motivating your message will be. To maintain accurate awareness of customer needs, develop a set of information sources by reviewing customer service complaints or regularly attending new customer presentations.

229. Become Anticipatory, Not Reactionary

Once every few months have your team step back from your business and hold a debate on where the market is going. Review market events along with trends in present and prospective markets. Outline a half-dozen scenarios that might happen within the next year. Simply conducting this "what-if" thinking exercise will enhance everyone's listening awareness. When team members encounter a customer situation that confirms a scenario, they will be much more likely to notice it and communicate it to others.

230. Leverage Strategic Partnerships for Knowledge

Look for opportunities to improve customer knowledge and communications by leveraging other members of your distribution channel. Seek customer insights from suppliers, comanufacturers, packaging suppliers, logistics, and other customer-linked partners. Your partners have a vested interest in your success. Leverage their wisdom by overtly asking them for ideas and insight.

231. Continuously Quantify Communications Effectiveness

Emphasize "management by fact" as a way to achieve continuous improvement in your customer communications. Continuously test your sales and marketing messages. On a perpetual basis test more effective methods for articulating your Meaningful difference.

DATA PROVEN TRUTH #59

The Power of Meaningful Brand Management

Brand management is a critical business success skill.

An Australian research study found that companies that had greater sales growth, profitability, customer satisfaction, and new product/service success rates also had significantly stronger brand management abilities.

Brand management means effective and coordinated advertising and promotion programs. It also means effective targeting and coordination of corporate resources to best serve customer needs.

For the quickest assessment of your organization's brand management skills, ask what quantitative measurements are taken on the company's advertising and promotions. Just as salespeople's results are quantified versus objectives, so, too, the effectiveness of advertising and promotion programs must be quantified if you wish to learn more and sell more with less effort.

Great brand management is about outstanding communications. It's about listening closely to end consumers, channel customers, and then focusing company resources on what really matters.

Great brand management is about continuously discovering new ways of looking at existing offerings. It's about thinking deeply about what you do and why you do it.

Important: Brand management is not about managing the brand; rather, it's about organizing the company's resources to service the customers' needs. And consequently from this, your brand grows stronger.

PRACTICAL IDEAS

232. Define What's Changed in Three Years, Five Years, Ten Years

Gather samples of your sales promotions and advertising campaigns from today, three years ago, five years ago, and ten years ago. Study how the content has changed. Are you communicating the same or virtually the same message as you did in years past? If so, it's time to evolve. Markets and customers are continuously growing. If you're doing the same promotions or running virtually the same advertising, then you're dying and you just haven't noticed yet.

233. Learn Both the What and the Why of Your Brand

Every week, make a conscious effort to learn more about "what" your brand does and "why." Become a master at understanding not just what but also why you do as you do. In the stories of why exist the drama to excite new customers to purchase.

234. Focus on What Really Matters

A survey of top sales and marketing executives indicated that developing new products or services was the most important marketing action that a manager could take. For inspiring growth, new product or service development was twice as important as managing pricing, and eight times more important than managing trade promotions.

235. Sharpen Your Brand's Thirty-Second Message

The complexity of today's products and services requires the involvement of many people both inside and outside of your organization. To maximize the effectiveness of your entire team, it's critical that everyone be focused on the same objectives. Spend time crafting a tight thirty-second message of your Meaningful benefit difference that can be communicated to anyone at any time. By keeping it simple and clear, your brand strategy will stay in the minds of all involved.

Big Changes Create Big Stress for Your People

Dramatic changes can cause significant stress within your organization, resulting in poor performance.

In life, critical events such as a marriage or a new house are seen as positives. Events such as death in the family or the loss of a job are negatives. The accumulation of events, even positive events, has been found to predict vulnerability to heart attacks or other health problems.

A research study of 526 sales representatives found that critical sales events follow a similar pattern. Critical sales events were defined as winning or losing a major customer, assignment to a different sales territory, new product introductions, major pricing changes, major change in the company's management team, or the entry of a major new competitor.

The study found a direct link between the critical events a salesperson had faced in the previous three months and his level of role conflict and role ambiguity. Recall, research has found that role conflict and ambiguity have a direct negative impact on sales success.

Even moving from Mindless to Meaningful Marketing can be a critical sales event that can create significant stress—stress that fuels uncertainty, lack of personal confidence, and poor job performance.

Encouragingly though, the research also found that training interventions can have a dramatic impact on reducing salesperson stresses. With education, role-playing, sales meetings, and one-on-one coaching, the salesperson's confidence can be enhanced and stress reduced.

A growing business is one that changes to exploit new technological and customer opportunities. However, our success at exploiting the opportunities may well lie in how well we help our team make the transition.

PRACTICAL IDEAS

236. Teach Your People Why

Often we tell our people "what" to do but neglect to tell them "why." By providing an in-depth explanation of why, you build a foundation of trust and commitment to your cause. Couple the why with the overt benefits that the change will bring about. Doing so doesn't guarantee everyone's agreement but simply gives you something to manage change against.

237. Explain the Consequences of Not Changing

The real workers in your organization likely have their heads down and eyes focused on accomplishing the specific assignment before them. To them, change is a disruption to their daily routine. As the visionary, it's your job to clearly explain why continuing your current path of action is not sustainable.

238. Use Major Changes to Speed Meaningful Growth

Human nature is to dislike the uncertainty and chaos that come with change. However, when change does occur, for whatever reason, it provides an opportunity to make even more Meaningful changes. For example, the change associated with adding new products to your sales staff's responsibilities can be used as a time to add a more reliable customer-needs reporting system. Use change as an opportunity to realign or set new goals.

239. Stay in Touch With Everyone

When major change happens to a group, a department, or an entire organization, the old adage "no news is good news" just doesn't apply. The best way to unleash employees' strengths is to empower them with knowledge. Everyone is affected by critical events; use communication to keep everyone on track.

DATA PROVEN TRUTH #61

The Importance of Reducing Customer Stress

There is tangible value in being the easiest company to do business with.

Stress has a direct impact on decision quality. "Frozen in fear" is a true occurrence. When crises like a heart attack, hurricane, or tornado occur, it's not uncommon for adults to delay taking appropriate action. Fear-focused stress reduces the ability to think rationally.

A study involving 101 students documented the negative impacts of stress on thinking ability. Students were presented with fifty word problems to solve on a computer with no time limit. The control group was simply asked to complete the problems. Students in the test groups had a hand wired to an electronic device that they were told would deliver a mild and harmless shock. One test group was told that the shock was uncontrollable and could occur at the start, middle, or end of the test. The other test group was told that the shock was controllable and would be delivered whenever they made a mistake.

After participants had answered fifteen questions the test was stopped and their results checked. Note, stopping after fifteen questions instead of the anticipated fifty questions made it possible to conduct the test without delivering shocks to any of the students.

Participants who were under no stress were significantly more accurate in their responses to the word problems. Overall those under no stress had an accuracy rate of 59 percent, compared to 36 percent for those under any type of stress.

Another study of 463 retail shoppers found that customers' intentions to shop a store again are based on the merchandise value they will receive minus the stress, time, and effort costs they perceive. Merchandise value (what you're selling) was the primary driver of intentions to revisit. However, as the customer's perception of shopping stress, time, and effort increases, the net intentions to shop again decrease.

PRACTICAL IDEAS

240. Total Value Equals Value Received Minus Hassles

To maximize total value, focus your energy on improving what customers receive as well as decreasing their cost and hassles involved with purchase and usage. The easier it is for customers to do business with you, the greater their likelihood of repurchasing.

241. Help Customers Consider All Information

Stress has been found to cause people to make a decision before reviewing all of the important information. Develop sales materials that lay out the options in simple side-by-side comparisons. Seek ways to make it nearly impossible for your customers to make a mistake when evaluating your offering versus your competition.

242. Help Customers Think in a More Organized Fashion

Stress has been found to cause people to review alternatives in a disorganized and ineffective fashion. Make your retail store, your brochure, your Web site easy for your customers to understand, to search, and to find what they are looking for.

243. Help Customers Reduce Impulsive Decisions

Stress has been found to cause people to make short-term impulsive decisions without considering the longer-term consequences. When your offering has long-term advantages, make that clear to customers at the start of the conversation. Explain that your company's mission is to "reduce total cost" or to "reduce long-term cost." More importantly, provide the data that confirms what you promise.

244. Use a Phased Approach to Reduce Stress and Conflict

A phased approach to big changes can help reduce customers' stress and internal corporate conflict. Develop programs of step-by-step tests and validations of the Meaningful difference that your product or service offers. Then, when broad-scale change occurs, it's already been validated as reliable in your customers' situation.

The Life Stages of Sales and Marketing

The role and impact of a salesperson varies with the life stage of a customer's relationship with the company.

It's been reported that a 1 percent increase in sales force productivity is capable of generating a 6.7 percent increase in revenue. A powerful way to increase productivity is to understand and adapt to the needs of customers based on what life stage they are at with regards to their relationship with you and your company.

Research with approximately fourteen hundred customers of an industrial products company finds that the impact of a salesperson varies with the customer life stage. The four life stages and salesperson's roles are as follows:

> *Exploration:* During this "search, compare, and trial" phase, the customer reviews the costs, benefits, and trade-offs of doing business with you. The salesperson's primary role is to efficiently provide information and make connections between the customer's needs and the company's capabilities.

> *Buildup:* The relationship deepens in this time of growth, and both sides share information. The salesperson's role is to nurture trust through facilitating mutual understanding of business goals and building a common vision for growth.

> *Maturity:* The firms have made a pledge to continue collaboration on a regular basis. The customer believes that pricing ups and downs will even out over the long term and no longer aggressively looks at alternatives. The salesperson's role is to direct and configure the relationship to best leverage joint investments.

> *Decline:* One or both firms experience dissatisfaction and consider ending the relationship. Through honest communication and flexibility, a trusted salesperson may be able to repackage the relationship to restore satisfaction.

PRACTICAL IDEAS

245. Enhancing Exploration Efficiency

Energy should be focused on clear communication of how your company can meaningfully fulfill the customer's needs. Lay the foundation for future trust by going above and beyond what is expected with regards to sharing information and assistance.

246. Enhancing Buildup Efficiency

Create a trusting relationship. Make a major investment in actions that help reduce your customer's risks and uncertainties about you and your company's motives and intentions. Outline actions for creating a long-term, mutually beneficial relationship.

247. Enhancing Maturity Efficiency

At this point, the relationship goes on "autopilot." Trust building has been replaced by long-term contracts. Your primary role as salesperson is to continue delivering on the existing promises. Be on the outlook for ways to make Meaningful adjustments in the relationship whenever challenges arise.

248. Enhancing Decline Efficiency

At this stage, the relationship is nearing an end. As the sales rep, you can make the end process orderly or take aggressive action to repair customer perceptions or past mistakes. As with the exploration stage, it's best that actions be focused on Meaningful, tangible changes in the relationship rather than trying to simply exploit emotional trust.

249. Restage Sales Relationships

Use the introduction of major new products or services as an opportunity to freshen and revitalize your sales relationship. Consider changes to established rituals and routines. Consider rotating sales coverages to connect the customer with a new person. Use changes to freshen and lengthen the relationship.

Talk to Customers in Real Words

For the masses of customers it is over twice as effective to tell them the story of your data than it is to provide a chart of numbers.

Meaningful Marketing is about translating raw data into knowledge and wisdom that customers can use to make smart decisions.

Researchers showed 250 consumers varying forms of nutritional information on two food products. One test cell utilized a chart of hard data on the percentage of the recommended daily allowance the food had of various nutrients. The other test cell was given the same information but in simple, storytelling language.

The results indicate that the storytelling approach is over twice as effective as the numerical chart in communicating the food was more nutritious (37 percent versus 18 percent). It also prompted nearly three times more customers to say they intended to purchase (16.8 percent versus 5.8 percent). Lastly, the storytelling format also generated significantly more accurate recall of the information presented.

When you tell your story with simple words, you make it easier for customers to understand and comprehend your Meaningful difference. Telling customers you have 40 percent of the recommended daily allowance of protein requires customer processing for relevance. Alternatively, a description of excellent protein content relative to the competition provides an actionable frame of reference.

Opportunities exist for combining the two techniques. By explaining that your product offers nearly twice as much as the competition does of the body-building protein your child needs, you have translated the hard data into a Meaningful benefit difference.

PRACTICAL IDEAS

250. Transform Data Charts Into Words

Translate data charts into simple words. Explain your core benefit to customers using simple language. Record yourself talking through the data chart as part of a presentation to identify the best words. The words you use could well be what you need to make the point. If you must provide a chart, place your verbal description below the chart itself to add clarity to your message.

251. Transform Technologies Into Words

We appreciate the fact that your technological wonder is considerable. However, you will increase your odds of success if you can tell it in a simple story. Translate your "techno-speak" into a simple explanation—using analogies where necessary. The benefit to you is customers who understand and better recall your Meaningful difference.

252. Be a Storyteller

Turn your marketing message into storytelling. Tell the story of what led you to develop your offering as it is. Create drama through the tension of the challenge; that is, the problem you addressed and the discovery of your solution.

253. Synthesize to Simplify

Today's customer has no shortage of data, information, and knowledge. The challenge is to discern the Meaningful versus the meaningless information. Seek ways to condense masses of information into simple analogies.

DATA PROVEN TRUTH #64

Quality Is for Customers

Quality improvements that improve customer satisfaction are more profitable than those focused on cost cutting.

Quality improvement projects can improve customer satisfaction, reduce company expenses, or do both simultaneously.

Research with 186 executives has found that a strategy of focusing quality improvements on improving customer satisfaction is dramatically more effective than either a cost-focused or dual strategy. Only the customer-satisfaction quality strategy correlates with overall company financial performance, company return on assets, and long-term stock returns.

Success in business is simple. To grow, you need to provide more Meaningful differences for customers. And quality improvements are a prime means of delivering Meaningful customer differences.

Cost savings is not a viable strategy for significant growth. We understand that some readers may be getting violent at this stage—saying, "Yes, but you don't understand our category" or "Yes, but our industry is different."

To you nonbelievers we say, "Get over it." If your life revolves around cost, you've lost the game and just don't know it yet. A study of the commodity price index for grain, milk, steel, plastic, and oil indicates that from 1845 to 1999 commodity prices have dropped an average of 80 percent! Net: If commodity pricing is your strategy, you can safely assume that over the long term, a 1.5 percent decrease in price per year will be the unrelenting average you must beat—just to stay even.

254. Think Offense, Not Defense, With Marketing Costs

As you seek to improve your sales and marketing cost effectiveness, focus energies first on how you can more meaningfully connect with customers' needs. Instead of saying what you can eliminate, focus first on what else you can do to make a more Meaningful articulation of the virtues of your offering. Instead of mindlessly advertising to millions, send a product sample to a subset of higher-probability customers. Instead of making millions of prospecting calls for your professional service, create a lecture or a book that can provide an in-depth display of your wisdom.

255. Enroll Everyone in Customer Satisfaction

Enroll the entire company in quality improvement. Make satisfying customer needs the primary focus of all departments. Create measurement systems that align each department's output with real customer satisfaction. Challenge each department to identify ideas that they can implement to improve customer satisfaction.

256. Define What You Would Spend Money On

Challenge your team to define how they would spend an additional 20 percent on product or service to improve customer satisfaction. What would be the specific impact for customers? Having defined a specific benefit, now find ways to pay for it through quality improvement programs.

257. Break the Commodity Cycle

If you're caught in a commodity marketplace, split your brand into two. Maintain the current brand to keep paying the bills. Then develop an alternative value-added, premium-margin option. Keep the overhead costs on the new initiative low so that you stay in the market long enough to learn, change, adapt, and grow successfully.

The Value of Being the Underdog

Smaller companies are perceived to have greater quality than highly successful market leaders.

Customers have a natural confidence and faith in smaller companies.

Research was conducted with a cross section of some eighty-five types of brands (products and services) over a five-year period. It found that the more successful a brand becomes, the more customers perceive its quality to slip.

Bigger brands are perceived to offer poorer quality. In fact, this perception is often reality, as what was once handled with craftsman care is now handled by inflexible systems built for mass efficiency. What was also once led by a passionate entrepreneur, whose name is on the door, is now an efficient and dispassionate corporate system.

Larger size can offer tremendous cost advantages. However, the same systems that empower cost savings can also result in delays in order delivery, timing, and delays in answering customer service lines.

Sadly, even when growth has not resulted in reduction in actual quality, it is still a natural perception of customers that you should be aware of.

The one exception to this rule is with premium-priced products. The research found that when customers pay a premium, they are less likely to perceive sales growth as a quality decline. Inherent in a premium price is a core belief of higher quality that mass-market, commodity-priced brands don't enjoy. Again, the higher margin of premium-priced goods versus commodities may result in this being as much a factual truth as a customer perception.

258. When You're Small, Leverage It as an Asset

Don't apologize for your small size. Rather, use it as an asset. Articulate and deliver customer service that exceeds expectations. Use your nimbleness and responsiveness as a major advantage versus the market leader.

Quantify the differences between you and your competition by conducting independent tests of the time it takes for your staff to answer customer service phone calls versus theirs. Show side-by-side the fine print and bureaucracy in competitive purchase order systems and/or warranties versus your simpler and more customer-centric approach.

259. When You're Big, Articulate Continuing Quality Growth

When you're highly successful, don't forget what sparked your success. Don't assume that customers accept you as high quality. Knowing your name and trusting your quality are two different things.

Make continuous improvement in your customers' experience with your goods or services a cornerstone of continuing growth. If competition is weak, compete with yourself; proclaim proudly the Meaningful improvements you've made in the past one, three, or five years.

260. Articulate How Higher Price Allows Greater Quality

In a portion of your communications, define the measurable differences inherent in your product or service. Quantify the technology and the higher quality of raw materials built into your offering.

DATA PROVEN TRUTH #66

Confronting False Customer Knowledge

Customers often think they know more than they do. Fortunately, sources of error are not totally random.

When evaluating your new offering, customers will often overestimate the effectiveness of their current choice.

A portfolio of studies on the accuracy of customer knowledge finds that the errors adults make tend to follow predictable patterns. By understanding the patterns of errors, you are better able to make a Meaningful sales and marketing connection.

In general, adults overstate their knowledge level. They think they are more accurate than they actually are. This is a natural tendency that has been shown in dozens of studies. This is why with a new product or service you must meaningfully exceed, not just meet, the performance of competitive offerings.

The harder the task, the greater the overstatement is. Studies have found that when given a more difficult task, adults' overstatement is significantly greater than with easy tasks. Thus, the greater the difficulty of objectively assessing performance dimensions in your category, the more likely customers are to overstate the performance of their existing choice—in effect creating an artificially high standard that you need to exceed to win their business.

Over time, adults' confidence in their knowledge grows, when in fact the accuracy of their knowledge declines. This means that the longer customers have been using a certain product or service, the more difficult it will be to get a fair comparison between your new offering and the truth about their current choice.

Successful sales and marketing requires that you respect the fact that customers believe that their current product or service choice is significantly better than it really is in truth.

PRACTICAL IDEAS

261. Ask for Confidence Levels

To probe for truth, ask customers to define on a scale of 0 percent to 100 percent, how confident they are about the various conclusions or facts before them. The research indicates greater accuracy when confidence levels are added to judgments. In addition, the act of thinking consciously about confidence levels can cause a shift from mindlessness to mindfulness. And the more you get customers to stop and think, the greater the likelihood that you'll get a response to your more Meaningful message.

262. Ask How They Measure and Assess Performance

To encourage conscious thinking by customers, ask them to define what their performance criteria are. You can then use these criteria to compare and contrast your superiority on objective dimensions. When you ask for performance criteria, you help organize the existing decision process so to give yourself higher odds of success.

263. Show Respect for History

The longer a customer has used an established process, the greater his commitment to it, even when today's reality does not match his historical perceptions. To confront this, utilize a presentation that respectfully details the wisdom of the past yet articulates the natural progression of improvement that your offering represents. Use the customer's established thinking patterns as the fuel to move to your offering.

264. Shock Customers Into Awareness

Amplify the total cost of continuing on the current path. For example, multiply the amount of extra time required to write checks by hand versus using electronic bill paying times the number of times checks are written in a ten-year period to quantify the advantage. Further, quantify the average number of mistakes through each system.

Eliminate the Irrelevant

The presence of irrelevant information lowers customers' perceptions of performance excellence.

When customers evaluate a product or service, they seek information to help them make informed decisions. Your sales and marketing message is the primary source of this information. Research has repeatedly found no correlation between the length of a message and its effectiveness. However, this assumes that the additional information is relevant to the decision the customer faces.

When irrelevant information is added to communications, customer interest declines.

Marketing information can be directly related to the task. For example, in looking for a fast computer, a customer could evaluate the speed of the computer's processor and the amount of RAM (random-access memory), features that can help with speed.

Marketing information can also be irrelevant to the task. In the fast computer example, irrelevant information could include "as seen in a recent movie," "as advertised on television," "made in the U.S.A." Each of these detracts from the main message of speed you want to communicate.

Ten separate experiments have found that when irrelevant information was added to a highly relevant marketing message, customer interest declined significantly. As an example, in one study, purchase interest in the target concept declined from 53 percent to 38 percent when irrelevant information was added to the concept.

Irrelevant information reduces customers' beliefs in the ability of your product or services to deliver on the promised benefit. It causes confusion and distraction, reducing focus and faith in your true Meaningful difference.

PRACTICAL IDEAS

265. Follow the Advice of Stephen King

Best-selling novelist Stephen King recommends that second drafts should equal the first draft less 10 percent of the words. You can do the same with your marketing. Cut the less relevant 10 percent of the ideas from your marketing message.

Even more powerfully, put aside your marketing materials and, with a fresh computer screen, rewrite them in a natural voice. When we talk to customers, we tend to naturally synthesize our message so to not bore our customers and to get to the point more quickly.

(Authors' note: Stephen King's advice is not easy. We vigorously cut the second draft, but in the end it had only 6 percent less words.)

266. Eliminate Advertising Gimmicks and Smoke and Mirrors

Focus your advertising message on providing relevant yet unexpected news about your brand. Mindless humor, video gimmicks, outrageous shock, and esoteric philosophy is for Hollywood movies, not capitalist advertising.

Great advertising is easy. It starts with a simple Meaningful benefit difference that resolves a real customer problem or enables a genuine customer desire. Lastly, it provides real reason to believe that the promise will be truly delivered.

267. Ignore Options

Many products and services come in a multitude of customized options. Rarely are these options a reason for purchase. The core brand offering is usually the real driver of persuasion. Options of form or format are simply executional details. Eliminate discussion of them to simplify your message. Focus your marketing communications on the one thing that you do really great.

DATA PROVEN TRUTH #68

Respect the Risk Factor

Respect what it takes to reduce customers' perceptions of risk.

Buyers often want to make a purchase, but they hesitate because it involves taking the risk of some kind of loss. To mitigate the chances of loss, they evaluate the relative credibility of various information sources.

Research was conducted with 472 customers on how effective various methods were in reducing the risk associated with new purchases. In the survey, risk was articulated in four manners: risk of time loss (wasting time with poor product), hazard loss (danger to health or safety), ego loss (feeling foolish for buying), and money loss (the bottom-line cost of failure).

The average effectiveness of each risk reduction method is shown below on a 0 to 200 scale.

Brand Loyalty: Bought and used before. . . . 194

Major Brand: Large, well-known brand. . . . 156

Free Sample: Trial size 113

Word of Mouth: From friends or family. . . . 106

Endorsements: By expert or celebrity 85

Money-Back Guarantee 81

The data shows that real, first-person experience is orders of magnitude more credible than manufactured marketing methods like endorsements and money-back guarantees.

Personal experience is the most real and reliable of any method of reducing fear.

PRACTICAL IDEAS

268. Be Overt in Leveraging Your Customers

Be aggressive in leveraging your existing customers. Use their knowledge, faith, and commitment to your brand as a spring-board for generating trials and recommendations for your new product.

269. Validate Customers' Real Fears

Openly acknowledge and validate customers' fears. Don't belittle them as unimportant. Fears are deeply personal. What customers perceive as a fear is real to them. It's also a real barrier to you if you wish to make a sale. Validate the fear, then show how your company has thought through the issue and dealt with it. Show how your offering is designed to reduce the fear, risk, and uncertainty.

270. Empower Greed

Fear is emotional. The only business emotion stronger than fear is greed. You can often defeat customers' fear by evoking greed through defining the Meaningful, quantitative, and substantial benefit that they will receive. The bigger the promised benefit, the less likely customers are to worry about potential fears or losses.

271. Provide Overt Reasons to Address Real Issues

Review the four types of risk to identify fears that may exist but that are not articulated by customers. Address these issues directly.

- *Hazard Loss:* Safety testing results and expert endorsements.

- *Time Loss:* Testimonials that it was worth the effort to change.

- *Money Loss:* A side-by-side balance sheet of the advantage.

- *Ego Loss:* Documentation of popularity with key customers.

DATA PROVEN TRUTH #69

The Dramatic Dilution of Marketing Messages

Due to the natural dilution effects of modern marketing, your end results can be as much as fourteen times smaller than forced-viewing situations led you to expect..

From your conference room to the marketplace, a dramatic dilution occurs. Most marketing messages are rarely noticed, seldom comprehended, and almost never acted on.

The truth is your customers don't spend significant time pondering your marketing messages. Tracking research on the step-by-step effectiveness of a direct mail marketing campaign documented the dilution effect.

1. *Didn't Notice:* When called later, only 60 percent of those who the mailing had been sent to remembered receiving it.

2. *Didn't Bother:* Only 47 percent of those who noticed the message actually bothered to read it.

3. *Didn't Understand:* Only 25 percent of those who read the marketing piece could accurately state the primary benefit of the new offering.

The total dilution effect is multiplicative. Thus, the actual number of customers who were in a position to make a Meaningful decision—that is, were aware of and correctly understood the offer—was only one-fourteenth, or 7 percent, of the 100 percent who were sent the mailing.

```
100  percent (were mailed new product message)
 60  percent (customers who remembered receiving it)
 47  percent (customers who read it)
 25  percent (customers who correctly understood it)
=  7  percent (number in a position to make Meaningful decision)
```

Sadly, in our consulting work, we've seen even worse than this.

PRACTICAL IDEAS

272. Measure the Effectiveness of Each Marketing Step

Quite simply, measure the dilution effect at each stage of your marketing. Conduct phone, mail, or E-mail surveys to measure the effectiveness of each step. Hard data empowers you to make Meaningful improvement. Focus your energies on those areas with the greatest opportunities for improvement.

273. Leverage the Multiplicative Impact of Meaningfulness

The dilution impact is yet another reason to focus on making your message as Meaningful as possible. Just as investing time to think deeply about architectural plans reduces the cost and time of construction, so, too, does adding more meaningfulness to your marketing.

Step back from your business and assess if what you are doing now will be recalled with pride when you're retired. Or will it blend into the Mindless blur of life? If you don't think your current marketing will be a Meaningful memory tomorrow, then it's probably not Meaningful to your customers today.

274. Look at Your Materials in Context

When you review your marketing materials, look at them in context. Place twelve direct mail envelopes in a pile with yours. Watch a collection of commercials with yours in the middle. Flash your billboard on a screen for the seconds it takes to drive past it. When you look at your message in context, you look at it through the same diluted eyes that customers see it with.

The Three-Legged Stool of New Product Success

New products fail for three reasons: (1) poor idea, (2) poor product, and/or (3) poor marketing programs.

New products are like a three-legged stool consisting of the idea, the product, and the marketing program. Mathematically, the three have a direct and multiplicative impact on success.

No matter how great your product performance and marketing plan, without an idea that makes a Meaningful difference to customers, few if any will bother to purchase it.

No matter how great your idea and marketing program, without a great product, no one will make a repeat purchase and you will fail.

No matter how great your idea and product performance, without a marketing plan that generates awareness and distribution, no one will know to purchase or be able to purchase your product.

Tracking forty-eight new products from entry into the marketplace found that, on average, they generated 58 percent awareness, and of those aware, 9 percent actually purchased, and of those who purchased, some 38 percent made a repeat purchase. If we subtract each of these results from the theoretical 100 percent that could have been achieved, we find that the idea is the largest source of lost customers. A remarkable 91 percent of those aware of a new product didn't purchase it.

When your volume is lower than expected, first look at improving your core idea. The Meaningful benefit difference offered by your brand is the single largest source of lost customers.

To succeed without a big idea, you should be prepared to spend lots of money on discounts, promotions, and advertising to coerce customers into purchasing.

PRACTICAL IDEAS

275. It's the Idea, Stupid

Step back and ask yourself what Meaningful difference you offer to customers. Often companies take one idea and spend 99 percent of their money, time, and energy optimizing marketing efficiencies—through reviewing media buys, sales force coverage, and mail-order list selections. At best, the net improvement is maybe 2 percent to 5 percent on but one area of the marketing mix.

Alternatively, research with small businesses has found that committing resources to finding a more Meaningful Marketing message can result in a 10 percent to 50 percent improvement in all areas of the marketing mix.

276. Play "King of the Hill" With Marketing Messages

There is no such thing as a marketing message that can't be made more effective. Challenge yourself and your staff to perpetually discover new and more effective ways to articulate your Meaningful Marketing message.

Develop low-cost test systems, such as direct mail or point-of-purchase testing systems, to quantify improvement. On a regular basis review the collection of tests you've conducted to identify patterns and trends regarding what's working and what's not.

277. Improve Marketing By Spending More on Product

Most marketing spending is a meaningless, Mindless waste. Challenge yourself to consider what level of product or service improvement you could deliver if you dramatically cut marketing expenses. Short term, the volume may take a hit, but long term, when word of mouth from customers kicks in, you could realize substantial growth.

Relevant Expertise

The effectiveness of your sales and marketing pitches is directly related to the relevance of your expertise.

Customers are intelligent. When you get their attention, they evaluate the relevance of your messages more than you may think. And when what you say doesn't make sense, they are significantly less likely to make a purchase.

A study was conducted on the importance of relevant expertise. A print ad of a new sports energy bar was designed that featured a photo of a man described as either a former U.S. Olympic track and field athlete or as a leading Broadway actor who has starred in two movies.

Consumers were significantly more likely to indicate they would purchase the new sports energy bar when an athlete was used versus an actor.

It just makes sense. An athlete has relevant expertise for a sports bar. An actor is irrelevant noise.

The sales and marketing industries may have more irrelevance than any other. Sales and marketing magazines, books, and conference speakers are filled with the equivalent of get-rich-quick schemes.

In general these schemes focus on credibility. They involve ways to trick customers into believing that your meaningless offering is more meaningfully different than it really is.

What the Mindless marketing charlatans offer is magic. These stage magicians show many ways to trick a customer once. During the first presentation, the customer is easily distracted through misdirection. However, few magic tricks are strong enough to survive a repeat performance. With repeat viewings the customer is more aware and observant of truth. Mindless marketing works once but rarely survives a repeat performance.

PRACTICAL IDEAS

278. Testimonial Relevance

Use testimonials that speak directly to your Meaningful benefit and that are given by an independent or expert authority who is credible. The "point of drama" in the testimonial should link directly to your Meaningful Marketing message. For example, an award-winning chef can speak to the ability of your wine to enhance the taste of food. A production supervisor can speak to the improvement in production efficiency he's noticed from your industrial lubricant.

279. Demonstration Relevance

Use demonstrations that speak to the "moment of drama" inherent in your Meaningful Marketing message. Even exaggerated demonstrations can be effective if they speak to the challenge. For example, when a floor cleaner cleans Grand Central Station in New York City, it gives you confidence that it can really clean stubborn dirt in your kitchen.

280. Product and Service Variations Relevance

Irrelevant product or service options are a cancer that, once it takes hold, is hard to stop. It's driven by a Mindless search for incremental volume. Asking your distributor to sell irrelevant options or your retail customers to stock them creates a culture of distrust and failure. Step back and consider what items make up 80 percent of your volume. Conduct a test market with just those items.

When Doug was at P&G, he introduced a new product line in only two sizes instead of three and realized 125 percent of his sales objective as a result of improved marketing focus.

Your Customers' Three Wishes

Retail trade customers' most important wishes for new products are (1) generate incremental sales, (2) offer an exciting and unique consumer advantage, and (3) receive substantial marketing support from the producer.

Businesses that sell to resellers—be they product retailers, service providers, or even restaurateurs—have the double challenge of selling the reseller and helping the reseller sell the end consumer.

The good news is that the findings from the research conducted with 145 buyers on "what is most important" is very similar to what drives success for new products from an end customer basis. On a ten-point importance scale, the following are the three top wishes of retail buyers when evaluating new products:

Generate Incremental Sales (8.6 importance): The new product should generate significant net extra volume and not just cannibalize existing volume.

An Exciting and Unique Consumer Advantage (8.4 importance): Trade customers look for big ideas that generate big volume. They make their evaluations by looking for evidence that your offering meets an unmet need, provides a unique advantage to consumers, or offers the potential for genuine shopping excitement.

Substantial Marketing Support (7.9 importance): Your level of marketing support is evidence of your confidence that your new product will generate significant sales. In addition, trade customers know that when one manufacturer makes a significant marketing investment, it causes healthy competition that results in more total category spending and overall category growth.

PRACTICAL IDEAS

281. Genuinely Grow Retail Sales Volume

Develop the products and/or the merchandising concepts that can meaningfully grow the sales of your retail customers. Create higher-value product offerings that spark customers to "trade up" to higher-revenue-producing options. Develop merchandising programs that deliver incremental sales. For example, quantify the incremental category growth that occurs when products are shelved in multiple locations in the store or the customer's catalog.

282. Prove Your Advantage With Comparisons

Make your difference overtly clear. Develop promotional materials that bring your point of difference to marketing and display materials. Show your advantage with boldness and clarity. If possible, bring a live taste test, demonstration, or other real-world experience to your meeting with the customer. Don't shy away from demos that take some work. Your willingness to put in the effort is evidence of your personal belief in your offering.

283. Bring Alive Your Customer Excitement

Utilize video of customers speaking to the wonder and the impact your new product delivers. Don't worry about the fact that the tape is edited. If your testimonials speak with relevance and authenticity, they will be convincing. Alternatively, what do you think it says to a buyer when you don't have testimonials declaring that the new offering is great?

284. Lead a Revolution Toward Smarter Spending

Document the Meaningful impact of your smarter marketing methods. Detail the effectiveness of your approach to sampling, trial generation, and targeted marketing. Estimate the translation of your smarter approach to equivalent dollar spending under older, less efficient marketing approaches.

DATA PROVEN TRUTH #73

Leverage a Customer's Natural Rhythms

Adults have natural rhythms that make a significant difference in their likelihood to make Meaningful decisions.

Customers have natural circadian rhythms. Some people are morning people. Some people are evening people.

Research indicates that when approached about making a decision during their "off time," humans are less likely to make an independent and Meaningful decision. Rather, they are significantly more likely to make a decision based on simplistic stereotypes.

Two studies involving a total of 248 participants were conducted. Participants were tested either early in the morning or later in the evening.

In the first study they were asked to choose which of two descriptions (one stereotypical, the other nonstereotypical) were most likely to be true of a person whose picture and name they were shown. When morning people were tested in the evening, 32 percent more chose the stereotypical response than those tested in the morning. When evening people were tested in the morning, some 31 percent more chose the stereotypical response than those tested in the evening.

In the second study, participants read descriptions of various defendants in criminal cases. Again, when outside of their best time, participants were more likely to judge defendants described in stereotypical ways as guilty than participants who made the same evaluations during their best time of day.

Bottom line: To make a Meaningful connection with your customers, be sensitive to their personal rhythms.

PRACTICAL IDEAS

285. Be Polite and Respectful

First and foremost, be polite and respectful of your customers' time and schedules. Ask them directly when the best time is to connect with them to discuss new opportunities. Be honest and upfront about how much time it will take you to review what you have to say. The more respectful you are to customers, the more respectful they will be to you in honoring commitments to meet.

286. Ride Ahead of the Wave

Customers have natural buying and planning cycles. Retailers make purchases in advance of the holiday season, consumers make summer vacation plans in the spring, and industrial buyers make commitments as part of annual budget planning processes. By planning your marketing push to begin ahead of natural purchasing times, you are able to steal a greater share of your customers' minds by influencing their thinking early.

287. Create Your Own Rituals and Sales Rhythms

Industrial and business-to-business salespeople seek to establish regular traditions with customers—from medical sales reps bringing doughnuts when they arrive at the doctor's clinic the first Monday of every month, to winter slide shows of last year's children's summer camp as a tool for signing up new and repeat customers. Look to your business dynamics to find ways to create unique opportunities to make Meaningful connections with customers.

288. Collect and Document Funky Habits

Be observant of customer rituals. Most adults are creatures of habit. By observing when they place orders and how they deal with the stress inherent in corporate cultures, you can start to identify the right times to make new pitches and close significant sales.

The Ever Dynamic Customer Loyalty

Customer loyalty is an ever changing dynamic that must be nurtured or else it will be lost to competition.

Customer purchasing is driven by dynamic probabilities rather than certainties. Customers start with a perception of what they wish to purchase. They then process promotional messages designed to influence them.

As they are exposed to new ideas and information in the form of sales and marketing messages, word-of-mouth advice, promotional offers, and first-person product experience, they increase and decrease the purchasing probabilities for various brands.

The following example of Brands X, Y, and Z provides understanding of dynamic customer loyalty.

Prepurchase Intentions

Brand X: 50 percent probability; positive previous experience with brand.

Brand Y: 30 percent probability; popular brand but never purchased.

Brand Z: 20 percent probability; low-price brand, rarely purchase.

At Point of Purchase

At the point of purchase the customer is presented a promotional offer for Brand Y, sparking a purchase.

Usage Experience—and Plan for Next Purchase

Customer has a bad experience with Brand Y—adjusting probabilities:

Brand X: 50 percent probability; old faithful.

Brand Y: 5 percent probability; bad experience—buy only if cheap.

Brand Z: 45 percent probability; consumer reads article about how price brands perform the same as established brands.

The probabilities are now shifted with a greater likelihood toward Brand Z and lower toward Brand Y. However, the shift remains dynamic, always open to adjustment, as news is acquired.

PRACTICAL IDEAS

289. Accept the Certainty of Uncertainty

Accept that customer loyalty is a dynamic variable, as opposed to the rigid definition that each customer is either loyal or not loyal to you. Even if they are totally satisfied with your performance, a random desire for novelty can cause even loyal customers to purchase a competitive product or service. When you appreciate the dynamic nature of buying, then you will fully appreciate the importance of always freshening your articulation of your Meaningful benefit difference.

290. Always Market to Established Customers

Remember that current customers are never fully yours. Competition is continually marketing to them too. Neglected by you, they will slowly but surely become the customer of another. Regularly telling them that you love them and are working hard to fulfill their needs can help you immunize them against the messages of your competition.

291. Regularly Deliver News to Keep Your Brand Fresh

Customers are always learning something. Better it be about the wonder of what you have to offer. The worst happens when your customer becomes bored with your offering and leaves for no good reason. Develop a regular cycle of delivering news to customers. At your annual trade show, announce new product upgrades and ideas. Better yet, at your annual customer-planning meeting, provide advance previews of what will be coming out soon.

292. Increase Your Frequency of Marketing Messages

Purchasing a new product or service requires that customers understand and believe in your offering, plus have a need at that moment. By increasing the frequency of marketing communications, you improve your odds of getting lucky. What you are attempting to do is reinforce in customers' minds your Meaningful message at the very moment that they have the greatest need for your offering.

DATA PROVEN TRUTH #75

Pictures Tell the Story

What customers see is what gets into their minds.

The classic saying that a picture is worth a thousand words has some evidence of truth. In their desire to simplify the processing of information, customers regularly rely on pictures and images to speed the decision-making process.

Consumers were shown advertisements for the same brand of frozen meals. The only variation was the photographs that were shown.

Consumers' interpretations of the product varied widely depending on the visual.

When a close-up of the food was shown, consumers viewed the brand as "appetizing and delicious."

When a collection of six dishes was shown, the brand was seen as "having larger variety."

When a variety of people was shown, the brand was perceived as "everyone likes."

Simply changing the visual could double consumer ratings on key attributes such as "good for families" and "good for everyday meals."

In the absence of listening and reading, pictures tell the story. Many years ago a series of experiments conducted by Doug at Procter & Gamble found that results of consumer testing for new food and beverage concepts could be predicted with about 70 percent accuracy by simply viewing the concepts from a distance—looking at the visual and the headline and not reading any of the descriptive body copy.

PRACTICAL IDEAS

293. Be Sure That What You Show Is Most Important

When you show your product front and center, that communicates that your product is what is most important. When you show your service people, it says that service is your most important asset. Stop now and look at what you see in your brochure, your Web site, or behind the counter of your retail store. Is what you see what you feel is the most important dimension for customers to know? If not, then change it. Show the story of your offering.

294. Tell Your Story Without Words

With digital cameras there is no excuse for not having high-quality images. When you snap a photo, you can check the photo quality immediately. If the lighting or the framing is not right, you can take it again and again until you get it right.

Bring your ease-of-use benefits to life by showing customers how to use your product through a sequence of visuals. Bring your emotional benefit to life by showing the excitement, pleasure, or joy through descriptively dramatic images. Use your Web site as a storyboard from which to educate your customers.

295. Ask Customers What Images They Recall

When you don't know what to show, ask your customers. Visual image recall is often a powerful means to identify what is most Meaningful to customers.

To gain insight into consumers' habits and practices, have them E-mail you images or take pictures with a disposable camera of when and where they would use your product.

The Tension of News vs. Confusion

Success comes to those who can balance the excitement of uniqueness with simplicity of explanation.

By its very nature, news is different from what we already know. And as the news increases, complexity does too.

A research study found that when explaining customers' recall of the details of a sales and marketing presentation, the two key dimensions, each with equal and significant correlations, were news and lack of confusion.

There is little doubt of the value of news. The greater the new information presented, the more likely customers are to meaningfully remember your offering's genuine value.

The more mental effort it takes customers to comprehend and follow your description, the less likely they are to take the time to process it.

Clearly, there is an inherent tension between uniqueness and confusion. The more dimensions of news—uniqueness of product, uniqueness of packaging, uniqueness of performance attributes—the greater the probability of confusing customers.

In today's high-technology world, this is even more challenging. Few customers really understand or wish to learn how the automatic pilot in an airplane works or the physics behind how our car achieves better road handling.

However, at the same time, if they can't understand it, they are left with a lack of trust and acceptance of what is promised.

Our challenge is to provide a relevant yet simple story of what's in it for the customer, and how it works, yet maintain an unexpected dimension that supplies uniqueness.

PRACTICAL IDEAS

296. Use Analogies

When your technology is genuinely complex, find ways to use analogies to help the uneducated understand your approach. Step back from your product or service and draw examples from other industries, Mother Nature, or other simple comparisons to make the complex appear to be simple.

297. Go Over the Edges

To describe the complex in a simple way, first force yourself to put in writing what your product is and does. Having completed this, rewrite it twice, each time forcing yourself to use fresh language and to avoid repeating yourself. Do this once a day for five days. At the end of the fifth writing, give a friend five versions to review and edit into one concise and impactful message.

298. Shorten the Benefit Feedback Loop

Find ways to accelerate the realization of your Meaningful benefit. Shorten the amount of time it takes to install and understand your offering before a significant portion, if not all, of your benefit is realized by the customer.

299. Depict the Magic Moment

Instead of a war of words, depict the "magic moment" that defines your benefit. If you're selling tutoring to help with college entrance exams, show the image of a child successfully graduating from college. If you're selling cakes and frosting, show a scrapbook with a picture of a gap-toothed four-year-old ready to blow out the candles. If you sell water pollution prevention systems, show clean crisp water. By powerfully visualizing the end benefit, the customer will find it easier to accept complexity in delivery.

DATA PROVEN TRUTH #77

The Double Negative of Negative Reviews

Negative reviews about your offering impact both your marketing ability and perceptions of actual product performance.

In an ideal world, what your product or service offers and actually does should transcend the noise of the world.

Research was conducted on potential customers' perceptions of a pair of reviews for a consumer electronics device tested by an "independent consumer-testing laboratory." For half the subjects, the evaluation reported favorably on the product. For the other half, a negative review was provided.

As expected, a negative review caused customers' preuse product expectations and purchase intent to decline significantly.

Customers were then provided with an opportunity to personally try the product. After usage of the same product, consumers gave lower purchase intention ratings (1.7 versus 2.4) when they had viewed the negative review, even though the product performed satisfactorily.

In effect, the negative review by an independent third party was trusted more than the consumer's own personal experience with the product.

A second part of this same study documented how a positive marketing message couldn't help a bad product. The product was modified to purposely perform poorly. In this case, it made no difference if a positive or negative review was seen; purchase intent declined significantly.

The marketing messages and information customers receive have an impact that goes beyond simply persuading customers to purchase. What customers perceive about a product or service directly impacts how they evaluate their product experience.

PRACTICAL IDEAS

300. Fast Response

When a negative product review or customer service incident occurs, move quickly. Speed of response reduces the potential for damage to your brand and also communicates your concern and commitment to customers. The passage of time with no response is quickly elevated in customers' minds as justification of their growing dissatisfaction.

301. Admit Mistakes Quickly and Take Specific Action

In the course of normal business, mistakes will happen. Customers understand this. The key is how you react to them. When mistakes happen, admit them quickly and explain what you are going to do to make it right. If you don't know the cause of the mistake, say so. And explain clearly when you will get back to the disgruntled customer or the member of the media with additional information.

302. Manage Positive Momentum

Momentum is the elusive fuel for driving your sales and marketing. When your momentum is positive, everything you do has an extra boost of energy behind it. Momentum is built through a series of unexpected positives. The size of the positive news isn't as important as its frequency. Manage for positive momentum by metering out the good news. But do not get tempted into a cycle of news for Mindless news' sake. Your customers will soon tune you out.

303. Create Your Own Positive News

Positive news can create positive momentum. You can and should create your own positive news by entering contests, celebrating industry awards received by your staff, seeking endorsements, pitching the news media on feature stories, as well as applying for and receiving patents.

DATA PROVEN TRUTH #78

Managing Customers' Stereotypes of Your Category

Customer perceptions of category complexity directly impact where to focus your communications.

Consumers have preexisting stereotypes about their ability to understand and comprehend various categories of new products and services.

A study was conducted among 140 adults who were shown alternatives for low-complexity products (refrigerators and washing machines) and high-complexity products (personal computers and digital cameras).

When novel benefits and features were added to the low-complexity products, they caused a statistically significant increase in customer appeal.

When novel benefits and features were added to the high-complexity products, they caused a significant decline in appeal.

Communication of new benefits is directly impacted by the stereotypes customers have of your category.

When a category is perceived to be complex and hard to understand, customers give up before they even begin considering new information. They become Mindless in their buying because they feel they are incapable of making a Meaningful evaluation of the category.

Alternatively, when customers feel that they understand fully what drives a category, they are more likely to believe they have the capability of understanding Meaningful differences. This empowers their ability to become more consciously involved in the decision process.

The indicated action for complex categories is not that we should avoid new technologies. Rather, it points to the need to find ways to document and define Meaningful differences in a manner that overstressed customers can comprehend.

PRACTICAL IDEAS

304. With High-Tech Help, Customers Believe They Can

When your offering is in an advanced technology category, be sympathetic to customers' lack of technological self-esteem. A friendly, educational approach to your marketing will win you their understanding and trust. Avoid the fancy jargon and instead, use simple analogies to shine a spotlight on your Meaningful difference. Tell customers that your new artificial intelligence system is like having a 24/7 expert assistant. Use photos and illustrations to show differences so that customers can see them as they read about them.

305. Proclaim How Your Technology Simplifies Everything

Make ease of understanding and operation an overt and Meaningful benefit. Design ease of operation into your offering. Quantify how much easier it is to use your offering. A research study found that when customers were told that a new technology was automatic versus manually operated, they were significantly more interested. This finding reinforces the earlier truth that reported on the importance of reducing customer stresses.

306. Be Daring in Old And Stable Categories

When your category is old, be bold and brash about your technological innovation. Customers fully understand what your core product is about; now push the news. Don't allow yourself to be held back by naysayers who don't believe that change is possible; old categories can and must reinvent themselves.

307. Focus on Advanced Customers in Tech Categories

When your category is technologically complex and your improvement or product is complex, target initial marketing efforts on leading-edge customers. Customers with advanced understanding and technical experience will most appreciate and applaud your technological advancements.

DATA PROVEN TRUTH #79

The Trust Power of Saying, "No, We Don't"

When you are honest about a weakness, you increase your credibility.

Customers understand that everyone, every product, and every service offers strengths and weaknesses. They realize that the creation of a great skill in one area results in trade-offs in other areas.

A research study was conducted on five products' ads that claimed either excellence in five different product dimensions or superiority in three areas and lack of superiority in two. The advertisements that disclaimed superiority for two dimensions were found to be significantly more persuasive than those that claimed perfection on all dimensions.

Another study found that trust was the primary driver of increased persuasion when features were disclaimed. A set of consumers was shown advertisements for two products containing either claims of excellence in all areas, or claims of excellence in most areas and statements that the competition was superior in two areas. Research found that the advertisements that disclaimed performance in two areas were perceived by potential customers to be significantly more truthful.

Customers have become numb to marketing that promises miracle cures. When you make statements that you "are not the choice if you are looking for _____," you increase your credibility for the next buying cycle when they might truly need something you can supply a Meaningful difference for.

When you honestly articulate your weakness, you are in effect helping customers make a decision. You help relieve them of the need to discover your flaw—which past experience tells them is present in all brands.

PRACTICAL IDEAS

308. Be Open About What You're Not Great At

Research has found that customers actually trust more when you honestly and openly state what you're not the best at. Think about your offering. What are your strengths and weaknesses? When you add them together, do you still win? If your combination of traits is superior, why not make the differences open and easy for customers to see for themselves?

309. Pursue a Philosophy of Underpromising

Develop a reputation for delivering more than you promised with regards to delivery timing, customer service response time, quality, etc. Get known as a sales or marketing person who exceeds expectations as opposed to one who regularly exaggerates.

310. Makes Sales Contingent on Your Evaluation

When there is even the smallest doubt in your mind about the appropriateness of a certain product or service for your customer, say so. Offer to make the sale contingent on you personally checking to make sure that your product works right and/or that the customer is happy with the purchase.

311. Tell Your Offering's History of Success and Failure

With experience, you will learn the strengths and weaknesses of your product or service. Without telling competitive secrets, relate your experience about when your offering has been most effective and least effective. The mere fact that you admit to less than spectacular results in any situation or condition at all will dramatically increase customers' trust.

Don't Cut Your Price

Introducing products or services at a lower-than-usual price is harmful to final sales.

Customer expectations of value received and cost paid are set when they make a purchase. When customers make initial purchases at a discounted price, they develop a lower value perception of the product than if they purchase at a regular price.

A study was conducted of matched sets of stores for five new products. In one set of stores, during the first few weeks of availability, the initial price was set about 20 to 30 percent lower than the regular price. In these stores, the price was eventually moved up after the initial period to the regular list price. In the other stores, the products were introduced at regular list price.

Across all five of the new products, long-term volume was higher when the brand was not sold at artificially cheap prices upon introduction.

The data was not available, but if we were able to calculate cumulative profit, it is likely that we would find an even more dramatic negative impact on bottom-line profits.

Artificially low prices "rent" customers, and what is rented must eventually be returned. When you sell on price, you mindlessly train customers to perceive low price as the primary benefit of your offering.

Meaningful Marketing means customers make a conscious choice for good reasons. It means that they have perceived real and tangible value. The net result is a deeper, more Meaningful connection with customers and longer-term sales and profits.

PRACTICAL IDEAS

312. Provide Proportional Trial-Size Offerings

Lower price reduces customer risk, but it also creates an artificially low price/value relationship. To prevent this, offer miniature sizes of your product or service. A trial size that is proportionally priced—single use or limited supply—reduces the absolute price while still maintaining the appropriate price/value relationship.

313. Pursue Exclusive Distribution Arrangements

When your offering has a Meaningful difference, it can become a tool to help retailers build customer traffic by using it as a loss leader. And when one retailer discounts your price, soon all do, resulting in an artificially low price perception by customers. If you utilize exclusive distribution agreements in specific areas, you reduce the chances that competitive forces will cause damaging low pricing.

314. Market Free Samples or Bonus Discounts With a Partner

Generate sampling yet maintain pricing integrity by jointly promoting your new product or service with another brand. The combination of your product with another will enhance the special "one-time-only" aspect of the promotion and not allow customers to tie the deal they got on your product to your brand's price.

315. Encourage Customers to Use Competitive Discounts

If you're feeling really bold, tell your customers when your competition is offering special discounts. Especially in business-to-business situations this can be an effective way to provide proof positive that you really believe in the value of your Meaningful difference.

MINDLESS MARKETING
Data-Proven Truths &
Practical Ideas

The Mindless Momentum of "Yes, Yes, Yes"

When adults say yes, they are more likely to say yes again.

Humans have a need for personal consistency. Once they say yes to a path of action, they are much more likely to feel good about the decision and to continue to say "yes" to additional requests.

In the field of persuasion research this is known as the "foot-in-the-door" or the "low-ball" technique. The strategy is simple: Get a customer to say yes to a small and harmless request, and he is much more likely to say "yes" to additional, larger requests.

This truth has been validated hundreds of times by academic researchers. A study found that when participants were asked to answer five research questions (small request), they were 28 percent more likely to answer a second twenty-question survey (larger request) than if they were asked to answer only the twenty-question survey.

In another study, conducted on fund-raising for the American Heart Association, participants were asked to answer four questions (small favor), then asked to make a donation. Of those asked to do the favor first, 34 percent made a donation versus 19 percent of those who were asked just to donate.

Even seemingly harmless concessions by customers can dramatically improve your odds of sales success. When customers make even a small commitment to you, they subconsciously become more favorable toward you.

When you gain any commitment from a customer, you dramatically increase your chances of gaining further commitments.

PRACTICAL IDEAS

316. Use the Franklin-in-France Wisdom-Selling System

When Benjamin Franklin was ambassador to France, he gained influence with a key thought leader by first asking to borrow a book from his library (small request). He returned the book promptly and borrowed another. Having proven his reliability, he then initiated discussions on larger requests.

Seek an opportunity to gain knowledge and wisdom—by sharing a book, suggesting a good training program, or asking customers' opinions. A customer who has shared his mind with you will be more willing to share his wallet.

317. Even a Penny Will Help

In the American Heart Association survey detailed earlier, the simple phrase "even a penny will help" was added to the small-request then big-request test sequence. The result was a 50 percent donation rate versus 19 percent for the donation-only request. Think about your business. What is the smallest, tiniest thing a customer can do—"just take a test drive," "just taste our new beer," "just answer a few questions," "just put down a $5 deposit." The smallest commitment will generate the largest persuasion impacts.

318. Get It in Writing—Any Writing

When students filled out a form after volunteering to help a charity, they were three times more likely to actually show up than those who simply gave verbal commitment. Seek ways to get your customers to send you E-mail or letters, fill out questionnaires—anything. The simple act of putting words to paper can be the start of a continuing relationship.

The Power of Having History Repeat Itself

A customer's past decisions are a powerful source of motivation for making a purchase from you.

Customers are Mindless creatures of habit. They are most likely to follow previous behaviors even when there is no demand or cause for doing so.

A study of young adults found that, in the four years after they left home, over 50 percent of their purchases of a set of eight household products (common products like pain reliever, detergent, tissue, and toothpaste) were the same as what their parents bought.

Rather than think for themselves, youths carry their parents' choices for products with them. They do so because the path of consistency requires less mental effort. This simple fact is why it is so important that you make Meaningful connections with customers early in their lives—before Mindless patterns set in.

Decisions made in the past tend to become amplified in consumers' minds in the present. Racetrack bettors were asked, on a seven-point scale, what they thought their chances of winning the next race were. Before placing a bet, the average rating was 3.5. After placing their bet, their rating rose to 4.8. The simple aspect of making a firm decision, by placing a bet, had amplified their confidence.

Customers have a natural gravitational pull toward repeating past actions. The sooner you can make a Meaningful connection regarding how your offering can make a real difference in their lives, the greater your chances of creating a long-term customer. Conversely, the longer they've been committed to another brand, the greater your challenge in getting them to switch.

PRACTICAL IDEAS

319. Make Connections With Past Precedents

Find ways to connect what you are selling with past precedents of customers' habits. Do this no matter how dramatically different what you have to offer is. Find points of connection to existing beliefs: "If you liked shopping at _____ for your _____ needs, then you'll love shopping at _____."

320. Connect to Past Habits

"You've always valued greater _____. Here's an offering that takes _____ to a higher level."

321. Connect to Past Requests

"You've always asked for a way for us to _____. We've listened and here's an opportunity that directly delivers on your request."

322. Connect to Previous Purchasing

"You loved the original as a teenager. Here's a version for your adult needs."

323. Leverage Transition Points

Transition points of any kind—graduations, marriages, or new jobs—offer an opportunity to break the Mindless purchasing consistency that is inherent in life.

324. Evoke a Memory That Connects Family and Friends

The past can be a great trigger point for retrying a product long forgotten. Connections to familiar times and faces can bring strong points of consumer attraction: The "good old days" or "Your mom used _____, the same _____ that has been improved for the demands of your life."

Initiation Power

The greater the initiation endured, the greater the commitment to further action.

When a customer goes through a great deal of trouble to find or buy something, they develop an enhanced sense of its value.

Studies have shown the impact of varying intensities of initiation rites on commitment to a group. College students were put through varying levels of personal embarrassment to become part of a group. The research found that those who endured the greatest initiation stress had the most favorable attitude toward the eventual group and its members.

The greater the intensity of stress and effort required to acquire something, the more positive the attitudes toward the end result. Marine boot camp and college fraternities both leverage this fundamental human dynamic. The more a person "owns the effort," the greater the commitment that develops.

In a similar manner, after we have spent a lot of time learning how to operate high-technology hardware or software, we are reluctant to throw away that investment. Or after we've spent significant time learning a trade, a craft, a hobby, or a system of any kind, we are reluctant to leave it.

The key to leveraging the power of initiation is that there must be a Meaningful payoff from the pain endured. The end result—be it a product, a service, or a new vendor—must offer something that is Meaningful to the participant. If the end result offers nothing special, then it is unlikely that many will endure the initiation stress.

Initiation doesn't have to always be a singular pain. A series of small, incremental initiations can get customers to mindlessly commit their time and energy so that they are less likely to walk away from their "investment."

PRACTICAL IDEAS

325. Leverage Longtime Members

Seek out those who are long-term members of your trade association. Leverage their commitment to the industry. This can be especially helpful if what you are offering has the potential to improve, enhance, or grow the industry.

326. Tour and Educate

Get your customers involved in learning and studying about your product. Engage them in the process of understanding deeply what makes you uniquely valuable. Do whatever it takes to get them to tour your production facility. Ideally, get them to visit in person. If you get them to physically visit your factory for a day, they will be mentally with you forever.

327. Purposely Leave Information out of Materials

When you have a Meaningful difference, make it overtly clear. But avoid the temptation to detail all information—terms, pricing, etc. Rather, require customers to call you for details. The simple act of making a phone call to you to gain additional information tilts your odds of sales success significantly.

328. Aggressively Pursue Customer Inquiries

Customers who make even a small investment of their time on your business have dramatically greater chances of becoming a customer than those who you make a cold call on. This is why it's important to promptly follow up on every customer inquiry.

329. Seek Those With the Biggest Problems

Those customers who have the greatest problems offer a special opportunity for you to create a Meaningful connection. The greater the pain they feel, the greater the bond they'll feel when they realize relief with your solution.

The Power of Positive Statements

Getting customers to verbalize positive feelings significantly improves sales results.

Customers follow Mindless consistency. If you can get them to make a positive statement about themselves, their work, their company, their life, you can dramatically improve your sales chances.

Research finds that simply asking someone how they are feeling, and listening to their response, can have a dramatic impact on your sales success.

Researchers phoned consumers asking for permission to visit their house to sell cookies for charity. When directly asked if they could visit, only 10 percent of the respondents said "yes." When asked how they were feeling before being asked to visit, 25 percent said "yes!"

In addition, customers' responses to how they were feeling were coded for degree of positive response. Response rates were nearly double (46 percent) among those who gave highly favorable responses such as "great" or "wonderful" to the question of how they were feeling.

Positive momentum creates positive momentum. When customers state they are feeling good, they are more inclined to give you a positive response to your request so to keep positive feelings flowing.

Quite simply, when customers take a "public position," they tend to behave in a manner that reinforces their words. This is the thinking behind behavior-modification programs like Alcoholics Anonymous and weight-loss programs that require participants to make public declaration of their weaknesses and faults. What is publicly stated is more likely to be done.

PRACTICAL IDEAS

330. Remember to Smile

Even when you are on the phone with a customer, the simple act of smiling when you talk is infectious. If you smile, people will respond in kind and be more open to your message.

331. Ask What You Can Do for Them

Consumers want to be happy. To help them achieve greater happiness, ask them directly what you can do to make their lives better. Ask them to verbalize what they need and have them confirm the need by defining, on a scale of 0 to 10, how important the need is to them.

By simply getting customers to publicly commit to a point of view, you can influence their purchasing behavior. A fundraising study found that adults who had signed a petition supporting the handicapped were twice as likely to make a donation when asked to give a week later.

332. Listen More Than You Talk

Ask clients open-ended questions regarding "why"—as in: "Why is it important that you increase production efficiency?" "Why is it important that you find new ways of training?" "Why is it important that you look at new vendors? Once they've spoken "why," it will be easier to get them to think "why not" and to do as you ask.

333. Make Their Day

Don't forget that everyone is entitled to a bad day. Don't lose a customer because he is not in the mood to see your benefit. Keep your tone upbeat and be a positive force. When customers hear your name, you want a smile to come to their minds. Make a point to elevate everyone you come in contact with.

Giving Something to Get Something

When you make a meaningful concession, customers feel an obligation to reciprocate.

Giving something to get something in return is one of the oldest and most reliable of persuasion tactics. Giving something to get something can be seen in client dinners at gourmet restaurants, donations to political campaigns, and even foreign aid to third-world countries.

The success of this tactic has been quantified in academic studies dozens of times. The most classic form of concession tactic is called the "door-in-the-face" persuasion tactic. The salesperson makes an extreme demand and upon receiving a negative response, gives up on the extreme request and makes a smaller demand. The smaller demand is seen as a concession to the customer. The customer then feels obligated to reciprocate by saying "yes."

A study of the effectiveness of fund-raising tactics confirmed the power of making a concession. When potential donors who had said "no" to the extreme request of becoming part of a long-term monthly donor program were then asked to simply make one donation, some 34 percent said "yes" compared to 19 percent of those who were asked only to make one donation. (Yes, the numbers were numerically the same as for Truth 81.)

In another study, college students were first asked an extreme request—to donate their time, two hours a day per week for two years, helping younger children. When they said "no," they were then asked the smaller request, to help chaperone one two-hour trip to the zoo. Of those asked the extreme request followed by the small request, 50 percent agreed to chaperone versus only 17 percent when asked only the small request.

When you make a Meaningful concession, it can cause a potential buyer to feel a responsibility to give something back to you by responding positively.

PRACTICAL IDEAS

334. Move From Pushing for the Sale to Gaining Leads

When a customer can't buy or won't buy, fall back and ask for names of those who might have an interest. By releasing sales pressure, you can create an environment where the potential customer voluntarily gives you names and phone numbers of quality leads. Then you can approach the sales leads with a personal recommendation: "Bill suggested that I call."

335. Give Something Away

A mail-order catalog company gave their customers overstock items that they would normally sell at warehouse sales. The free gifts had an average value of fifteen dollars. Response rates from those receiving the free gift rose from 5 percent to 25 percent and their average purchase rose from $100 to $300. Think about your business. What can you give away to hook customers?

336. Sell From High to Low

Present your most expensive option first, then move to lower-cost options. A study by a manufacturer of expensive billiards tables found that when customers were first shown low-cost then higher-cost tables, the average sale was for $550. When they were shown the $3,000 tables first then lower-cost options, the average price of the billiards table purchased was over $1,000!

337. Give Price Discounts or Free Bonuses to Close Sales

Persuade uncertain customers through introduction of special offers or free bonuses if they make an immediate decision. The momentum of your concession can tip customers toward making a commitment.

338. Make a Concession to Get Customers to Trade Up

After a customer has made a purchase decision, offer a special deal on the higher-grade model or service option.

DATA PROVEN TRUTH #86

Be Likable

Customers are three times more likely to purchase when they like the message form and/or the messenger.

We prefer to buy from people we like. And we really like people who are like us.

Being likable is as simple as helping customers feel happy, feel relaxed, or even just feel good about themselves.

When customers feel good, they're more likely to purchase. When students were shown commercials for nearly identical products, they were three times more likely to select the one that featured likable music.

All things being equal, we would rather do business with those we like. Unlikable people can be successful when they have a monopoly. However, when the natural cycles of the marketplace create greater parity, customers will buy from someone they like better.

A key element of likability is similarity. When customers view you as similar to them, they are more likely to cooperate. A study involving 450 students found average attraction to a stranger rose from 6.4 to 11.9 when they were paired with someone who, based on personality tests, had higher similarity.

In another study, when asked to borrow money to make a phone call, over two-thirds of the time, participants said "yes" when the requester was dressed like them and less than half the time, when he was dressed differently. Connecting with customers based on common hobbies, feelings, or attitudes is one of the oldest sales tactics on earth.

Amazingly, studies have found that even when customers know you are complimenting them on purpose or are wrong in your compliment, they still feel better about you. As Ben Franklin once said, "A flatterer never seems absurd: The flatter'd always takes his word."

PRACTICAL IDEAS

339. Be Observant and Understanding

It's in the little details of your customer's office that connections can be made. Know the lives of your customers. The more you make a relevant, yet unexpected connection with their lives, the greater your chance of gaining their interest.

340. Show Solidarity

Analysis of recordings of phone sales calls found that when the seller gave overt statements of solidarity—approving of a customer's choice, laughing at a customer's joke, acknowledging a customer's opinion as valid—they were significantly more likely to close a sale.

341. Talk Less and Listen to Customers More

Encourage your customers to talk as much as possible. Few sounds are as appealing to adults as the sound of their own voice. Studies indicate that the average person speaks at about 150 words per minute, but the average person thinks at 600 words a minute. The more you talk, the more your customer has time to think of objections to your proposal.

342. Mimic Your Customers

Customers tend to respond to those who think, act, and believe as they do. Make yourself a mirror to your customers. In a gentle way mimic their feelings, tone, and attitude. Help them feel that you are in this with them. View the world from your customers' viewpoint and you improve your ability to persuade them to see things as you want them to.

DATA PROVEN TRUTH #87

Monkey See, Monkey Do

Customers rely on the opinions of others in making their decisions.

This truth is powerful and frankly a little scary. Research has confirmed that what we see, feel, and perceive dictates how we react. We voluntarily give up our judgment and follow the masses.

A set of classic studies conducted in New York City showed how the size of a group had direct impact on the behavior of others. When one person stopped on the sidewalk and looked upward, 4 percent of those passing by looked up also. When five test subjects stopped and looked up at the same time, 18 percent of passersby did too. Finally, when a group of fifteen looked up, some 40 percent of those walking by looked up too.

The most disturbing evidence of imitation is a series of large-scale research studies that have documented the impact of news stories on increasing suicides, murders, and even crashes of airplanes or cars. Analysis has found that the bigger the news coverage, the greater the impact on numbers of imitative incidences.

Leveraging mass acceptance as a marketing tool is especially valuable when customers are uncertain. The greater their uncertainty, the more likely they are to follow the path trodden by the masses. In effect, customers run on autopilot, foregoing Meaningful thinking for mindlessly following.

The social proof set can be a broad-based mass of people or a more focused set. Teenagers act distinctly from their parents, yet in near total alignment with fellow teens.

Following the crowd is a means of reducing one's perception of risk. It guarantees that "I won't lose. I won't do worse than most people." Given the risk-averse nature of the masses, this approach has some definite advantages as a trial method.

PRACTICAL IDEAS

343. Leverage Testimonials

Leverage testimonials from satisfied customers who share similarities. Testimonials reinforce that others were willing to take risks so that your customer doesn't have to. Make it easier for your target audience to accept your product by finding those testimonials from people who overcame the major hurdles they most identify with.

344. Build Momentum

Take advantage of momentum. Traders on Wall Street know that a fast-moving stock either up or down means it's possible that someone knows something that they don't. Create your own sense of "buzz" by drawing attention to your product's growing popularity. Overtly declare your growth in customers. Directly draw attention to the number of customers who have switched to you from the competition.

345. Avoid Negative Opinions

Negative opinions have been found to cause customers to back off making decisions. Analysis of recordings of phone sales calls found that when sellers stated negative opinions—"I think that might be a problem and you should consider _____"—they were significantly less likely to close a sale.

346. See Themselves in the Action

Emulation is a standard human trait. Endorsements by celebrities your target audience emulates can attract new consumers. We may not be able to jump as high, run as fast, or drive like our heroes, but we love to wear, eat, or do those normal things they do.

347. Tell a Story

Develop case studies that show the human side of your consumers' experiences with your product or service. Use these case studies of personal stories to reduce fear.

DATA PROVEN TRUTH #88

Scarcity as a Sales Tool

When your customers perceive your product or service as being in short supply, they view it as more valuable.

The more scarce an item is, the more valuable it feels. Marketers of collectibles (from baseball cards to coins to antiques) understand the profit potential in marketing items that are rare.

A range of studies has validated the impact of scarcity on customers' perceptions. One study found that ratings of a college cafeteria's food quality increased significantly when students were told that a fire had occurred in the kitchen, causing the cafeteria to be closed for several weeks. Another study found that when students were given a jar containing just two cookies instead of ten, they rated the quality and value of the cookies significantly higher.

Scarcity is yet another component that customers use to simplify their decision-making process. When something is sold out, they make the simplistic assumption that it is because other customers have found it to be of high quality.

In addition, when we lose access to something, we perceive the loss as a loss of freedom. This causes a passion for restoring our freedom by purchasing or acquiring the restricted item.

Basic economics tells us that when demand exceeds supply for goods or services, the result is upward pressure on pricing. When more people are interested in purchasing than there is product availability, the net impact is an increased sense of product worth.

In effect, the marketplace is one giant auction. When supply exceeds demand, the buyers retain control of pricing. When demand exceeds supply, the sellers have freedom to price higher.

PRACTICAL IDEAS

348. Expand Demand Beyond Supply

If your offering provides a Meaningful difference, you have a simple means for increasing profitability—overmarket. Utilize more marketing than you have the ability to support. Ideally, target for 20 percent extra demand than you can supply to maintain or increase pricing.

The challenge with increasing demand is greed. Manufacturers feel that the loss of even one sale, because of lack of availability, is a loss of revenue. Stop and reassess the reality of the situation. If you dramatically increase your supply, you will end up losing profit margin.

349. Be Genuine With Scarcity

In today's world of instant communication, customers are far more savvy at discovering false claims of scarcity. The Internet makes it easier for them to discover when you're lying. Make sure your claims of scarcity are truly that, otherwise you will be labeled a cheat.

350. Create a Buzz About Demand

Don't let product supply issues stop the momentum caused by the very consumer demand that sparked the scarcity to begin with. Fuel the buzz by "apologizing" publicly for the lack of demand. Long after supply catches up with your demand, you will have set in customers' minds the clear understanding that your company creates "wow" demand. This can be of great help the next time you introduce something new.

351. Remember Supply vs. Demand Determines Profitability

An aggressive marketing campaign can be a profitable way to increase demand and thus your ability to raise your price or at the very least reduce your price discounting. In this case, marketing serves two purposes: It generates sales and provides protection against discounting through increased customer demand.

DATA PROVEN TRUTH #89

The Power of Authority

When your customers perceive you as an expert
or authority, they are more likely to purchase.

Customers are inclined to follow the directions and advice of authorities. An authority can be a specific person or the perception of a company's or brand's expertise.

Authority can come from a perception of power or prestige. In one classic study, a man walked on the "wait" light at a city intersection. Over 3.5 times more people went with him—against the instructions of the light—when he wore a high-status suit and tie than when he was dressed in lower-class clothing. Other studies have found overt stereotypical responses to those dressed as doctors, ministers, and members of the military.

Similar behavioral changes have been seen in reaction to automobiles. In one study, a high-priced black sedan or a beat-up station wagon drove up and stopped at a red light. When the light turned green, they waited at least fifteen seconds before moving. With the low-status car, 84 percent of the time the car behind it honked to get the driver's attention. The high-status car was honked at only 50 percent of the time.

Authority can be as simple as a type of dress, type of car, or a person's job title. It can also come from a person's knowledge or experience in the area of exploration.

As with many other Mindless marketing truths, the key dimension is that customers are influenced by authority when they assume that they don't know or are unable to make a decision by themselves. When customers are confused or uncertain, they are most likely to follow the opinions and actions of those they perceive know more.

PRACTICAL IDEAS

352. Gain Authority By Knowing More

When you know more, you have genuine authority. Collect data and opinions of people that matter to the lives of your target consumer. Be the "go-to" person when others are looking for direction.

The shady side of knowing more is using gossip and secrets as your knowledge currency. We don't doubt its potential as a tool for making connections with customers; however, we do have concerns about potential ethical conflicts.

353. Use Closed Questions

Consciously listening is critical to the early stages of selling. However, at the midpoint of the sales process, closed-ended questions can be more effective. Analysis of recordings of phone sales calls found that when the seller utilized closed-ended questions—"Would you like option A or B?" "Is option C or D more important to you?"—they were significantly more likely to close a sale. When you present fixed options, you provide a voice of authority as you have distilled the key issues into a simple choice.

354. Publish

The power of the written word as a source of authority is immense. When your writing becomes an academic paper, trade publication article, or even a book, it takes on a new level of significance. Even in today's multimedia world, the written word is king!

355. Make Your Brand the Expert

Sponsor research. Fund educational programs. Make your brand the perceived expert when it comes to knowledge in your field.

DATA PROVEN TRUTH #90

The Power of Food

Meeting over food and drink has a positive impact on customers' reactions to your presentation.

Breaking bread and sharing a meal has a significant impact on customers' attitudes. This finding reinforces the merits of expense account meals.

Studies were conducted asking participants to rate various people or marketing slogans. In the test variables, participants rated the stimuli while having a free lunch. In the test controls, the evaluations were made while not eating. In each case, significantly more positive attitudes were recorded when participants were eating.

Sharing a meal creates a sense of community among participants. It also softens the we/they barrier that can be created in classic buyer/seller interactions. When we have a meal together, we are forced to slow down and connect with others.

The positive impact of food has elements of the famous experiments conducted by Russian psychologist, Ivan Pavlov. Pavlov found that it was possible to connect the ringing of a bell to a dog's salivation response. By always connecting the bell to food, Pavlov conditioned the dog to act in a preconditioned manner.

So, too, when customers are hungry, they are more likely to digest and politely accept what you're selling if you feed them. The roots of this may well go back to our childhood. The dinner table is often the center stage for teaching children politeness and manners. This teaching carries forward to our adult lives.

Another psychological driver of positive feelings during meals is related to the need for reciprocation. When we are given food or drinks, we feel thankful and develop a feeling of "owing" the giver.

PRACTICAL IDEAS

356. Dine Like Europeans

Dine, listen, talk, and connect with your customers in a more leisurely manner.

357. Make Dining Unexpectedly Wonderful

Look for ways to make the dining a particularly memorable experience. Dining at a restaurant where you are well known by the chef and wait staff can make a positive impression. When the chef brings special appetizers for your table alone, it lets your customers know that you consider them special.

Even more effective, you cook and serve—either at your home or simply bring home-baked muffins to your breakfast meeting. Your grandmother's blueberry muffin recipe can be a powerful sales tool.

358. Make the Everyday Special

We all live in a busy, time-compressed world. Taking the time to make a meeting or a hurriedly scheduled meeting special doesn't have to be that difficult. Paying simple attention to details and the little things can speak volumes for you. For example, making sure the bread is fresh, the ice cubes are not melted, the coffee is hot and freshly brewed are small but noticeable efforts that build connections.

359. Show Your Human Side

Certainly, if it is an important day in the life of a customer, celebrate it. We all have times when a birthday, anniversary, or other important date lands on a business day. Everyone enjoys a certain amount of attention.

Also, learning about small, yet important eating habits of a customer can be just as powerful. Be aware of special needs such as a vegetarian diet or food allergies or even simple food no-no's, like no brussels sprouts, please!

DATA PROVEN TRUTH #91

Remember Customer Names and They'll Remember to Purchase

Remembering a potential customer's name can increase sales by up to 239 percent.

Today's managers have many high-tech sales tools available to them. However, research indicates that the simple act of remembering a customer's name can have a dramatic impact on your ultimate success.

A professor conducted a set of three experiments involving ninety students to determine what impact remembering people's names has on persuading them to make a purchase.

Students were asked to introduce themselves during the first class of the semester, stating their full name and briefly indicating their background or interests. At the end of the class, the students were asked to individually meet with the professor in his office.

As each student entered the office, the professor made it a point to remember some of the students' names. He then asked a predetermined collection of questions about each student's background. At the end of the meeting, the professor offered the student the opportunity to purchase cookies his wife was selling to raise money for their church.

Of the students whose names were remembered, 92 percent bought cookies, versus 57 percent of those whose names were not remembered. And among those that bought cookies, students whose names were remembered bought an average of 2.1 cookies versus 1.6 cookies for the others.

Net: In total, remembering a potential customer's name generated a 239 percent increase in sales!

360. Remember Customers' Names

Right now, make a tangible commitment to remember the names of your customers. Find a reason to state your customer's name at least three times during the conversation when you first meet. Always end a conversation by repeating the customer's name to seal that lasting impression.

361. Recall Everyone's Name to Get Everyone's Help

Make it a point to remember names beyond your direct contact. Remember the names of office staff, assistants, and receptionists. Ignore these people and they will ignore your requests for help. Treat them as important and they will treat your future requests with equal importance.

362. Record and Remember All Customer Details

Just as names are important so, too, are the other personal details of your customers' lives. Remembering personal details tells your customers that you value them as a person, not just as a customer.

363. Become a Master at Handwritten Notes

Speaking a customer's name creates a point of connection. The same effect can be generated through the use of handwritten notes. In today's voice mail, E-mail world, the handwritten note is becoming a scarce commodity.

364. Make One-on-One Marketing a Reality

One-on-one communication with customers is often more dream than reality. After great expenditure of funds, the net result of many programs is simply a custom-addressed letter. A great opportunity exists for those who make a commitment to genuinely connect with their customers.

The Power of a Person's Word

*When people give their word, they are over four times
more likely to follow through as requested.*

When people give you their personal commitment, they are far more
likely to follow through.

A series of studies was conducted to measure the number of times
bystanders took action when they observed what they perceived was
a theft. In one set of experiments bystanders on a beach were asked
to keep an eye on a radio and other valuables while the owner went
for a swim. While the owner was away, an accomplice came by and
"stole" the radio. The reaction of the bystander was then observed.

Bystanders who had made a commitment to help stopped the thief
95 percent of the time. Only 20 percent of the time did bystanders
stop the thief when a prior commitment had not been made.

The inherent human desire for consistency sets up a conflict
within the bystanders. When they say yes, they'll keep an eye on the
radio, they create a bond. It's difficult to follow through and inter-
vene when the theft occurs; it's even more difficult to face the owner
of the radio who would return to find it missing.

A restaurant reduced its no-shows for reservations from 30 percent to 10 percent by simply asking, "Will you please call if you have
to change your plans?" instead of stating, "Please call if you have to
change your plans."

In your sales and marketing efforts, asking for and receiving a
commitment can be a powerful tool when setting up meetings or gaining customer commitment to purchase.

PRACTICAL IDEAS

365. Gain Approval One Small Step at a Time

The sales process is a step-by-step process. At each step along the way we move closer to a sale. Break your purchase sequence into a series of steps that are small and unthreatening. Ask customers for thirty minutes to provide a presentation of your capabilities. Follow the meeting with a request to conduct a product demonstration. Offer to do a free survey of the company's situation to quantify the benefit of using your services. Each small step moves the client closer to buying.

366. Nurture a Skeptical Client

When you give your word to a skeptical client who has yet to commit to you, it signals your willingness to commit to them. People instinctively know that it is human nature to rise to meet the expectations of those closest to them. Giving your word— and then keeping it—signals a change in the customer/supplier relationship that can make the difference in winning future sales.

367. Ask Them to Tell You About Opportunities

Directly ask your customers to tell you when there is a significant change in the company's needs. Directly ask customers to call you when an opportunity to bid on new business occurs. Ask them to send you an E-mail when they hear of anyone who needs your product or service.

368. Give With No Strings Attached

You cannot lead customers where they do not want to go. Reinforce the overt benefit of your product or service together with your word and make sure to reinforce that no strings are attached. This signals that you are giving a customer-focused benefit without hidden expectations in return.

DATA PROVEN TRUTH #93

The Power of Deadlines

By setting a specific deadline, you can dramatically speed customer decision making.

Time is money. And when a customer is unable or unwilling to make a decision, it creates a cost for the salesperson. The salesperson utilizes time and energy, the most precious assets available, chasing a customer for resolution.

Many times the delay is due to multiple purchasing options. This is the case when more than one option is available and each offers a distinct set of Meaningful benefits. For example, technology product A might be ultra easy to operate, while product B is more complicated but with higher performance characteristics. When we have a clear vision of our needs, the energy to resolve the conflict is minimal and we simply decide.

However, in many cases the "right answer" is not self-evident. In these cases, a new option C to delay the decision and seek more information becomes the preferred choice. A test of 121 college students found that 46 percent chose to wait until they learned more about the various models when presented with a conflicting choice.

One of the most powerful decision-making systems is to create a sense of loss. Specifically, in the case outlined, if only two units of product A were available in the store, the fear of loss would drive decisions.

Anytime we give a deadline or conscious restriction, we speed action. A study was conducted where students were paid a few dollars to complete a questionnaire with varying requests of completion time. When they were given no deadline, 25 percent completed the questionnaire; with a three-week deadline, 42 percent completed it; and with a five-day deadline, some 60 percent completed the questionnaire. Net: The more flexibility in timing, the less likely customers are to take action.

PRACTICAL IDEAS

369. Be Specific in Your Requests

When seeking to persuade, use a deadline in decision-making to influence the customer's direction. Be direct and specific about your request. And define clearly the costs of delaying a decision.

370. The Power of Silence

Silence in a meeting is a form of deadline. When you don't speak, you create a need for customers to talk. One of the most common mistakes that salespeople make is to talk too much. When you stop speaking, you put pressure on the customer either to make a decision or to share information with you that could be helpful.

371. Deadline Reinforcement and Reminders

Deadlines can easily be forgotten. When you take a stance on a deadline, make it clear. Then hold to it. Reinforce and warn of the consequences. And when the time's up, it's up. Be firm in following through on your deadlines or you lose all future credibility.

372. Crossing the Cost Threshold

Use deadlines to quantify the cost/value relationship in a transaction. Illustrate how a missed deadline affects the bottom line and you have a clear leverage tool when dealing with a rational left-brain customer. Instill a sense of emotional loss or fear with the right-brain customer.

373. Reward Good Customers With Deadline Flexibility

One of the greatest benefits you can give longtime customers is flexible deadlines and details of operation. It's a way to show that you trust them as a result of your long-standing relationship. It's also an effective way to solidify customer loyalty.

DATA PROVEN TRUTH #94

Never, Ever, Ever Give Up

*Customers' opinions about purchasing are not
absolute predictors of behavior.*

There is little doubt that customers' opinions are not absolute determinants of their behavior. When customers are asked their opinions,
they often avoid deep thinking and instead answer based on what they
perceive is the "politically correct" answer.

A sample of 4,707 customers' intentions, versus actual purchases,
was tracked for a wide variety of products sold in grocery stores. Of
those who indicated there was virtually no chance of them purchasing a product, some 19 percent actually did. And of those stating they
definitely would purchase, only 43 percent actually did.

Customers' intentions have a clear relationship with behavior.
Customers who are more interested are more likely to purchase.

However, in the absolute, customers have a poor ability to predict their actual behavior. When asked to project their opinion, they
don't appear to think deeply about the benefits and costs of the option
presented to them.

The importance of this with regards to sales and marketing is that
we must not give up too early. When selling, never, ever, ever give up.

Just because customers state that they are not likely to do something doesn't mean that, with additional information or perspective,
they won't change their minds.

PRACTICAL IDEAS

374. Make the Unfamiliar Familiar

The more unique your offering, the more likely a customer is to give a stereotypical response to your request. However, as the research shows, a "no" is not necessarily a "no." And the more times they consider your request, the more familiar it becomes and the more likely they are to feel comfortable saying "yes." The key is to not create annoyance with your repeated presentations.

375. Delivering News

When you bring news, you open the door for reconsideration. Each time you present your offer, showcase another piece of news. Consumers respond to news. Leverage the revelation factor when communicating newness to capture attention.

376. The Power of Simplicity

When dealing with seemingly complex products or ideas, translate them into simple steps to circumvent a "no" response. Often a "no" is really a plea for more information or clarity. The simpler and clearer the overt benefits of your offering, the easier it is for customers to say "yes."

377. Manage Your Return on Investment

Measure the return you get on each presentation. Classify customers according to their current stage of sale—and quantify the cost and return on each subsequent marketing effort. You can also increase your profitability by learning how to eventually cut customers from your call list, database, and target marketing when the return no longer justifies the expense.

The Halo of Attention to Personal Details

When you look successful, customers perceive you as successful.

When you make a presentation or create an advertisement, attention to little details means a lot.

Multiple studies have shown that customers make a direct connection between attention to detail and competence.

Research was conducted of job applicants who had equal qualifications but whose pictures either showed a poorly groomed applicant (wrinkled shirt) or a well-groomed applicant (fresh pressed clothing). The results indicated that the well-groomed applicant was hired more frequently than the poorly groomed applicant. Interestingly, this was found even though the research subjects initially rated grooming as the least important decision criteria. Clearly what the research respondents thought was important and what they acted on were different.

Another test involving 124 subjects varied both grooming and qualifications. Mathematical modeling found that good grooming had as great an impact on hiring decisions as did qualifications.

Other studies have shown that good-looking political candidates receive 2.5 times more votes than unattractive candidates, and that good-looking employees are better paid. Another study found that good-looking defendants in court cases were assessed average damages of $5,623 versus $10,051 for unattractive defendants.

The natural way of adults is to be lazy when it comes to making decisions. Instead of meaningfully evaluating criteria, we rely on stereotypes—cues like grooming, looks, and attention to detail—to make our decisions for us.

PRACTICAL IDEAS

378. Pay Attention to Details

Nothing can be more aggravating or distracting to the sales process than the erroneous little details that go undetected. Simple miscues like spelling errors, color mismatching, or an out-of-place line or margin can destroy customer confidence.

379. The Look of Success

When you project an image of success, people assume that you are successful. Akio Morita, one of the founders of Sony, made it a point to always stay in high-quality hotels on sales visits—even in the early days, when money was tight. He felt that staying at a quality hotel projected an image of success to customers and also enhanced his personal confidence.

380. Get a Fresh Perspective

Make sure that fresh eyes review and look at all aspects of your sales and marketing materials and presentations. One of the simplest ways to see the seemingly unseeable is to look at it in a fresh way. As an example, proofreaders are taught to read materials in reverse order to more easily find typos and mistakes.

381. Ask the Experts About Their Pet Peeves

Your established customers are your biggest experts when it comes to details because they are the actual users of your product or service. Ask them for the little things that annoy them, the seemingly unimportant details that make their lives more difficult. Watch your customers use or interact with your products under real-world conditions. Simply spending time watching gives insight into unspoken details that matter.

The Power of Suggestion

The simple act of asking a customer to buy sets off a chain reaction resulting in a small but significant increase in purchasing.

When a customer is asked to make a purchase, it sets off a chain reaction of thinking and consideration.

This finding comes from a study of forty thousand households. A portion of the panel was asked their likelihood of purchasing an automobile or a personal computer within the next six months. Subsequently, the actual purchase of a car or a computer by those surveyed was compared to those who had not been surveyed.

Analysis found a 37 percent increase in automobile purchasing and an 18 percent increase in computer purchasing among those who had simply been asked their likelihood of purchasing.

The impact of the question is clearly small. However, the huge size of the study makes clear the power of suggestion. The simple act of asking customers if they would like to purchase increases their odds of doing so.

When asked to make a purchase, customers are required to think more deeply about their actual needs. It also results in a greater awareness of the meaningfulness of your offering.

When customers think more meaningfully, they become more aware of their situational needs and desires.

A related study found that merely asking consumers to consider a scenario in which they would become cable television subscribers significantly increased the rate at which they subscribed to cable TV.

When we ask customers to think about or to purchase our offering, it sets off a mental discussion that lights a spark, resulting in a significant increase in actual purchasing—even among those who are not planning to purchase.

PRACTICAL IDEAS

382. Ask Customers If They Ever Expect to Make a Purchase

Once they agree that they will be in the market sometime for your product or service, you're halfway to a sale. Once they make a commitment to buying sometime, they set off a chain reaction toward an eventual sale. The only issue remaining then is timing.

Timing can be accelerated by increasing their dissatisfaction with their current purchasing option and by increasing their perception of your value. The more they see your offering as solving a Meaningful need that they have, the more they will accelerate their decision.

383. Use Market Research as a Sales Tool

Survey attitudes about purchase interest as part of the sales process. When customers browse, they provide live market research as they consider their choices. Motivate browsing customers to buy by simply asking them which product is the most interesting to them. Overtly getting customers to display likability will increase the probability that they will purchase.

384. Consumers Run in Packs

While most people say they want to stand out from the pack, the reality is that consumers follow a herd instinct. Another way to ask them to buy is to reinforce that others like them are buying, too. This signals to them that they are indeed looking at the right product or service.

385. Assume Success

Start your conversations in marketing materials and live presentations with the presumption of success. Take the perspective that the customers have already made the purchase. Discuss how happy they will be with their decision. Talk about how they will never regret their purchase. Detail how, as they get used to the benefit of what you offer, they will find it hard to ever go back to the competition.

Make It Personal

*The more personal your connection to customers,
the more they are likely to spend.*

Research on restaurant tipping has provided a simple and easy way
to quantitatively measure the impact of interpersonal contact with
customers.

In one simple study, the server at a Sunday brunch buffet sometimes introduced herself by name: "Good morning. My name is Kim,
and I will be serving you this morning. Have you ever been to (restaurant name) before?" In the other condition she omitted her name.

Analysis found that when the server stated her name, and thus
made a personal connection, she received an average tip of 23 percent of the check versus 15 percent when she didn't give her name.

This study confirmed earlier studies that have shown that the level
of personal connection by restaurant staff has a dramatic impact on
tips. Other studies have shown similar results when the server physically touches a diner and when the server makes more visits to the
table that are not related to classic tasks such as serving food or taking orders. Interestingly, several studies have shown that the quality
of the service rendered by the server tends to be unrelated to tipping
rate both in a restaurant setting and in a taxi setting.

When you make a personal contact with a customer, you create
a sense of connection that goes beyond the commercial transaction.

PRACTICAL IDEAS

386. Connect Meaningfully

Stop and talk with genuineness. Discuss the weather and the state of the world or your small part in the world. Take the time to find out about your customers. Understand what brought them to your product or service. Understanding their true motivations can help you connect with them in a more personal manner.

387. Be Yourself

A powerful strategy for Mindless Marketing is getting customers to like you a lot by being overtly friendly. An alternative strategy that is equally effective is to focus your energy on competence, trustworthiness, and putting your customer's interests first. In this case, being a touch quirky but genuine will win you a deeper and more Meaningful connection.

388. The Common Denominator

People look to find associations with each other to reinforce trust and a sense of community. Find a common point between you and your customers. Ask where they're from, where they like to vacation, what their kids are into, what they like to do in their free time, etc. Seek and find a common connection to enhance the personal bond you create with your customers.

389. Use the Internet as a Connection Tool

For your key customers, set up an Internet news media tracker to follow their companies and areas of special interest. When a story pops up that might be of genuine interest to them, forward it with a note.

390. The Universal Power of Thank You

A simple bit of wisdom goes a long way, and one of the easiest Mindless Marketing tactics is to simply thank people for their time and interest. This simple connection reinforces that you value them and increases your chances of their valuing you in return.

DATA PROVEN TRUTH #98

Basking in Reflected Glory

Customers like to be perceived as being on winning teams.

Both internal and external dimensions determine our sense of self-worth. One way that people enhance their positive feelings is by making a connection with someone or something that has been successful.

When we are associated with the best, the brightest, the winner, it enhances our feelings of self-worth and personal pride.

In one study, the number of students wearing school logo clothing on the Monday following a weekend win or loss in football, was measured. Following a win, some 43 percent more students wore school logo clothing than following a loss.

These results were further confirmed in a phone survey of students asking them the results of the weekend's football game. When describing the results, students used the term "we" twice as often after a win than after a loss.

When you are associated with an organization that wins, that becomes part of you and what you are. When an athlete from your hometown wins an Olympic medal, you bask in the glory. When your company wins an award, you savor the victory.

In a sales and marketing situation, this reinforces the value of sparking a sense of belonging between your customers and your organization—and of celebrating victories together.

PRACTICAL IDEAS

391. Build a Sense of Belonging

Create a sense of belonging among your customers by enrolling them as members of a club. Use regular newsletters, special events, imprinted sportswear, and other premiums to reinforce customers' special membership status with your company.

392. Celebrate Wins

Invite customers to celebrate your milestones as victories that they made possible. Celebrate "one million cars sold" or "twenty-five years of service" as a broad statement of quality and performance. Think beyond the business dynamics and celebrate your people. Celebrate the winning of trade association awards, celebrate the hiring of your hundredth Ph.D. researcher, and celebrate your appearances on national television.

393. Build "Winner" Momentum

The perception of success can be achieved from major victories such as discovering patented breakthroughs, achieving market share leadership, or winning an award for outstanding quality. "Winner" momentum can also be achieved through a perpetual series of announcements of minor victories, that together, give the perception of a successful product or service brand. The management of Walt Disney World in Florida leverages this concept. Every year they identify something to celebrate, from the anniversary of Mickey Mouse's debut to the anniversary of one of the company's animated movies.

394. Celebrate the Extremes

Victories can be identified in the extremes. When a customer has an outrageous request and your company succeeds in filling it, celebrate it as a case study. Stories of customer service success in outrageously difficult, torture-test conditions can be motivating. Though customers may never face similar situations, they feel good knowing that if they did, you could help them.

Persuasion of Those With a Poor Sense of Self

When customers lack self-esteem, you can realize great success by addressing their personal needs.

Psychologist Abraham Maslow defined a ladder hierarchy of human needs. At the bottom rung are the physiological needs—air, water, food, sex. Then come safety needs—security, stability; social needs—belonging, love, acceptance; and ego needs—self-esteem, self-confidence, respect. At the top of it all are the self-actualization needs—the need to fulfill oneself, to realize one's true potential. Maslow said we must feel secure on each rung before we can move up the ladder.

A study was conducted of 560 new-car buyers' values and perceptions of the sales process. Modeling the data identified three distinct sets of consumer attitudes toward the sales process.

> *Low Self-Esteem and Self-Confidence:* These customers have a desire to be led. They prefer to purchase a vehicle that the salesperson recommends. They depend on the salesperson for help in making a decision. They even admit that they could be talked into making a purchase by a salesperson.

> *Low Sense of Belonging:* These customers consider themselves outcasts and crave connections with salespeople. They prefer salespeople with whom they can create a personal relationship. Their primary focus is on the relationship that develops—not the product facts or salesperson's recommendation.

> *Independent Decision Makers:* These are customers whose interaction with the salesperson is focused on learning information about the vehicles. They view themselves as not being directly influenced by a salesperson's recommendation.

PRACTICAL IDEAS

395. Ask Customers Their Opinions

Ask customers what they are looking for and what is most important to them. Be prepared to be amazed at how directly and honestly customers respond to direct and honest questions. Based on their responses, you will quickly understand the current state of their self-esteem with regards to the purchase decision at hand.

396. Leverage Preexisting Prejudices

Chameleons survive in nature because they adapted the ability to change color to fit their surroundings. The same is true with your advertising message. Research subjects were asked to judge messages that either supported or contradicted their preexisting personal viewpoint. Repeatedly, it was found that subjects rated arguments that aligned with their prejudices stronger even when they were, in truth, weaker than alternatives.

397. Leverage Others When Marketing Contradictions

New product or service breakthroughs that challenge existing ways of thinking can be particularly challenging to sell to low self-esteem customers. Bold changes can be seen as risky and as having the potential to expose their lack of ability to assess and examine your strengths and potential issues. The result can be a reflexive "no" under the guise of "waiting to see what others do." To confront this, bring the testimonials of thought leaders to your presentation. With the support of industry leaders the low self-esteem manager will now find it riskier to not change, than to change.

398. Use Color, Graphics, and Pictures to Reinforce Benefits

Research has found that people with low self-motivation have little ability to think through strengths and weaknesses. Often they base their attitudes on more visual cues such as pretty ads and visually striking imagery.

DATA PROVEN TRUTH #100

Making Irrelevant Differences Work

In a parity situation, distinguishing but meaningless differentiation can drive sales.

In many marketplaces, all brands are identical clones. This can be caused by legal regulations that restrict claims and formulation variations. It can be driven by an historical acceptance of commodity marketing by the category.

Meaningless differentiation can be used as a way to give your brand an excuse for differentiation. And in a world of sameness, anything different provides a convenient "excuse" for purchasing. For example, one brand of coffee may contain flaked crystals—a meaningless difference; a brand of pasta sauce may be meaninglessly described as being "authentic Milanese style."

Research studies involving 227 participants were conducted to quantify the impact of a meaningless addition. In one test, consumers were asked to rate descriptions of down-filled winter jackets that were said to contain either regular down filling or Alpine-class down fill.

The addition of the meaningless Alpine-class down fill caused product ratings to nearly triple from 3.1 to 9.1. Interestingly, in a separate test the meaningless difference was revealed. Participants were told, "Alpine-class fill is goose down, and although the age of a bird matters, the type of bird it comes from does not make a difference in a jacket." When asked the importance of Alpine down, participants now rated it as unimportant. However, they still gave an outstanding overall rating for the Alpine down product of 8.4.

Caution: Following this approach makes you vulnerable to competitive attack. Smart competitors will seek to use your leveraging of a meaningless differentiation as a means to bring all your claims into question.

PRACTICAL IDEAS

399. Don't Overthink Meaningless

When making much about nothing, do not try to confirm that it's Meaningful to consumers. You only raise the shadow of skepticism and ultimately distrust. Instead, straightforwardly articulate the perception of uniqueness without making it seem larger than life.

400. Be Meaningless on What Is Most Meaningful

Add meaningless differentiation in the area that matters the most. When selling a sports car, celebrate your Italian racing tires, not your ergonomic cup holders. When selling a new automobile insurance product, celebrate your advanced claims resolution system, not your Saturday office hours.

401. Just Add More and More and More

If you have nothing Meaningful to communicate, then just add more meaningless differences to your marketing communications. In this case, more is better. In studies of persuasion with college students in various mindless buying situations, simply having more arguments (nine statements versus three) as part of marketing messages was twice as persuasive.

402. Stop and Think About the Effort vs. Return

It is a fact that meaningless differentiation can work. However, this should be considered a tactic of last resort. Often the effort it takes to execute a Meaningful change versus a meaningless one is the same. Yet, the return on the investment of time and money is dramatically different.

BONUS TRUTHS & IDEAS

We define quality as "exceeding expectations."
In that spirit, the following truths are provided
to exceed the number promised on the front cover.

DATA PROVEN TRUTH #101

Meaningful Marketing Checklist

You know what you need to know; you simply need to be reminded.

The core concept that selling should be focused on customer satisfaction, as well as on closing the sale, was first articulated by E. K. Strong in an article in the *Journal of Applied Psychology*, (1925), titled "Theories of Selling." Today the concept lives on under various names from "relationship selling" to "one-to-one marketing."

A research study identified a set of traits that define a salesperson or marketer who has a genuine customer orientation. Together these traits define Meaningful Marketing.

- I try to help customers achieve their goals.

- I try to achieve my goals by satisfying customers.

- I have the best interests of my customers in mind.

- I try to get customers to discuss their needs with me.

- I try to influence a customer by information rather than by pressure.

- I offer the product of mine that is best suited to a customer's need.

- I answer customers' questions as correctly as I can.

- I try to bring a customer with a problem together with a product that helps him solve that problem.

- I am willing to disagree with a customer in order to help him make a better decision.

- I try to give customers an accurate expectation of what my offering will do for them.

- I try to figure out what a customer's needs are.

Importantly, following these traits is good business. The research found a significant positive relationship between presence of these traits and bottom-line sales success.

PRACTICAL IDEAS

A. Walk the Talk

You know what you need to do. You know the value of the statements articulated on the facing page. So do it. Pick two and focus on them for a week. In a month and a half, you'll have focused on each of them. And with repeated cycles, in six months, you'll notice that not only do you sell more with less effort, but you also feel better about marketing your offering in a more Meaningful manner.

B. What Not to Do

A set of negative traits were also identified as part of the survey of customer orientation.

- I try to sell a customer all I can convince him to buy, even if I think it is more than a wise customer would buy.

- I try to sell as much as I can rather than to satisfy a customer.

- I keep alert for weaknesses in a customer's personality.

- If I am not sure a product is right for a customer, I will still apply pressure to get him to buy.

- I decide what products to offer on the basis of what I can convince customers to buy, not on the basis of what will satisfy them in the long run.

- I paint too rosy a picture of my products, to make them sound as good as possible.

- I spend more time trying to persuade a customer to buy than I do trying to discover his needs.

- I pretend to agree with customers to please them.

- I imply to a customer that something is beyond my control when it is not.

- I begin the sales talk for a product before exploring a customer's needs with him.

- I treat a customer as a rival.

DATA PROVEN TRUTH #102

Be Bold; Be Brave

Whatever you can do or dream you can, begin it.
Boldness has genius, power, and magic in it.

—*Johann Wolfgang von Goethe*

The truths on these pages are designed to help you "know more," in the words of Drayton Bird. However, the success you will realize comes from your skill times your effort.

To make a Meaningful difference, you must run advertisements, knock on doors, or make sales calls. You must get yourself actively involved and take conscious action.

The rules of basic multiplication indicate that no matter how effective the truths in this book are in improving your skills, if you exert zero effort in applying them, the net result is still zero. *No action guarantees no result.*

The greater the change you act on, the greater your chances of realizing a Meaningful improvement in your sales and marketing results. In theory, this is easy. In reality, it's not. It's not, because fear holds us back. The greater the change, the greater your fear will be. And research finds a direct negative correlation between fear level and productive creativity.

Fear is rational and fear is emotional. Fear is social and fear is personal. Fear is conscious and fear is subconscious.

Sadly, when our sales and marketing results are at their absolute worst and our fear is at its highest that is exactly the time when we have the greatest need for bold, brave courage.

To make a difference in the world, you must get up, get out, read, listen, learn, and take action. And that takes courage. The following quote from Winston Churchill puts courage in perspective: "Courage is rightly esteemed the first of human qualities, because... it is the quality which guarantees all others."

PRACTICAL IDEAS

C. Make the Unknown Known

Fear of the unknown is one of the primary sources of fear. What we don't see or don't know scares us. Reducing this fear is as simple as opening ourselves to learning. Reading this book has taught you about the root causes of sales and marketing failure. Beyond this book you can learn more by talking to others, by analyzing data trends, and through first-person experiences with customers.

D. Fail Fast and Fail Cheap

We can reduce our fear by first, prototyping and then, testing our thinking in small-scale, low-cost environments. Test a new sales pitch with your next ten sales calls, in person, via the phone, at trade shows, or through your next direct mail campaign. Continuously seek opportunities to test, try, and learn.

E. Do the Right Thing

There is no more powerful way to find courage than when you focus your energies on making a Meaningful difference for your customers. When we serve others—meaningfully—we find the sort of authentic and genuine courage that helps us confront and defeat our biggest fears.

F. Take Responsibility for Your Life

Benjamin Franklin said many things. There is, however, one Franklin quote that precisely captures the essence of Meaningful Marketing and a Meaningful life. Live it and you will live your life to the potential for which it was intended:

> *Up, Sluggard, and waste not life;*
> *in the grave will be sleeping enough.*

Technical Appendix

We admit it. We are both data geeks. We love data and data discussions. However, our editor tells us that in the world of business, we are a minority group. He's given us this little section in the back to communicate further details on our research and data sources.

Overview of Data Philosophy
The articles referenced are a combination of laboratory experiments, marketplace experiments, and secondary data analyses of real-world results. We prefer studies that are conducted in real-world situations. However, in some cases, the noise and chaos of everyday life make laboratory studies the preferred research methodology.

Proprietary Data Sets
DARWIN 900 The Darwin 900 is a study by the Merwyn Technology division of the Eureka! Ranch. It involved tracking the survival rate of 901 products from their initial introduction over a period of five years.

In the development of this data set, we removed products that were seasonal, short-term promotions or were potentially undercapitalized efforts by small or start-up companies. Thus by their nature, products in the Darwin 900 were branded products from major consumer products companies. The products in this data set comprised a cross section of the grocery category and included food and beverages, health and beauty aids, and cleaning products. While greater differences were seen in our previous work with data that was corrected for distribution and awareness (see Truth 5 et al., Kahle, Hall, and Kosinski, 1997), significant differences could were observed even in the uncorrected, raw data.

One of our greatest challenges in working with this data was agreeing to a reliable definition of success versus failure. In other studies, we found that success was typically a self-reported response by the manufacturers (see Truth 42, Cooper and Kleinschmidt, 1993). However, as the old corollary warns, one company's definition of success is another's definition of failure, so we desired a more real-world definition.

After considering many options, we settled on a Darwinian survival definition. We defined success as "still being in production and distribution after five years." We can't say for sure that all products still on the shelf are successful for their manufacturers. However, it is a reasonable assumption that discontinued products were unsuccessful.

To determine if the products were alive or dead, we visited major chain grocery stores. If the products were not found, we then checked the brand or corporate Web site, or in cases where additional uncertainty existed we called the corporation directly for resolution.

The general analysis method utilized for the Darwin 900 was to score the products on a secondary variable and then use t-tests to quantify significant differences between products that were still alive (on the shelf) versus those that were dead (discontinued). Having determined statistical significance, we conducted a secondary sorting to provide the simplified description of results for this book. The process involved sorting the concepts into tertiles based on the secondary variable. Then the percentage surviving was calculated within each of the three groups, and the results from the top versus bottom tertile group were indexed. Thus, if 45 percent of the products in the top tertile survived and 30 percent in the bottom tertile survived, we reported that you had a 50 percent greater chance of success by following the researched approach.

The primary source of the secondary data was ratings of marketing materials content by multiple raters on more than two hundred archetype attributes related to Meaningful or Mindless dimensions (for example, the number of benefits promised). The raters were validated for standardized accuracy and reliability.

Another source of secondary data was consumer research results. This data had been gathered among a nationally representative set of consumers within the first few weeks of introduction. Consumers rated the products in concept form from either the original marketing materials, package copy, point-of-sales copy, or print advertising, on such variables as purchase interest, product uniqueness, and price sensitivity. This data was utilized to calculate the impact of Meaningful versus Mindless marketing. Specifically, the difference was empirically derived as the combination of purchase interest and uniqueness perception scores from consumer ratings. We then looked at the significance of various levels of each archetype trait that comprised the top and bottom 10 percent of the Meaningful difference distribution. Concepts in the top 10 percent were defined as Meaningful, the bottom 10 percent as Mindless. In the case of the Mindless concepts the primary customer selling points were the classic Mindless approaches of "foot in the door" (low initial price) and "consistency and authority" (leveraging a major brand name).

Note to researchers: The Darwin 900 data set contains proprietary client data that is covered under confidentiality agreements. We are legally restricted from sharing it publicly. However, we are committed to continuing research and are interested in partnering on further academic studies as resources allow. Please E-mail DougHall@DougHall.com with your proposal or area of interest in joint research.

SCANNER 9000 The Scanner 9000 is a study by the Merwyn Technology division of the Eureka! Ranch. This data set utilizes information from the 1999 marketing fact book, *Consumer Knowledge Suite*, produced by IRI (Information Resources, Inc., Chicago, IL). It contains annual purchasing data from some fifty thousand households that are provided with an in-home UPC scanner. The analysis conducted here utilized 9,804 carefully screened products. The data was analyzed by subcategories, categories, and brand basis, then evaluated by multiple regression to compare the relative importance of standardized regression coefficients for various marketplace variables of interest.

Overview and Part I References

Abraham, M. M., and L. M. Lodish. "Getting the Most out of Advertising and Promotion." Harvard Business Review, 30:3 (May–June 1990), pp. 50–60.

Ailawadi, K. L., D. R. Lehmann, and S. A. Neslin. "Market Response to a Major Policy Change in the Marketing Mix: Learning from Procter & Gamble's Value Pricing Strategy." Journal of Marketing, 65:1 (January 2001), pp. 44–61.

Albion, Mark. Making a Life, Making a Living (New York: Warner Books, 2000), p.17.

Anderson, R. E. "Personal Selling and Sales Management in the New Millennium." Journal of Personal Selling and Sales Management, 16:4 (Fall 1996), pp.17–32.

Bettman, J. R., M. F. Luce, and J. W. Payne. "Constructive Consumer Choice Processes." Journal of Consumer Research, 25:3 (December 1998), pp. 187–217.

Bettman, J. R., and C. W. Park. "Effects of Prior Knowledge and Experience and Phase of the Choice Process on Consumer Decision Processes: A Protocol Analysis." Journal of Consumer Research, 7 (December 1980), pp. 234–248.

Goodman, Nathan G., ed. A Benjamin Franklin Reader (New York, Thomas Y. Crowell Company, 1971) pp. 118–131.

Hoyer, W. D. "An Examination of Consumer Decision Making for a Common Repeat Purchase Product." Journal of Consumer Research, 11 (December 1984), pp. 822–829.

Lasn, K. "Ad Spending Predicted for Steady Decline." Adbusters, 45 (January/February 2003), www.adbusters.org/magazine/45/articles/ad_spending_predicted_for.html.

Lodish, L. M., and M. M. Abraham. "How T.V. Advertising Works: A Meta-Analysis of 389 Real World Split Cable T.V. Advertising Experiments." Journal of Marketing Research, 32:2 (May 1995), pp. 125–139.

Lodish, L. M., M. M. Abraham, J. Livelsberger, et al. "A Summary of Fifty-Five In-Market Experimental Estimates of the Long-Term Effect of TV Advertising." Marketing Science, 14:3, Part 2 of 2 (1995), pp. G133–G140.

Maidique, M. A., and B. J. Zirger. "A Study of Success and Failure in Product Innovation: The Case of the U.S. Electronics Industry." IEEE Transactions on Engineering Management, EM31:3 4 (November1984), pp. 192–203.

Marton, B. A. "Mastering the Art of Persuasion." Harvard Management Communication Letter, 3:7 (July 2000), pp.4–6.

Mela, C. F., and S. Gupta. "The Long-Term Impact of Promotion and Advertising on Consumer Brand Choice." Journal of Marketing Research, 34:2 (May 1997), pp. 248–261.

Petty, R. E., and J. T. Cacioppo. "Central and Peripheral Routes to Persuasion: Application to Advertising." Eds. L. Percy and A. G. Woodside. Advertising and Consumer Psychology (Lexington, Mass.: Lexington Books, 1983), pp. 3–23.

Data Source: Digital Scriptorium. "Emergence of Advertising in America: 1850–1920." http://scriptorium.lib.duke.edu/eaa/.

Data Source: Eureka! Ranch. Based on marketplace analysis of 900 new product launches: Merwyn Technology Internal Data Set: Darwin 900 Study (Eureka! Ranch, 2001).

Data Source: Information Resources, Inc. InFocus Report: New Product Trends 2002 Study (Chicago, 2002), pp. 6–7.

Data Source: Sahr, R. "Inflation Conversion Factors for Dollars 1665 to Estimated 2013." http://oregonstate.edu/dept/pol_sci/fac/sahr/sahr.htm.

TRUTH 0

Wood, S. L., and J. G. Lynch, Jr. "Prior Knowledge and Complacency in New Product Learning." Journal of Consumer Research, 29:3 (December 2002), pp. 416–426.

TRUTH 1

Kalyanaram, G., W. T. Robinson, and G. L. Urban. "Order of Market Entry: Established Empirical Generalizations, Emerging Empirical Generalizations, and Future Research." Marketing Science, 14:3, Part 2 of 2 (1995), pp. G212–G2212.

Robinson,W. T. "Sources of Market Pioneer Advantages: The Case of Industrial Goods Industries." Journal of Marketing Research, 25:1 (February 1988), pp. 87–94.

Robinson, W. T., and C. Fornell. "Sources of Market Pioneer Advantages in Consumer Goods Industries." Journal of Marketing Research, 22:3 (August 1985), pp. 305–317.

Urban, G. L., T. Carter, S. Gaskin, and Z. Mucha. "Market Share Rewards to Pioneering Brands: An Empirical Analysis and Strategic Implications." Management Science, 32:6 (June 1986), pp. 645–659.

Data Source: Information Resources, Inc. Client Study: How Advertising Works for New Products, (Chicago, 2001).

TRUTH 2

Lau, G. T., and S. H. Lee. "Consumer's Trust in a Brand and the Link to Brand Loyalty." Journal of Market-Focused Management, 4 (1999), pp. 341–370.

Data Source: Eureka! Ranch. Based on marketplace analysis of 900 new product launches: Merwyn Technology Internal Data Set: Darwin 900 Study (Eureka! Ranch, 2001).

TRUTH 3

Lau, G. T., and S. H. Lee. "Consumer's Trust in a Brand and the Link to Brand Loyalty." Journal of Market-Focused Management, 4 (1999) pp. 341–370.

Trout, J. "Differentiate or Die." Ad Age, November 22, 1999.

TRUTH 4

Anschuetz, N. "Why a Brand's Most Valuable Consumer Is the Next One It Adds." Journal of Advertising Research, 42:1 (January–February 2002), pp. 15–22.

Lau, G. T., and S. H. Lee. "Consumers Trust in a Brand and the Link to Brand Loyalty." Journal of Market-Focused Management, 4 (1999), pp. 341–370.

Data Source: Eureka! Ranch. Based on marketplace scanner data analysis of 9804 established brands: Merwyn Technology Internal Data Set: Scanner 9000 Study (Eureka! Ranch, 2001).

TRUTH 5

Ailawadi, K. L., and S. A. Neslin. "The Effect of Promotion on Consumption: Buying More and Consuming It Faster." Journal of Marketing Research, 35:3 (August 1998), pp. 390–398.

Kahle, L. R., D. B. Hall, and M. J. Kosinski. "The Real-Time Response Survey in New Product Research: It's About Time." Journal of Consumer Marketing, 14:3 (1997), pp. 234–248.

Mela, C. F., K. Jedidi, et al. "The Long-Term Impact of Promotions on Consumer Stockpiling Behavior." Journal of Marketing Research, 35:2 (May 1998), pp. 250–262.

Data Source: Eureka! Ranch. Based on marketplace scanner data analysis of 9804 established brands: Merwyn Technology Internal Data Set: Scanner 9000 Study (Eureka! Ranch, 2001).

TRUTH 6

Data Source: Eureka! Ranch. Based on marketplace analysis of 900 new product launches: Merwyn Technology Internal Data Set: Darwin 900 Study (Eureka! Ranch, 2001).

TRUTH 7

Vorhies, D. W., and M. Harker. "The Capabilities and Performance Advantages of Market-Driven Firms: An Empirical Investigation." Australian Journal of Management, 25:2 (September 2000), pp. 145–171.

Vorhies, D. W., M. Harker, and C. P. Rao. "The Capabilities and Performance Advantages of Market-Driven Firms." European Journal of Marketing, 33:11/12 (1999), pp. 1171–1202.

Data Source: Eureka! Ranch. Based on marketplace analysis of 900 new product launches: Merwyn Technology Internal Data Set: Darwin 900 Study (Eureka! Ranch, 2001).

TRUTH 8

Cox, D., and A. D. Cox. "Beyond First Impressions: The Effects of Repeated Exposure on Consumer Liking of Visually Complex and Simple Product Designs." Journal of the Academy of Marketing Science, 30:2 (2002), pp. 119–130.

TRUTH 9

Arndt, J. "A Test of the Two-Step Flow in Diffusion of a New Product." Eds. H. H. Kassarjian and T. S. Robertson. Perspectives in Consumer Behavior (Glenview, Ill.: Scott, Foresman & Co., 1973), pp. 331–342.

Daghfous, N., J. V. Petrof, and F. Pons. "Values and Adoption of Innovations: A Cross-Cultural Study." Journal of Consumer Marketing, 16:4 (1999), pp. 314–331.

Dwyer, S., J. Hill, and W. Martin. "An Empirical Investigation of Critical Success Factors in the Personal Selling Process for Homogenous Goods." Journal of Personal Selling and Sales Management, 20:3 (Summer 2000), pp. 151–159.

Keller, E., and J. Berry. The Influentials (New York: The Free Press, 2003), cover.

TRUTH 10
Cialdini, R. B. Influence: Science and Practice (Boston: Allyn and Bacon, 2001), pp. 147–148.

Dwyer, S., J. Hill, and W. Martin. "An Empirical Investigation of Critical Success Factors in the Personal Selling Process for Homogenous Goods." Journal of Personal Selling and Sales Management, 20:3 (Summer 2000), pp.151–159.

Data Source: Eureka! Ranch. Based on marketplace analysis of 900 new product launches: Merwyn Technology Internal Data Set: Darwin 900 Study (Eureka! Ranch, 2001).

TRUTH 11
McLaughlin, K., and C. Halsall. "Marketing Spending Effectiveness: How to Win in a Complex Environment." McKinsey Marketing Practice Working Paper (June 2000).

Data Source: Eureka! Ranch. Based on marketplace analysis of 900 new product launches: Merwyn Technology Internal Data Set: Darwin 900 Study (Eureka! Ranch, 2001).

TRUTH 12
Sharma, A., and R. Pillai. "Customers' Decision-Making Styles and Their Preference for Sales Strategies: Conceptual Examination and an Empirical Study." Journal of Personal Selling and Sales Management, 16:1 (Winter 1996), pp. 21–33.

Thomas, R. W., G. N. Soutar, and M. M. Ryan. "The Selling Orientation–Customer Orientation (S.O.C.O.) Scale: A Proposed Short Form." Journal of Personal Selling and Sales Management, 21:1 (Winter 2001), pp. 63–69.

Data Source: Eureka! Ranch. Based on marketplace analysis of 900 new product launches: Merwyn Technology Internal Data Set: Darwin 900 Study (Eureka! Ranch, 2001).

TRUTH 13
Hall, D. Jump Start Your Business Brain (Cincinnati: Brain Brew Books, 2001).

Herrmann, N. The Whole Brain Business Book (New York: McGraw-Hill, 1996).

Leonard, D., and S. Straus. "Putting Your Company's Whole Brain to Work." Harvard Business Review, 75:4 (July/August 1997), pp. 110–121.

TRUTH 14
Hall, D. Jump Start Your Business Brain (Cincinnati: Brain Brew Books, 2001).

Herrmann, N. The Whole Brain Business Book (New York: McGraw-Hill, 1996).

Leonard, D., and S. Straus. "Putting Your Company's Whole Brain to Work." Harvard Business Review, 75:4 (July/August 1997), pp. 110–121.

TRUTH 15
Hall, D. Jump Start Your Business Brain (Cincinnati: Brain Brew Books, 2001).
Herrmann, N. The Whole Brain Business Book (New York: McGraw-Hill, 1996).

Leonard, D., and S. Straus. "Putting Your Company's Whole Brain to Work." Harvard Business Review, 75:4 (July/August 1997), pp. 110–121.

TRUTH 16
Liu, A. H., and M. P. Leach. "Developing Loyal Customers With a Value-Adding Sales Force: Examining Customer Satisfaction and the Perceived Credibility of Consultative Salespeople." Journal of Personal Selling and Sales Management, 21:2 (Spring 2001), pp. 147–156.

Robinson, W. T. "Sources of Market Pioneer Advantages: The Case of Industrial Goods Industries." Journal of Marketing Research, 25:1 (February 1988), pp. 87–94.

TRUTH 17
Anderson, R. E. "Personal Selling and Sales Management in the New Millennium." Journal of Personal Selling and Sales Management, 16:4 (Fall 1996), pp. 17–32.

Liu, A. H., and M. P. Leach. "Developing Loyal Customers With a Value-Adding Sales Force: Examining Customer Satisfaction and the Perceived Credibility of Consultative Salespeople." Journal of Personal Selling and Sales Management, 21:2 (Spring 2001), pp. 147–156.

McLaughlin, K., and C. Halsall. "Marketing Spending Effectiveness: How to Win in a Complex Environment." McKinsey Marketing Practice Working Paper (June 2000).

Data Source: Eureka! Ranch. Based on marketplace analysis of 900 new product launches: Merwyn Technology Internal Data Set: Darwin 900 Study (Eureka! Ranch, 2001).

TRUTH 18
Kanouse, D. E. "Explaining Negativity Biases in Evaluation and Choice Behavior: Theory and Research." Advances in Consumer Research, 11 (1984), pp. 703–708.

Data Source: Eureka! Ranch. Based on marketplace analysis of 900 new product launches: Merwyn Technology Internal Data Set: Darwin 900 Study (Eureka! Ranch, 2001).

TRUTH 19
Gartner, W. B., and R. J. Thomas. "Factors Affecting New Product Forecasting Accuracy in New Firms." Journal of Product Innovation Management, 10:1 (January 1993), pp. 35–52.

TRUTH 20

Sullivan, M. "Brand Extension and Order of Entry." Report No. 91-105 (Boston: Marketing Science Institute, 1991).

Data Source: Eureka! Ranch. Based on comparison of Merwyn marketplace predictive models for established brands versus new brands: Merwyn Technology Internal Data Set: Merwyn Comparison Study (Eureka! Ranch, 2001).

TRUTH 21

Boyd, T. C., and C. H. Mason. "The Link Between Attractiveness of 'Extrabrand' Attributes and the Adoption of Innovations." Journal of the Academy of Marketing Science, 27:3 (July 1999), pp. 306–319.

Golder, P. N., and G. J. Tellis. "Will It Ever Fly? Modeling the Takeoff of Really New Consumer Durables." Marketing Science, 16:3 (1997), pp. 256–270.

TRUTH 22

Kahle, L. R., D. B. Hall, and M. J. Kosinski. "The Real-Time Response Survey in New Product Research: It's About Time." Journal of Consumer Marketing, 14:3 (1997), pp. 234–248.

Reinartz, W. J., and V. Kumar. "On the Profitability of Long-Life Customers in a Noncontractual Setting: An Empirical Investigation and Implications for Marketing." Journal of Marketing, 64:4 (October 2000), pp. 17–35.

Data Source: Eureka! Ranch. Based on marketplace scanner data analysis of 9804 established brands: Merwyn Technology Internal Data Set: Scanner 9000 Study (Eureka! Ranch, 2001).

TRUTH 23

Church, A. H. "Estimating the Effect of Incentives on Mail Survey Response Rates." Public Opinion Quarterly, 57 (1993), pp. 62–79.

James, J. M., and R. Bolstein. "Large Monetary Incentives and Their Effect on Mail Survey Response Rates." Public Opinion Quarterly, 56 (1992), pp. 442–453.

Marks, L. J., and M. A. Kamins. "The Use of Product Sampling and Advertising: Effects of Sequence of Exposure and Degree of Advertising Claim Exaggeration on Consumers' Belief Strength, Belief Confidence, and Attitudes." Journal of Marketing Research, 25:3 (August 1988), pp. 266–281.

TRUTH 24

Anderson, R. E. "Consumer Dissatisfaction: The Effect of Disconfirmed Expectancy on Perceived Product Performance." Journal of Marketing Research, 10:1 (February 1973), pp. 38–44.

TRUTH 25

Gouillart, F. J., and F. D. Sturdivant. "Spend a Day in the Life of Your Customers." Harvard Business Review, 72:1 (January/February 1994), pp. 116–125.

Hite, R. E., and J. A. Bellizzi. "Differences in the Importance
of Selling Techniques Between Consumer and Industrial Salespeople." Journal of Personal Selling and Sales Management, 5:2 (November 1985), pp. 19–30.

TRUTH 26

Hite, R. E., and J. A. Bellizzi. "Differences in the Importance of Selling Techniques Between Consumer and Industrial Salespeople." Journal of Personal Selling and Sales Management, 5:2 (November 1985), pp. 19–30.

TRUTH 27

Schoormans, J.P.L., R. J. Ortt, and C.J.P.M. de Bont. "Enhancing Concept Test Validity by Using Expert Consumers." Journal of Product Innovation Management, 12:2 (March 1995), pp.153–162.

Singh, M., S. K. Balasubramanian, and G. Chakraborty. "A Comparative Analysis of Three Communication Formats: Advertising, Infomercial, and Direct Experience." Journal of Advertising, 29:4 (Winter 2000), pp. 59–75.

TRUTH 28

Burn, S. W. "Social Psychology and the Stimulation of Recycling Behaviors: The Block Leader Approach." Journal of Applied Social Psychology, 21 (1991), pp.611–629.

Yu, J., and H. Cooper. "A Quantitative Review of Research Design Effects on Response Rates to Questionnaires." Journal of Marketing Research, 20:1 (February 1983), pp. 36–44.

TRUTH 29

Greenleaf, E. A., and D. R. Lehmann. "Reasons for Substantial Delay in Consumer Decision Making." Journal of Consumer Research, 22:2 (September 1995), pp.186–199.

TRUTH 30

Boatwright, P., and J. C. Nunes. "Reducing Assortment: An Attribute-Based Approach." Journal of Marketing, 65:3 (July 2001), pp. 50–63.

Iyengar, S. S., and M. R. Lepper. "When Choice Is Demotivating: Can One Desire Too Much of a Good Thing?" Journal of Personality and Social Psychology, 79:6 (December 2000), pp. 995–1006.

TRUTH 31

Gupta, S. "Impact of Sales Promotions on When, What, and How Much to Buy." Journal of Marketing Research, 25:4 (November 1988), pp. 342–355.

Kotler, P. "Mathematical Models of Individual Buyer Behavior." Eds. H. H. Kassarjian and T. S. Robertson. Perspectives in Consumer Behavior (Glenview, Ill.: Scott, Foresman & Co., 1973) pp. 541–560.

TRUTH 32

Charlett, D., R. Garland, and N. Marr. "How Damaging Is Negative Word of Mouth?" Marketing Bulletin, 6 (May 1995), pp. 42–50.

Maxham III, J. G., and R. G. Netemeyer. "A Longitudinal Study of Complaining Customers' Evaluations of Multiple Service Failures and Recovery Efforts." Journal of Marketing, 66:4 (October 2002), pp. 57–71.

TRUTH 33

Wansink, B. "Advertising's Impact on Category Substitution." Journal of Marketing Research, 31:4 (November 1994), pp. 505–515.

TRUTH 34

Carpenter, G. S., and K. Nakamoto. "Consumer Preference Formation and Pioneering Advantage." Journal of Marketing Research, 26:3 (August 1989), pp. 285–298.

Kuester, S., C. Homburg, and T. S. Robertson. "Retaliatory Behavior to New Product Entry." Journal of Marketing, 63:4 (October 1999), pp. 90–106.

TRUTH 35

Cox, D., and A. D. Cox. "Communicating the Consequences of Early Detection: The Role of Evidence and Framing." Journal of Marketing, 65:3 (July 2001), pp. 91–103.

Keller, P. A., and L. G. Block. "Increasing the Persuasiveness of Fear Appeals: The Effect of Arousal and Elaboration." Journal of Consumer Research, 22 (March 1996), pp. 448–459.

Meyerowitz, B. E., and S. Chaiken. "The Effect of Message Framing on Breast Self-Examination Attitudes, Intentions, and Behavior." Journal of Personality and Social Psychology, 52:3 (1987), pp. 500–510.

TRUTH 36

Keller, K. L., S. E. Heckler, et al. "The Effects of Brand Name Suggestiveness on Advertising Recall." Journal of Marketing, 62:1 (January 1998), pp. 42–51.

Data Source: Eureka! Ranch. Based on marketplace analysis of 900 new product launches: Merwyn Technology Internal Data Set: Darwin 900 Study (Eureka! Ranch, 2001).

TRUTH 37

Babakus, E., D. W. Cravens, M. Johnston, and W. C. Moncrief. "The Role of Emotional Exhaustion in Sales Force Attitude and Behavior Relationships." Journal of the Academy of Marketing Science, 27:1 (January 1999), pp.58–70.

TRUTH 38
Shimp, T. A., and W. O. Bearden. "Warranty and Other Extrinsic Cue Effects on Consumers' Risk Perceptions." Journal of Consumer Research, 9 (June 1982), pp. 38–46.

TRUTH 39
Adaval, R., and K. B. Monroe. "Automatic Construction and Use of Contextual Information for Product and Price Evaluations." Journal of Consumer Research, 28:4 (March 2002), pp. 572–588.

Simonson, I., S. Nowlis, and K. Lemon. "The Effect of Local Consideration Sets on Global Choice Between Lower Price and Higher Quality." Marketing Science, 12:4 (Fall 1993), pp. 357–376.

TRUTH 40
Bushman, B. J., and A. M. Bonacci. "Violence and Sex Impair Memory for Television Ads." Journal of Applied Psychology, 87:3 (June 2002), pp. 557–564.

Meyers-Levy, J., and L. A. Peracchio. "Understanding the Effects of Color: How the Correspondence Between Available and Required Resources Affects Attitudes." Journal of Consumer Research, 22 (September 1995), pp. 121–138.

Stieg, B. "Facts of Life." Men's Health (March 2003), pp. 52.

TRUTH 41
Anderson, R. E. "Personal Selling and Sales Management in the New Millennium." Journal of Personal Selling and Sales Management, 16:4 (Fall 1996), pp. 17–32.

Brock, T. C., and S. Shavitt. "Cognitive-Response Analysis in Advertising." Eds. L. Percy and A. G. Woodside. Advertising and Consumer Psychology (Lexington, Mass.: Lexington Books, 1983), pp. 91-116.

Dwyer, S., J. Hill, and W. Martin. "An Empirical Investigation of Critical Success Factors in the Personal Selling Process for Homogenous Goods." Journal of Personal Selling and Sales Management, 20:3 (Summer 2000), pp. 151–159.

Kahle, L. R., D. B. Hall, and M. J. Kosinski. "The Real-Time Response Survey in New Product Research: It's About Time." Journal of Consumer Marketing, 14:3 (1997), pp. 234–248.
Krugman, H. E. "Why Three Exposures May Be Enough." Journal of Advertising Research, 12:6 (December 1972), pp.11–14.

Pechmann, C., and D. W. Stewart. "Advertising Repetition: A Critical Review of Wearin and Wearout." Current Issues and Research in Advertising, 12 (1988), pp. 285–330.

Vakratsas, D., and T. Ambler. "How Advertising Works: What Do We Really Know?" Journal of Marketing, 63:1 (January 1999), pp. 26–43.

TRUTH 42

Cooper, R. G., and E. J. Kleinschmidt. "Major New Products: What Distinguishes the Winners in the Chemical Industry?" Journal of Product Innovation Management, 10:2 (March 1993), pp. 90–111.

TRUTH 43

Morris, M. H., R. W. LaForge, and J. A. Allen. "Salesperson Failure: Definition, Determinants, and Outcomes." Journal of Personal Selling and Sales Management, 14:1 (Winter 1994), pp. 1–15.

TRUTH 44

Lambert, D. M., H. Marmorstein, and A. Sharma. "The Accuracy of Salespersons' Perceptions of Their Customers: Conceptual Examination and an Empirical Study." Journal of Personal Selling and Sales Management, 10:1 (Winter 1990), pp. 1–9.

Strub, P., and S. Herman. "Can the Sales Force Speak for the Customer?" Marketing Research, 5:4 (Fall 1993), pp. 32–35.

TRUTH 45

Dowling, G. R., and M. Uncles. "Do Customer Loyalty Programs Really Work?" Sloan Management Review, 38:4 (Summer 1997), pp. 71–82.

Estell, L. "Loyalty Lessons." Incentive, 176:11 (Nov 2002), pp. 38–41.

Kearney, T. J. "Frequent Flyer Programs: A Failure in Competitive Strategy, With Lessons for Management." Journal of ConsumerMarketing, 7:1 (Winter 1990), pp. 31–40.

Timson, J. "Fliers, Airlines Love Their Point Programs." The Toronto Globe and Mail (February 1, 2003).

TRUTH 46

Wotruba, T. R. "The Effect of Goal-Setting on the Performance of Independent Sales Agents in Direct Selling." Journal of Personal Selling and Sales Management, 9:1 (Spring 1989), pp. 22–29.

TRUTH 47

Brown, S. P., W. L. Cron, and J. W. Slocum, Jr. "Effects of Trait Competitiveness and Perceived Intraorganizational Competition on Salesperson Goal Setting and Performance." Journal of Marketing, 62:4 (October 1998), pp. 88–98.

TRUTH 48

Williams, G. A., and R. B. Miller. "Change the Way You Persuade." Harvard Business Review, 80:5 (May 2002), pp. 65–73.

TRUTH 49
Sharma, A., and R. Pillai. "Customers' Decision-Making Styles and Their Preference for Sales Strategies: Conceptual Examination and an Empirical Study." Journal of Personal Selling and Sales Management, 16:1 (Winter 1996), pp. 21–33.

TRUTH 50
Plank, R. E., D. A. Reid, and. E. B. Pullins. "Methods in Sales Research: Perceived Trust in Business-to-Business Sales: A New Measure." Journal of Personal Selling and Sales Management, 19:3 (Summer 1999), pp. 61–71.

Swan, J. E., and J. J. Nolan. "Gaining Customer Trust: A Conceptual Guide for the Sales-person." Journal of Personal Selling and Sales Management, 5:2 (November 1985), pp. 39–48.

TRUTH 51
Lau, G. T., and S. H. Lee. "Consumers 'Trust in a Brand and the Link to Brand Loyalty." Journal of Market-Focused Management, 4 (1999), pp. 341–370.

TRUTH 52
Doyle, S. X., and G. T. Roth. "Selling and Sales Management in Action: The Use of Insight Coaching to Improve Relationship Selling." Journal of Personal Selling and Sales Management, 12:1 (Winter 1992), pp. 59–64.

Locke, K. D., and L. M. Horowitz. "Satisfaction in Interpersonal Interactions as a Function of Similarity in Level of Dysphoria." Journal of Personality and Social Psychology, 58:5 (May 1990), pp. 823–831.

Swan, J. E., and J. J. Nolan. "Gaining Customer Trust: A Conceptual Guide for the Sales-person." Journal of Personal Selling and Sales Management, 5:2 (November 1985), pp. 39–48.

Swan, J. E., I. F. Trawick Jr., D. R. Rink, and J. J. Roberts. "Measuring Dimensions of Purchaser Trust of Industrial Salespeople." Journal of Personal Selling and Sales Management, 8:1 (May 1988), pp. 1–9.

TRUTH 53
Vorhies, D. W., M. Harker, and C. P. Rao. "The Capabilities and Performance Advantages of Market-Driven Firms." European Journal of Marketing, 33:11/12 (1999), pp. 1171–1202.

TRUTH 54
Vorhies, D. W., M. Harker, and C. P. Rao. "The Capabilities and Performance Advantages of Market-Driven Firms." European Journal of Marketing, 33:11/12 (1999), pp. 1171–1202.

TRUTH 55
Vorhies, D. W., M. Harker, and C. P. Rao. "The Capabilities and Performance Advantages of Market-Driven Firms." European Journal of Marketing, 33:11/12 (1999), pp.1171–1202.

TRUTH 56
Vorhies, D. W., M. Harker, and C. P. Rao. "The Capabilities and Performance Advantages of Market-Driven Firms." European Journal of Marketing, 33:11/12 (1999), pp. 1171–1202.

TRUTH 57
Vorhies, D. W., M. Harker, and C. P. Rao. "The Capabilities and Performance Advantages of Market-Driven Firms." European Journal of Marketing, 33:11/12 (1999), pp. 1171–1202.

TRUTH 58
"Do You Talk Too Much?" The American Salesman, 47:12 (December 2002), pp. 26–27.

Hite, R. E., and J. A. Bellizzi. "Differences in the Importance of Selling Techniques Between Consumer and Industrial Salespeople." Journal of Personal Selling and Sales Management, 5:2 (November 1985), pp. 19–30.

Vorhies, D. W., M. Harker, and C. P. Rao. "The Capabilities and Performance Advantages of Market-Driven Firms." European Journal of Marketing, 33:11/12 (1999), pp. 1171–1202.

TRUTH 59
Cross, J., S. W. Hartley, and W. Rudelius. "Sales Force Activities and Marketing Strategies in Industrial Firms: Relationships and Implications." Journal of Personal Selling and Sales Management, 21:3 (Summer 2001), pp. 199–206.

Vorhies, D. W., M. Harker, and C. P. Rao. "The Capabilities and Performance Advantages of Market-Driven Firms." European Journal of Marketing, 33:11/12 (1999), pp. 1171–1202.

TRUTH 60
Russ, F. A., K. M. McNeilly, et al. "Exploring the Impact of Critical Sales Events." Journal of Personal Selling and Sales Management, 18:2 (Spring 1998), pp. 19–34.

TRUTH 61
Baker, J., A. Parasuraman, D. Grewal, and G. B. Voss. "The Influence of Multiple Store Environment Cues on Perceived Merchandise Value and Patronage Intentions." Journal of Marketing, 66:2 (April 2002), pp. 120–141.

Dwyer, S., J. Hill, and W. Martin. "An Empirical Investigation of Critical Success Factors in the Personal Selling Process for Homogenous Goods." Journal of Personal Selling and Sales Management, 20:3 (Summer 2000), pp.151–159.

Keinan, G. "Decision Making Under Stress: Scanning of Alternatives Under Controllable and Uncontrollable Threats." Journal of Personality and Social Psychology, 52:3 (1987), pp. 639–644.

TRUTH 62

Jap, S. D. "The Strategic Role of the Salesforce in Developing Customer Satisfaction Across the Relationship Lifecycle." Journal of Personal Selling and Sales Management, 21:2 (Spring 2001), pp. 95 108.

TRUTH 63

Keller, S. B., M. Landry, J. Olson, et al. "The Effects of Nutrition Package Claims, Nutrition Facts Panels, and Motivation to Process Nutrition Information on Consumer Product Evaluations." Journal of Public Policy and Marketing, 16:2 (Fall 1997), pp. 256–269.

Scammon, D. L. "Information Overload and Consumers." Journal of Consumer Research, 4:3 (1977), pp. 148–155.

TRUTH 64

Enriquez, Juan,. As The Future Catches You. (New York: Crown Business, 2001).

Rust, R. T., C. Moorman, and P. R. Dickson. "Getting Return on Quality: Revenue Expansion, Cost Reduction, or Both?" Journal of Marketing, 66:4 (Oct 2002), pp. 7–24.

TRUTH 65

Hellofs, L. L., and R. Jacobson. "Market Share and Customers' Perceptions of Quality: When Can Firms Grow Their Way to Higher Versus Lower Quality?" Journal of Marketing, 63:1 (January 1999), pp. 16–25.

TRUTH 66

Alba, J. W., and J. W. Hutchinson. "Knowledge Calibration: What Consumers Know and What They Think They Know." Journal of Consumer Research, 27:2 (September 2000), pp. 123–156.

Wood, S. L., and J. G. Lynch, Jr. "Prior Knowledge and Complacency in New Product Learning." Journal of Consumer Research, 29:3 (December 2002), pp. 416–426.

TRUTH 67

Bedell, G. "Persuading People to Buy Your Product." Incentive, 175:2 (February 2001), pp. 70–71.

Meyvis, T., and C. Janiszewski. "Consumers' Beliefs About Product Benefits: The Effect of Obviously Irrelevant Product Information." Journal of Consumer Research, 28:4 (March 2002), pp. 618–635.

TRUTH 68
Roselius, T. "Consumer Rankings of Risk Reduction Methods." Eds. H. H. Kassarjian and T. S. Robertson. Perspectives in Consumer Behavior (Glenview, Ill.: Scott, Foresman & Co., 1973), pp. 55–6564.

TRUTH 69
Clancy, K. J., and R. S. Shulman. Marketing Myths That Are Killing Business: The Cure for Death Wish Marketing (New York: McGraw-Hill, 1994), pp. 275–278.

TRUTH 70
Hall, D. Jump Start Your Business Brain (Cincinnati: Brain Brew Books, 2001).

Kahle, L. R., D. B. Hall, and M. J. Kosinski. "The Real-Time Response Survey in New Product Research: It's About Time." Journal of Consumer Marketing, 14:3 (1997), pp. 234–248.

TRUTH 71
Till, B. D., and M. Busler. "Matching Products with Endorsers: Attractiveness Versus Expertise." Journal of Consumer Marketing, 15:6 (1998), pp. 576–586.

TRUTH 72
Alpert, F. H., M. A. Kamins, and J. L. Graham. "An Examination of Reseller Buyer Attitudes Toward Order of Brand Entry." Journal of Marketing, 56:3 (July 1992), pp. 25–37.

TRUTH 73
Bodenhausen, G. V. "Stereotypes as Judgmental Heuristics: Evidence of Circadian Variations in Discrimination." Psychological Science, 1:5 (September 1990), pp. 319–322.

TRUTH 74
Bettman, J. R., M. F. Luce, and J. W. Payne. "Constructive Consumer Choice Processes." Journal of Consumer Research, 25:3 (December 1998), pp. 187–217.

Drolet, A. "Inherent Rule Variability in Consumer Choice: Changing Rules for Change's Sake." Journal of Consumer Research, 29:3 (December 2002), pp. 293–305.

TRUTH 75
Dwyer, S., J. Hill, and W. Martin. "An Empirical Investigation of Critical Success Factors in the Personal Selling Process for Homogenous Goods." Journal of Personal Selling and Sales Management, 20:3 (Summer 2000), pp. 151–159.

Edell, J. A., and R. Staelin. "The Information Processing of Pictures in Print Advertisements." Journal of Consumer Research, 10 (June 1983), pp. 45–61.

Percy, L., and J. R. Rossiter. "Mediating Effects of Visual and Verbal Elements in Print Advertising Upon Belief, Attitude, and Intention Responses." Eds. L. Percy and A. G. Woodside. Advertising and Consumer Psychology (Lexington, Mass.: Lexington Books, 1983), pp. 171–196.

TRUTH 76
Alwitt, L. F. "What Do People Mean When They Talk About Advertising?" Eds. L. Percy and A. G. Woodside. Advertising and Consumer Psychology (Lexington, Mass.: Lexington Books, 1983), pp. 273–286.

Weitz, B. A., and K. D. Bradford. "Personal Selling and Sales Management: A Relationship Marketing Perspective." Journal of the Academy of Marketing Science, 27:2 (April 1999), pp. 241–254.

TRUTH 77
Wilton, P. C., and D. K. Tse. "A Model of Consumer Response to Communication and Product Experiences." Eds. L. Percy and A. G. Woodside. Advertising and Consumer Psychology (Lexington, Mass.: Lexington Books, 1983), pp. 315–322.

TRUTH 78
Mukherjee, A., and W. D. Hoyer. "The Effect of Novel Attributes on Product Evaluation." Journal of Consumer Research, 28:3 (December 2001), pp. 462–472.

TRUTH 79
Settle, R. B., and L. L. Golden. "Attribution Theory and Advertiser Credibility." Journal of Marketing Research, 11:2 (May 1974), pp. 181–185.

Smith, R. E., and S. D. Hunt. "Attributional Processes in Promotional Situations." Journal of Consumer Research, 5 (December 1978), pp. 149–158.

TRUTH 80
Calder, B. "Cognitive Consistency and Consumer Behavior." Eds. H. H. Kassarjian and T. S. Robertson. Perspectives in Consumer Behavior (Glenview, Ill.: Scott, Foresman & Co., 1973), pp. 247–263.

Doob, A., J. M. Carlsmith, et al. "Effect of Initial Selling Price on Subsequent Sales." Journal of Personality and Social Psychology, 11:4 (1969), pp. 345–350.

TRUTH 81
Reingen, P. H. "On Inducing Compliance With Requests." Journal of Consumer Research, 5 (September 1978), pp. 96–102.

Reingen, P. H., and J. B. Kernan. "Compliance With an Interview Request: A Foot-in-the-Door, Self-Perception Interpretation." Journal of Marketing Research, 14:3 (August 1977), pp. 365–369.

TRUTH 82

Feltham, T. S. "Leaving Home: Brand Purchase Influences on Young Adults." Journal of Consumer Marketing, 15:4 (1998), pp. 372–385.

Howard, J. A., and J. N. Sheth. "A Theory of Buyer Behavior." Eds. H. H. Kassarjian and T. S. Robertson. Perspectives in Consumer Behavior, (Glenview, Ill.: Scott, Foresman & Co., 1973), pp. 519 540.

Knox, R. E., and J. A. Inkster. "Post Decision Dissonance at Post Time." Journal of Personality and Social Psychology, 8:4 (1968), pp. 319–323.

TRUTH 83

Aronson, E., and J. Mills. "The Effect of Severity of Initiation on Liking for a Group." Journal of Abnormal and Social Psychology, 59 (1959), pp. 177–181.

Cialdini, R. B. Influence: Science and Practice (Boston: Allyn and Bacon, 2001), pp. 75–80.

TRUTH 84

Cialdini, R. B., and K.V.L. Rhoads. "Human Behavior and the Marketplace." Marketing Research, 13:3 (Fall 2001), pp. 9–13.

Howard, D. J. "The Influence of Verbal Responses to Common Greetings on Compliance Behavior: The Foot-in-the-Mouth Effect." Journal of Applied Social Psychology, 20:14 (1990), pp. 1185–1196.

Sherman, S. J. "On the Self-Erasing Nature of Errors of Prediction." Journal of Personality and Social Psychology, 39 (1980), pp. 211–221.

TRUTH 85

Cialdini, R. B., J. E. Vincent, et al. "Reciprocal Concessions Procedure for Inducing Compliance: The Door-in-the-Face Technique." Journal of Personality and Social Psychology, 31:2 (1975), pp. 206–215.

Gruner, S. "Reward Good Customers." Inc. Magazine (November 1996), p. 84.

Mowen, J. C., and R. B. Cialdini. "On Implementing the Door-in the-Face Compliance Technique in a Business Context." Journal of Marketing Research, 17:2 (May 1980), pp. 253–258.

Reingen, P. H. "On Inducing Compliance With Requests." Journal of Consumer Research, 5 (September 1978), pp. 96–102.

TRUTH 86

Cialdini, R. B. Influence: Science and Practice (Boston: Allyn and Bacon, 2001), p. 152.

Gonzales, M. H., J. M. Davis, et al. "Interactional Approach to Interpersonal Attraction." Journal of Personality and Social Psychology, 44:6 (1983), pp. 1192–1197.

Gorn, G. J. "The Effects of Music in Advertising on Choice Behavior: A Classical Conditioning Approach." Journal of Marketing, 46:1 (Winter 1982), pp. 94–101.

Schuster, C. P., and J. E. Danes. "Asking Questions: Some Characteristics of Successful Sales Encounters." Journal of Personal Selling and Sales Management, 6:1 (May 1986), pp. 17–27.

Tracy, B. "Stop Talking . . . and Start Asking Questions." Sales and Marketing Management, 147:2 (February 1995), pp. 79 86.

TRUTH 87

Milgram, S., L. Bickman, and L. Berkowitz. "Note on the Drawing Power of Crowds of Different Size." Journal of Personality and Social Psychology, 13:2 (1969), pp. 79–82.

Phillips, D. P. "Airplane Accidents, Murder, and the Mass Media: Towards a Theory of Imitation and Suggestion." Social Forces, 58:4 (June 1980), pp. 1001–1024.

Phillips, D. P. "Suicide, Motor Vehicle Fatalities, and the Mass Media: Evidence Toward a Theory of Suggestion." American Journal Of Sociology, 84:5 (1979), pp. 1150–1174.

Schuster, C. P., and J. E. Danes. "Asking Questions: Some Characteristics of Successful Sales Encounters." Journal of Personal Selling and Sales Management, 6:1 (May 1986), pp. 17–27.

Whittler, T. E. "Eliciting Consumer Choice Heuristics: Sales Representatives' Persuasion Strategies." Journal of Personal Selling and Sales Management, 14:4 (Fall 1994), pp. 41–53.

TRUTH 88

West, S. G. "Increasing the Attractiveness of College Cafeteria Food: A Reactance Theory Perspective." Journal of Applied Psychology, 60:5 (1975), pp. 656–658.

Worchel, S., J. Lee, and A. Adewole. "Effects of Supply and Demand on Ratings of Object Value." Journal of Personality and Social Psychology, 32:5 (1975), pp. 906–914.

TRUTH 89

Bushman, B. J. "The Effects of Apparel on Compliance." Personality and Social Psychology Bulletin, 14:3 (September1988), pp. 459–467.

Doob, A. N., and A. E. Gross. "Status of Frustrator as an Inhibitor of Horn-Honking Responses." Journal of Social Psychology, 76 (1968), pp. 213–218.

Lefkowitz, M., R. R. Blake, and J. S. Mouton. "Status Factors in Pedestrian Violation of Traffic Signals." Journal of Abnormal and Social Psychology, 51 (1955), pp. 704–706.

Schuster, C. P., and J. E. Danes. "Asking Questions: Some Characteristics of Successful Sales Encounters." Journal of Personal Selling and Sales Management, 6:1 (May 1986), pp. 17–27.

TRUTH 90
Cialdini, R. B. Influence: Science and Practice (Boston: Allyn and Bacon, 2001), pp. 167–168.

Razran, G.H.S. "Conditioning Away Social Bias." Psychological Bulletin, 35 (1938), p. 693.

Razran, G.H.S. "Conditioned Response Changes in Rating and Appraising Sociopolitical Slogans." Psychological Bulletin, 37 (1940), p. 481.

Wyrwicka, W. "Classical Conditioned Reflexes." Conditioning (New Brunswick, N.J.: Transaction Publishers, 2000), pp. 5–10.

TRUTH 91
Howard, D. J., C. Gengler, and A. Jain. "What's In a Name? A Complimentary Means of Persuasion." Journal of Consumer Research, 22 (September 1995), pp. 200–211.

TRUTH 92
Cialdini, R. B. Influence: Science and Practice (Boston: Allyn and Bacon, 2001), p. 74.

Moriarity, T. "Crime, Commitment, and the Responsive Bystander: Two Field Experiments." Journal of Personality and Social Psychology, 31:2 (1975), pp. 370–376.

TRUTH 93
Dwyer, S., J. Hill, and W. Martin. "An Empirical Investigation of Critical Success Factors in the Personal Selling Process for Homogenous Goods." Journal of Personal Selling and Sales Management, 20:3 (Summer 2000), pp. 151–159.

Tversky, A., and E. Shafir. "Choice Under Conflict: The Dynamics of Deferred Decision." Psychological Science, 3:6 (November 1992), pp. 358–361.

TRUTH 94
Kahle, L. R., D. B. Hall, and M. J. Kosinski. "The Real-Time Response Survey in New Product Research: It's About Time." Journal of Consumer Marketing, 14:3 (1997), pp. 234–248.

Sherman, S. J. "On the Self-Erasing Nature of Errors of Prediction." Journal of Personality And Social Psychology, 39:2 (1980), pp. 211–221.

TRUTH 95

Chaiken, S. "Communicator Physical Attractiveness and Persuasion." Journal of Personality and Social Psychology, 37:8 (1979), pp. 1387–1397.

Cialdini, R. B. Influence: Science and Practice, (Boston: Allyn and Bacon, 2001), pp. 148–150.

Mack, D., and D. Rainey. "Female Applicants' Grooming and Personnel Selection." Journal of Social Behavior and Personality, 5:5 (1990), pp. 399–407.

Stieg, B. "Facts of Life." Men's Health (March 2003), p. 52.

TRUTH 96

Morwitz, V. G., E. Johnson, and D. Schmittlein. "Does Measuring Intent Change Behavior?" Journal of Consumer Research, 20 (Jun 1993), pp. 46–61.

TRUTH 97

Garrity, K., and D. Degelman. "Effects of Server Introduction on Restaurant Tipping." Journal of Applied Social Psychology, 20:2 (1990), pp. 168–172.

TRUTH 98

Cialdini, R. B., R. J. Borden, et al. "Basking in Reflected Glory: Three (Football) Field Studies." Journal of Personality and Social Psychology, 31:3 (1976), pp. 366–375.

TRUTH 99

Goff, B. G., D. N. Bellenger, and C. Stojack. "Cues to Consumer Susceptibility to Salesperson Influence: Implications for Adaptive Retail Selling." Journal of Personal Selling and Sales Management, 14:2 (Spring 1994), pp. 25–39.

TRUTH 100

Carpenter, G. S., and R. Glazer. "Meaningful Brands From Meaningless Differentiation: The Dependence on Irrelevant Attributes." Journal of Marketing Research, 31:3 (August 1994), pp. 339–350.

TRUTH 101

Saxe, R., and B. A. Weitz. "The SOCO Scale: A Measure of the Customer Orientation of Salespeople." Journal of Marketing Research, 19:3 (August 1982), pp. 343–351.

TRUTH 102

Hall, D., and D. Wecker. The Maverick Mindset (New York: Simon & Schuster, 1997), pp. 207–210.

Brain Brew Radio and Eureka! Ranch Services

BRAIN BREW RADIO is about ideas—ideas to help you think quicker, smarter and more creatively about your life and your business. Ideas to help you turn your invention into reality. Ideas to help non-profits turn a profit. Ideas to help your small business win more, lose less and make more money.

Brain Brew is hosted each week by Doug Hall and David Wecker of the Eureka! Ranch. It's long on humor and high on entertainment, giving listeners an engaging, eye-opening experience that's brimming with "wow!" moments. It's about what it takes to get anyone's American dream from the garage to the marketplace—and once there, how to sell it.

The program is nationally distributed by PRI, Public Radio International. Contact your local public radio station for details on when Brain Brew airs in your market. To hear last week's show or to apply to be a guest on the show, visit www.BrainBrewRadio.com.

BRAIN BREW LIVE is a theatrical version of the radio show designed for company meetings and industry trade shows. Live and unscripted, this special event program features the Brain Brew crew jump-starting audience members' brains. One by one, audience members bring their most difficult business problem to the stage. The Brain Brew crew has just ten minutes to diagnose and give each person a portfolio of solutions. Each event is filled with unexpected turns, humor, drama, and learning. Profits from Brain Brew Live are used to help fund and support Public Radio. For more information, e-mail Events@EurekaRanch.com.

EUREKA! is a marketing and innovation consulting service focused on helping clients discover and develop meaningfully effective ideas for growing their brands. It's available in a range of formats for consumer, business-to-business, and industrial businesses. Scholarships are available to help small businesses and nonprofits receive assistance at reduced cost.

EUREKA! EVENTS feature practical wisdom, backed by data and delivered with caffeinated energy. Programs include classic keynote lectures by Doug Hall and the Ranch staff, as well as interactive business theater training events—ranging from Brain Brew Live to competitive marketing simulations (where audience teams bet million-dollar poker chips) to Capitalist Creativity® innovation shootouts.

MERWYN is a patented concept research system that benchmarks the "meaningfulness" of core customer concepts. The basis for the Merwyn system is the *Meaningful Marketing* truths that you have just learned. Merwyn is an efficient and effective way to quantify the strengths and weaknesses of your marketing, advertising, new product or service concepts. The system has been validated versus AcuPOLL®, BASES® and marketplace survival results.

To learn about any Eureka! Ranch service
Visit: www.EurekaRanch.com
Call: 513-271-9911
E-mail: DougHall@DougHall.com

We Love to Receive E-mail From Readers

Thank you for letting us into your life for this short time.

We'd like to know your thoughts, reactions, and comments about Meaningful Marketing.

We'd also like to know the truths and ideas you like the most, which you didn't, and what effect, if any, this book has had on your sales and marketing success.

Most importantly we'd like to hear your data-proven truths and practical ideas. Great ideas will be posted at the Meaningful Marketing section of the DougHall.com Web site.

LAWYER NOTE: When you submit a truth or an idea, you are giving us permission to publish it on the Web or in future editions of the book. Our only obligation to you is to identify the source on our Web site and in the Geek Appendix section of future versions of *Meaningful Marketing*.

Please E-mail us at
DougHall@DougHall.com
    or
Jeff@EurekaRanch.com

We promise to make every effort to personally respond to each message.

To check on updates to the book as well as to review additional data-proven truths and practical ideas visit www.DougHall.com.

Thank You

When the book was coming to an end, we sat back one night with some of Scotland's finest nectar to ponder who was the marketer who most embodied the spirit of Meaningful Marketing. Our first nomination was Sergio Zyman. When it comes to courage, authenticity, overtness and commitment to marketing quantification no one else comes close. Thank you Sergio for the Foreword, but even more importantly, thank you for blazing the trail of Meaningful Marketing with your work at The Coca-Cola Company and now with the Zyman Group.

Thanks to the thousands of Eureka! Ranch clients who over the years have challenged us to think quicker, smarter, and more creatively about business.

Thanks to the Eureka! Ranch staff and the Trained Brain Posse: Kari McNamara, Bruce Hall, Matt Kirk, Zach Sorrells, Lorrie Paulus, Corie Roudebush, Hannah Buchanan, Anne Badanes, Tracy Duckworth, Juliann Gardner, Benjamin Franklin, Colleen Harris, Craig Kurz, Sondra Kurz, Mike Katz, Jane Portman, Matthew Fenton, Laura Rolfes, David Wecker, Tod Gentile, Scott Wells, Tom Wilson, Kevin McNamara, Jason Saunders, Billay Brooks, Chris McMahon, Mark Twist, Pam Twist, Julie Phillipi, Bruce Forsee, Margaret Henson, Negia York, and Les Moermond.

Thanks to the friends of the Ranch, whose never-ending support helped make this book possible: Richard Hunt, Tom Ackerman, John Altman, David Cassady, Steve and Mary Friedberg, Ann Herrmann, Patty Hogan, Chris Hylen, Kip Knight, Copthorne MacDonald, Thane Maynard, Austin McNamara, Kevin McNamara, Jerry McNellis, Dave Owens, Tim Riker, Eric Schulz, Renee Steele, Dick Steuerwald, Chic Thompson, Tracie Tighe, and Andy Timmerman. Thanks to Chris Stormann for statistical help.

Thanks to public radio stations across America for your support of our efforts to help entrepreneurs turn their dreams into reality.

Special thanks to the world-class team at PRI Public Radio International: Alisa Miller, Ann Phi-Wendt, Barbara Eisinger, Brian Wald, Brooke Anthony, Cathy Twiss, Cheryl Luebke, Chris Morlock, Claire Adamsick, Clinton Forry, Dale Spear, Dan Jensen, Denise Andrews, Eleanor Harris, Ellen Widmark, Ellie Zimmerman, Emma Marshall-Cerqueira, Gennise, Heather Marchant, Heidi Schultz, Jennifer, John Neupauer, Julie Mears, Kathy Jeong, Kelli Jackson, Kristi George,

Kristine Holmgren, Kyle Lerfald, Laura DiLodovico-Weigenant, Leslie Wolfe, Linda Sue Anderson, Lori Haskell, Marilyn Murray, Mark Kausch, Mary Brennan, Melinda Ward, Michelle Kornowski, Mike Pfeifer, Morgan Church, Patty Johnson, Rene Rosengren, Richard Ruotolo, "Rocky" Rothrock, Ruth Goettig, Sara Sneddon, Sonia Krinke, Stephen Salyer, Sue Winking, Tim Engel, Valerie Ascher, Vidal Guzman.

Thanks to the Brain Brew Radio team at WGUC - Mark Perzel, Robin Gehl, Bruce Ellis, Rich Eiswerth, Gordon Bayliss, Don Danko, Tim Lanter, Andrew Lucyzyn, Sherri Mancini, Coleen Tracey, Chris Phelps.

Thanks to the entire F&W team of true publishing professionals. David Lewis, Budge Wallis, Jerry Jackson, Sara Dumford, Clare Finney, Phil Sexton, Mary Schuetz, Sharon Daugherty, Steve Koenig, Michael Murphy, Jennifer Johnson.

Special Thanks From Doug

Thank you to the people of Prince Edward Island, Canada who continuously teach me how to live life meaningfully. Special thanks to those who provided good food and never-ending support to nourish me when I was hidden away at our farmhouse in Springbrook: Mike and Margaret England, Copthorne Macdonald and Beverly Mills Stetson, Scott MacAulay, Don Groom and Mary and Mel Crane.

Special Thanks From Jeffrey

A special thanks to our academic friends that helped review and provide comments on this book: Ted Labuza, University of Minnesota; Al Lieberman, New York University; Michael Morris, Syracuse University; John Altman, Babson College; Lynn Kahle, Oregon University; Paul Farris, University of Virginia; Terri Barr, Miami University; Tim Heath, Miami University; Roger Blackwell, Ohio State University, Chuck Matthews, University of Cincinnati; Shai Vyakarnam, Cambridge University; Neal Hartman, MIT; James Davis, Notre Dame; Don Kuratko, Ball State University; Carl Vesper, University of Washington.

To those whose names we missed, we apologize.
We will seek to correct our mistake in future editions.

Index